Management Processes and Functions

Michael Armstrong graduated from the London School of Economics, and is a Fellow of the Institute of Personnel Management and a member of the Institute of Management Consultants. From 1976 to 1988 he was general manager and a member of the executive board of a major UK publishing organization. He has now returned to management consultancy, specializing in strategic management skills. He has written a number of successful management books including *A Handbook of Management Techniques*, *A Handbook of Personnel Management Practice*, *How to be a Better Manager* and *Personnel and the Bottom Line*.

Management Studies Series

Series Editors: Michael Armstrong and David Farnham

Today's business environment demands that managers possess a wide range of knowledge, skills and competencies. The Professional Management Foundation Programme is a major initiative developed by a group of forward-looking professional institutes to help them meet these needs. This series of practical, introductory texts, while ideally suited to students on the Programme, will be equally useful for anyone wishing to enhance their understanding of contemporary management techniques and methods.

Other titles in the series:

The Corporate Environment
David Farnham

Finance and Accounting for Managers
David Davies

Management Information Systems and Statistics
Roland and Frances Bee

Managing Human Resources
Jane Weightman

MANAGEMENT STUDIES

Management Processes and Functions

Michael Armstrong

Institute of Personnel Management

First published in 1990

Phototypeset by Wessex Typesetters
Frome, Somerset

and printed in Great Britain
by Short Run Press, Exeter.

British Library Cataloguing in Publication Data
Armstrong, Michael, *1928–*
    Management processes and functions.
    1. Management
    I. Title   II. Institute of Personnel Management   III.
    Series
    658

    ISBN 0–85292–438–0

Contents

List of Figures

Editors' Foreword

Today's business environment demands that managers possess a wide range of knowledge, skills and competencies. As well as a sound understanding of management processes and functions, managers need to be able to make the best use of their time and talents, and of other people's, and to work with and through others to achieve corporate objectives. They also need to demonstrate a full understanding of the business environment and of their organization's key resources: its people, finance and information.

Management education in Britain has at last begun to take full account of these business realities. In particular, the Professional Management Foundation Programme is a major initiative developed by a group of forward-looking professional institutes to meet these needs. They recognize that a synthesis of knowledge and skills, and theory and practice, is vital for all managers and those aspiring to management positions.

For many years, the Institute of Personnel Management has been strongly committed to developing professional excellence. This major new series reflects this ideal. It covers five key areas: management processes and functions; the corporate environment; managing human resources; management information systems and statistics; and finance and accounting for managers. In drawing on the expertise of experienced teachers and managers, this series provides all students of management with an invaluable set of practical, introductory and informed texts on contemporary management studies.

MICHAEL ARMSTRONG
DAVID FARNHAM
April 1990

1

The Framework of Management

The Role of Management

Management is a process which exists to get results by making the best use of the human, financial and material resources available to the organization and to individual managers. It is very much concerned with adding value to these resources, and this added value depends on the expertise and commitment of the people who are responsible for managing the business.

The overall process of management is subdivided into a number of individual processes which are methods of operation specially designed to assist in the achievement of objectives. Their purpose is to bring as much system, order, predictability, logic and consistency to the task of management as is possible in the ever-changing, varied and turbulent environment in which managers work. These processes will be concerned with planning, organizing and controlling activities, information flows, and helping managers to make better decisions.

Management functions are the activities that take place in organizations and the things that the people who manage these activities do, which involves using the processes, responding to instructions, allocating work, getting teams into action and seeing that the required results are obtained.

Effective management requires an understanding of how the processes are applied and how they can be used. It also demands certain skills. Management is more art than science in that managers are constantly having to use their judgement and expertise. Experimentation and testing, which is what science is based on, play relatively little part in the day-to-day work of managers. Information technology, financial analysis techniques such as discounted cash flow, management science in the form of operational research, decision theory, modelling and sensitivity analysis techniques, are all available to take some of the guesswork

1

out of problem solving and to help make more logical decisions on the basis of better data. But they cannot replace judgement developed through experience, or the skills needed to manage what can be the most expensive but at the same time least tractable resource, namely people. Faced with the need constantly to make decisions under pressure, management becomes the art of the possible rather than a cool and collected science, although it will always involve the use of analytical skills.

The Management Framework

Management takes place within the framework of the organization – its strategic mission, its corporate culture, its structure and the environment in which it exists. Because this framework is constantly changing and differs widely between organizations it is dangerous to generalize on how management should be applied in any circumstances.

Mary Parker Follet,[1] one of the pioneers of management thinking in the 1920s, and one of the wisest, calls this the law of the situation – the work to be done and the decisions to be made must be based on the objective requirements of the situation in which managers or the organization find themselves. This 'law' was rediscovered 50 years later by those such as Lawrence and Lorsch,[2] who developed contingency theory, which says that what managers do and how businesses are organized is contingent or dependent on the situation and not on any abstract principles of management.

The Context of Management

The law of the situation, contingency theory and systems theory as developed by Miller and Rice[3] all, in their different ways, emphasize the importance of the environment of the organization, the context within which managers operate. Systems theory lays particular stress on the belief that organizations are essentially open systems, which transform inputs into outputs but are always under the influence of their environment, with which they are continually making transactions. The environment will include the internal technology and organization climate (the working atmosphere). Externally, the environment will consist of all those factors that impinge on the organization, such as competition, market developments, government edicts, economic trends and societal pressures.

The phenomenon of change

The economic and business environment has become much more turbulent, uncertain and demanding. Tom Peters[4] refers to 'an era of unprecedented change' and suggests that 'predictability is a thing of the past.'

Environmental change has taken place in a number of ways.

- Economic and political change has seen a rise in recent years of the enterprise culture and its associated phenomenon, the market economy.

- Social change has produced a trend towards individualism and away from collectivism.

- Consumer expectations are higher than ever before. They want value for money, as always, but they are now demanding, quite rightly, higher standards of quality and service.

- The business environment is changing significantly with an emphasis on growth, a rash of takeovers and acquisitions and increased competition from Europe and Japan and from multinational firms.

- Product life cycles are shorter and leading-edge firms must innovate to remain competitive and to establish and maintain their position in increasingly segmented markets.

- New technology is playing a much greater part in the management process in so far as that process is largely concerned with information flows.

The impact of change on attitudes

A new managerial revolution has taken place over the last decade. Attitudes have changed in the following directions:

- *The market place.* It is at last recognized that organizations are market-driven and that management must be market-orientated.

- *Customers*. Customer care and service has become a major feature in marketing strategies.

- *Excellence*. Peters and Waterman[5] initiated what has become almost a cult of excellence. ICL, for example, in its message to all employees has stated that 'ICL's sights are now set on world success. That demands excellence in everything we undertake. And excellence will be achieved only by adopting "can do" attitudes and the highest levels of co-operation and commitment throughout the organization.'

- *Turbulence*. Managements are beginning to accept turbulence as a way of life. Tom Peters[4] redefines his original definition of excellence to read:

  Excellent firms don't believe in excellence – only in constant improvement and constant change. That is, excellent firms of tomorrow will cherish impermanence and thrive on chaos.

The impact of change on the firm

Environmental and technological developments have resulted in fundamental changes to the ways in which firms are structured and managed.

We now have:

- *The responsive firm* which has to react quickly to changes in the market place and in customer needs and preferences.

- *The pro-active firm* which has to make markets as well as adapt itself to them.

- *The flexible firm* which has to adjust its structure, its product range, its marketing strategies and its manufacturing facilities quickly to respond to and, more importantly, anticipate change.

- *The information-based firm* which will be knowledge-orientated and composed largely of specialists who direct and discipline their own performance through organized feedback from colleagues, customers and the strategic business units into which the organization is divided in accordance with the markets it serves.

- *The compact firm* which has a flatter organization structure because superfluous layers of management have been stripped out.

- *The decentralized firm* which consists of strategic business units placed firmly in their market niches and capable of responding quickly to opportunities. These units are tightly managed to achieve well-defined goals with the minimum of interference from above.

The impact on managers

Managers have to learn to exist with change, like the organizations in which they work. They have to be more flexible and more responsive to new and challenging demands.

In the decentralized organization of today they must be able to operate independently – the very essence of effective managers is that they achieve the goals they set themselves. But in the flatter organization they also have to be good team workers able to deploy a wider range of skills in working with others across organizational boundaries.

These demands can result in role conflict and role ambiguity, which can produce stress. People generally prefer to work in an orderly structure which provides a framework within which they have a fair degree of autonomy. They prefer to know where they stand and where they are going. They like a certain amount of predictability, and although they welcome variety, it has to be within reasonable bounds. But life in organizations is not like that. Change, uncertainty and ambiguity are ever-present. Organizations are supposed to behave rationally, progressing steadily from A to B. But they do not. They consist of webs of power and politics and proceed by fits and starts.

The balancing act practised by all managers is between the need for order and continuity, and the demands of the situation, which involve flexibility and discontinuity. Organizations suffer too. As Rosabeth Moss Kanter[6] points out:

Resource-conserving management stifles innovators, the argument ran, while 'undisciplined' entrepreneurial management wastes resources. But now I see business struggling to do both simultaneously. This constitutes the ultimate balancing act. Cut back and grow. Trim down and build. Accomplish more, and do it in new areas, with fewer resources.

What Managers Need to Know and Do

To achieve their objectives, cope with change and carry out their balancing act managers need to learn how to manage themselves, which involves:

- understanding the nature of management work in their environment and under conditions of turbulence, ambiguity, diversity, pressure and organizational politics and power plays
- understanding the management processes they can use to cope with these conditions and with their environment
- practising and developing the skills of management required to ensure that these processes operate effectively
- appreciating the approaches required to manage performance, time, stress and their own careers.

These aspects of management are dealt with in Chapters 2–9.

Managers must also understand how to work with other people, which involves working in groups, managing change, and the use of communicating and interpersonal skills. These areas are considered in Chapters 10–14. Additionally, they must learn how to work in the organization, which means understanding about organization structure and development, organization culture, the different functions within businesses, and the strategic planning process which sets goals to be achieved and directions to be followed by the enterprise and its managers (Chapters 15–18).

Finally, managers have to learn to work with the various stakeholders of the organization, its shareholders, employees, customers, suppliers and the community at large. Organizations have responsibilities to each of those stakeholders and it is management's duty to fulfil them. This important aspect of management today is considered in Chapter 19.

References

1 FOLLET Mary Parker. *Creative experience.* London, Longman, 1924
2 LAWRENCE P. R. and LORSCH J. W. *Organization and environment.* Cambridge, Mass., Harvard University Press, 1967
3 MILLER E. and RICE A. K. *Systems of organization.* London, Tavistock Publications, 1967
4 PETERS Tom. *Thriving on chaos.* London, Macmillan, 1988
5 PETERS Tom and WATERMAN Robert. *In search of excellence.* New York, Harper & Row, 1982
6 KANTER Rosabeth Moss. *When giants learn to dance.* London, Simon & Schuster, 1989

2

The Nature of Managerial Work

The purpose of this chapter is to provide a conceptual framework within which the various managerial activities of managing oneself, working with other people, managing within the organization and formulating strategies can be placed. This conceptual framework consists of:

- An overall definition of the process of management
- An examination in general terms of the nature of managerial work
- A study in practical terms of what managers actually do
- An analysis of the distinguishing characteristics of managerial work and the roles of managers

What is Management?

Essentially, management is about deciding what to do and then getting it done through people. This definition emphasizes that people are the most important resource available to managers. It is through this resource that all the other resources – knowledge, finance, materials, plant, equipment etc. – will be managed.

However, managers are there to get results. To do this they have to deal with events and eventualities. They may do this primarily through people, but an overemphasis on the people content of management diverts attention from the fact that in managing events managers have to be personally involved. They manage themselves as well as other people. They cannot delegate everything. They frequently have to rely on their own resources to get things done. These resources consist of experience, know-how, skill and, importantly, time – all of which have to be deployed not only in directing and motivating people but also in understanding situations and issues, analysing and defining problems, making decisions and taking direct action themselves, as well as acting through other people. They will get support, advice and assistance from their staff, but in the last analysis they are on their own. They have to make the decisions and they have to initiate and sometimes take the action. A chairman fighting a takeover bid will get lots of advice but he or she will personally manage the crisis, talking directly to the financial institutions, merchant banks, financial analysts, City editors and the mass of shareholders.

The basic definition of management should therefore be extended to read 'deciding what to do and then getting it done through the effective use of resources'. The most important part of management will indeed be getting things done through people, but managers will be concerned directly or indirectly with all other resources, including their own.

Models of Managerial Work

Over the years many attempts have been made to define the nature of managerial work as a model consisting of a number of well-defined but interrelated activities which together provide a framework for the analysis and conduct of the managerial task. This analytical model, which could be described as the classical approach, has been challenged by those who take an empirical view of management as a much more fragmented activity, the nature of which depends more on the demands of the situation and the people concerned than on any theoretical division of the task into clearly differentiated elements.

Let us look more closely at these two views – the classical and the empirical.

The classical model

The classical model was first constructed by a pioneer writer on management, Henri Fayol[1] who analysed managerial activity into five elements:

- planning

- organizing
- commanding (or directing)
- co-ordinating
- controlling

He argued that, to be effective, management should be founded upon fourteen principles, which were as follows:

1   Division of work and specialisation
2   Authority to match responsibility
3   Discipline
4   Unity of command (one person, one boss)
5   Unity of direction
6   Subordination of individual interest to the general interest
7   Fair remuneration in relation to effort
8   Centralization
9   The scalar or hierarchical principle of line authority
10 The principle of order (a place for everyone and everyone in his or her place)
11 Equity
12 Stability of tenure of personnel
13 Importance of initiative
14 Importance of esprit de corps ← Team Spirit

A later classical theorist was Luther Gullick[2] who developed Fayol's ideas into the acronym POSDCORB which stands for:

- *Planning*, working out in broad outline the things that need to be done and the methods for doing them to accomplish the purpose set for the enterprise
- *Organizing*, establishing the formal structure of an organization through which work subdivisions are arranged, defined and co-ordinated for the whole enterprise

- *Staffing*, the personnel function of bringing in and training the staff and maintaining favourable conditions of work

- *Directing*, the continuous task of making decisions and embodying them in specific general orders and instruction and serving as the leader of their enterprise

- *Co-ordinating*, the all-important duty of interrelating the various parts of the work

- *Reporting*, keeping those to whom the executive is responsible informed as to what is going on, which includes keeping himself and his subordinates informed through records, research and inspection

- *Budgeting*, financial planning, accounting and control

In more recent times this list has been narrowed down to four basic management functions.

- *Planning*, deciding on a course of action to achieve a desired result and focusing attention on objectives and standards and the programmes required to achieve them

- *Organizing*, setting up and staffing the most appropriate organization to achieve the aim

- *Motivating*, exercising leadership to motivate people to work together smoothly and to the best of their ability as part of a team

- *Controlling*, measuring and monitoring the progress of work in relation to the plan and taking corrective action when required

This classical model has been around for some time and has become deeply embedded in the minds of many managers. They may not consciously follow it but they feel they ought to try, and they worry if their attempts to operate in accordance with the model in their day-to-day work fail, which they are bound to do.

The empirical model

The empirical model has been developed by those who have actually studied managers at work, such as Sune Carlsson,[3] Leonard Sayles,[4] Rosemary Stewart,[5] Henry Mintzberg[6] and Peter Lawrence.[7]

Sune Carlsson sums up the empirical view as follows:

> If we ask a managing director when he is coordinating, or how much coordination he has been doing during the day, he would not know, and even the most highly skilled observer would not know either. The same holds true of the concepts of planning, command, organization and control.[3]

The empiricists observed that the work of the manager is fragmented, varied, subjected to continual adjustment and governed to a large degree by events over which the manager has little control, and by a dynamic network of interrelationships with other people. Managers exist to control their environment but sometimes it controls them. They may consciously or unconsciously seek to plan, organize, direct and control but their days almost inevitably become a jumbled sequence of events.

Managers have to cope with ambiguity and turbulence, indeed chaos. The ordered world within which the classical theorists developed their model has vanished.

To the empiricists, management is a process involving a mix of rational, logical, problem-solving and decision-making activities and intuitive, judgemental activities. It is therefore both science and art. As Philip Sadler says, 'The important thing is to recognise which problems and decisions fall into which category and to treat them accordingly.'[8]

How do Managers Spend Their Time?

The empiricists rightly reject the classical concept of managers sitting down and dividing their day into neat segments labelled planning, organizing, motivating and controlling (POMC). They know by observation what every manager knows by experience – life is not like that. These activities are indeed carried out, but they are jumbled up in the fragmented pattern of events that make up the typical manager's day. Conscious attention to the need to carry out the POMC processes helps to produce order out of chaos, but it is no good telling aspiring managers that these processes should govern their day. Management has to be approached the other way round. It starts from an understanding of what actually happens – how managers spend their time. This empirical evidence can then be used as the basis for analysing the distinguishing characteristics of managerial work and the various roles that managers play in the different situations in which they find themselves.

We can now examine the findings of a number of key research projects in this area.

Sune Carlsson

Sune Carlsson[3] studied the work of nine Swedish managing directors and his findings can be summarized under three headings:

1 *Working time.* Executives were alone for not more than one hour a day but the typical 'alone' intervals were only of 10–15 minutes' duration. They spent their days being constantly interrupted and they had remarkably little control over how they spent their time.

2 *Communication patterns.* Chief executives initiate far fewer letters a day than they receive. The average time spent with visitors was three and a half hours a day.

3 *Work content.* One of the main activities of the chief executives was to keep themselves informed.

Leonard Sayles

Leonard Sayles[4] interviewed 75 lower- and middle-level managers in a large American corporation. He identified three aspects of managerial work in his analysis.

1 *The manager as a participant in external work flows*, which leads to seven basic relationships with people outside his immediate managerial responsibility:

- trading relationships: making arrangements with other members of the organization to get work done

- work-flow relationships: making contacts concerning the work preceding or following that supervised by the manager

- service relationships: contacts concerning the giving or receiving of services or support by specialist groups, for example market research or maintenance

- advisory relationships: provision of counsel and advice to line managers by experts, for example industrial relations

- auditing relationships: contacts with those who evaluate or appraise organizational work, for example management accounts or quality control

- stabilization relationships: contacts with those who are empowered to limit or control the manager's decisions in accordance with organizational policy, for example production planning and control

- innovative relationships: contacts with groups specially isolated to perform a research function

2 *The manager as leader*, which results in three basic types of leadership behaviour:

- Leadership as directions: getting subordinates to respond to the requests of the manager

- Leadership as response: responding to initiatives from subordinates who are seeking aid or support

- Leadership as representation: representing subordinates in contact with other parts of the organization

3 *The manager as monitor*, in which the manager follows the progress of work through the system, detects variations and initiates action as required.

Rosemary Stewart

Rosemary Stewart[5] studied 160 senior and middle managers for four weeks each. Her main findings on how they spent their time were:

- The managers worked an average of 42 hours per week.

- Discussions took 60 per cent of their time – 43 per cent informal, 7 per cent committee, 6 per cent telephoning and 4 per cent social activity.

- They spent 34 per cent of their time alone, 25 per cent with their immediate subordinates, 8 per cent with their superiors, 25 per cent with colleagues and 5 per cent with external contacts.

- Fragmentation in work was considerable. In the four-week period, managers averaged only nine periods of 30 minutes or more without interruption and averaged 20 contacts a day, 12 of them fleeting ones (less than five minutes' duration).

Rosemary Stewart established five basic work profiles from her research.

1 *The emissaries*. These managers spend much of their time away from the company, dealing with and entertaining outsiders. They work longer hours but their days are less fragmented than most. Typical of this group are senior executives who act as public figures and sales managers.

2 *The writers*. These managers spend a greater share of their time in writing, reading, dictating and figure work. They are solitary only by comparison and include accountants and other staff specialists.

3 *The discussers*. These are the most typical managers. They spend much of their time with other people, particularly colleagues, and they carry out a diverse range of activities.

4 *The trouble-shooters*. These managers spend much of their time coping with crises, hence their work is much more fragmented. They spend a lot of time with subordinates and less with peers. Production managers tend to fall into this group.

5 *The committee people*. These managers are mainly to be found in large organizations and spend much of their time in meetings. Their contacts are both vertical and horizontal within the company.

Henry Mintzberg

Henry Mintzberg[6] observed five chief executives over a period of five weeks. He found that the proportion of time they spent on different activities was:

	Average %	Range %
Desk work	22	16–38
Telephone calls	6	4–9
Scheduled meetings	59	38–75
Unscheduled meetings	10	3–18
Tours	3	0–10
Proportion of activities lasting less than 9 minutes	49	40–56
Proportion of activities lasting longer than 60 minutes	10	5–13

The managers' days were characterized by a large number of brief informal two-person contacts (telephone calls and unscheduled meetings) and relatively few scheduled meetings, which nevertheless took most of their time. Subordinates consumed about half the managers' contact time and were involved in two-thirds of the contacts. The managers initiated less than one-third of their contacts and only 5 per cent were scheduled regularly.

The variations in the work of the managers can be ascribed to:

- the nature of the industry
- the nature of the organization
- the nature of the individual's style
- the needs of the moment

The broad conclusions emerging from this study confirmed that management is:

- highly interactive
- very much concerned with communication
- about getting things done with or through other people

- not much about office work

Peter Lawrence

Peter Lawrence[7] observed the work of 16 German and 25 British general and production managers. His analysis of the proportion of time spent on different activities was as follows:

	German %	British %
Formal scheduled recurrent meetings	9.78	15.5
Convened special-purpose meetings	12.62	14.46
Ad hoc discussions	20.07	17.93
Time spent in works	16.87	17.35
Telephoning	10.56	7.23
Office work	11.56	11.16
Explanations to researcher	10.45	13.08
Miscellaneous	8.02	4.08

The Distinguishing Characteristics of Managerial Work

The nature of every manager's job will be influenced by its function, its level and the circumstances of the firm. Individual managers will adapt to these circumstances in different ways and will operate more or less successfully in accordance with their own perceptions of the behaviour expected of them, their experience of what has or has not worked for them in the past and their personal characteristics. The factors that affect managerial behaviour are analysed in more detail in Chapter 3.

The classical concept that all managerial jobs are basically the same because all managers plan, organize, motivate and control grossly overemphasizes the similarities of the manager's job at the expense of the differences, which are many and important. As Rosemary Stewart says:

> They [the management theorists] could talk about *the* manager's job because their description of his functions was so general as to be universally valid; but such a level of generalisation has a very limited usefulness in practice.[8]

A more helpful approach is to follow the empiricists who analyse the work that managers actually do in terms of its main characteristics and then consider the different roles that managers play.

The main characteristics of managerial work

The activities of managers are characterized by brevity, variety and fragmentation. Because of the open-ended nature of the work, managers feel compelled to perform a great variety of types of work at an unrelenting pace. As Henry Mintzberg comments:

> The manager actually appears to prefer brevity and interruption to his work. He becomes conditioned by his workload; he develops an appreciation of the opportunity cost of his own time; and he lives continuously with an awareness of what else might or must be done at any time. Superficiality is an occupational hazard of the manager's job . . . The manager gravitates to the more active elements of his work – the current, the specific, the well-defined, the non-routine activities.[6]

Managerial roles

During the course of a typical day a chief executive may well meet the marketing director to discuss the programme for launching a new product, the personnel director to decide how best to reorganize the distribution department, the production director to ask why costs per unit of output are going up and what is going to be done about it, and the finance director to review the latest set of management accounts before the next board meeting. These activities could be categorized under the headings of planning, organizing, directing and controlling, but the chief executive would not have attached these labels when deciding how to spend his or her day (in so far as there was any choice). The fact that these processes took place was imposed by the situation and the need to exercise one or more of the roles inherent in the manager's job. These roles are fundamentally concerned with:

- getting things done – maintaining momentum and making things happen

- finding out what is happening
- reacting to new situations and problems
- responding to demands and requests

They involve a great deal of interpersonal relations, data processing and decision making.

Henry Mintzberg[6] suggests that managerial activities can be divided into ten roles within three broad groups: interpersonal roles, informational roles and decisional roles.

Interpersonal roles

1 *Managers as figure-heads* who, because of their formal authority, are obliged to perform a number of duties

2 *Managers as leaders*, providing guidance and motivation

3 *Managers as liaison officers*, maintaining a web of relationships with many individuals and groups

Informational roles

4 *Managers as monitors*, continually seeking and receiving information as a basis for action

5 *Managers as disseminators*, passing factual information to supervisors, colleagues and subordinates and transmitting value statements to guide subordinates in making decisions

6 *Managers as spokespeople*, transmitting information into their organization's environment

Decisional roles

7 *Managers as entrepreneurs*, acting as initiators of controlled change in the organization

8 *Managers as disturbance handlers*, dealing with involuntary situations and change beyond their control

9 *Managers as resource allocators*, making choices about scheduling their own time, authorizing actions and allocating people and finance to projects. These plans are seldom explicit or documented in detail. Rather, crude and often highly flexible plans exist in the managers' minds in the form of visions about

the direction they want to go and the resources they need to get there.

10 *Managers as negotiators* with other organizations or individuals

References

1 FAYOL Henri. *General and industrial administration.* London, Pitman, 1949
2 GULLICK Luther. 'Notes on the theory of organizations' *in* GULLICK Luther and URWICK Lyndall *eds. Papers on the science of administration.* New York, Columbia University Press, 1937
3 CARLSSON Sune. *Executive behaviour: a study of the work load and the working methods of managing directors.* Stockholm, Strombergs, 1951
4 SAYLES Leonard. *Managerial behaviour.* New York, McGraw-Hill, 1964
5 STEWART Rosemary. *Managers and their jobs.* London, Macmillan, 1967
6 MINTZBERG Henry. *The nature of managerial work.* New York, Harper & Row, 1973
7 LAWRENCE Peter. *Management in action.* London, Routledge & Kegan Paul, 1984
8 SADLER P, and BARRY B. A. *Organizational development.* Longman, 1970

3

The Managerial Environment

The nature of managerial work will depend largely on the organizational environment within which managers operate. To function
effectively as a manager it is necessary to understand the environmental factors that affect your work. This means appreciating:

- the nature of the organization itself as an open system
- the impact which the environment can make – contingency
  theory
- the effect of technology
- the key processes and features of organizational life which
  impact on managers – turbulence, change, variety, politics,
  power and conflict

The Organization as an Open System

An organization can be described as an open system which is
continually dependent on and influenced by its environment. The
basic characteristic of the enterprise as an open system is that it
transforms inputs into outputs within its environment as illustrated
in Figure 1.

Figure 1
The organization as an open system

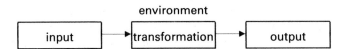

environment

| input | transformation | output |

Open system theory is useful in analysing managerial work because

21

it emphasizes two things: first, that organizations are dynamic; and secondly, that the dynamic processes they follow are strongly influenced by their environment, which is itself usually turbulent.

British Aerospace, for example, transforms inputs in the shape of raw materials into outputs in the form of aircraft, missiles and space vehicles. It operates, however, in two business environments: first, the national, British, environment, where defence policy and the buying strategies of the airlines will influence everything that happens within the organization; and secondly, the international or global environment where joint ventures and individual requirements will again be dependent on the thrusts and shifts in national defence and airline strategies. These external pressures and changes, together with competitive forces, will affect the work of every manager, indeed every employee, in the organization. Those, such as commercial and sales managers and designers, who have to carry out direct transactions in the environment will be affected most, but the variety and unpredictability of everyone's work will also be influenced to varying degrees.

In a large retailing organization such as W. H. Smith, the inputs will be the goods and materials bought in from suppliers, which will be transformed by marketing and merchandising activities to be sold at retail outlets. The external environmental factors will include the activities of competitors, suppliers, the Government, the City and, importantly, customers. The chairman of W. H. Smith probably has to spend much of his time looking outwards from the organization and dealing at top level with the issues which are continually arising with the innumerable organizations and interest groups that affect the firm. The managing director will spend more of his time looking inwards and managing the business, but he will always be under the influence of the environment. The division between a primarily outward-looking chairman and a more inward-looking managing director is, incidentally, a fairly typical arrangement in British industry and reflects the importance of the external environment. There are, of course, many managers below the top level in an organization – buyers, sales managers, shop managers – who will spend most of their time relating to outsiders, and this will certainly add much variety to their work.

An organization can therefore be described, in the words of Lawrence and Lorsch as 'the co-ordination of different activities of individual contributors to carry out planned transactions with the environment'.[1] This means that there are continual interfaces taking place – between people within and people outside the organization, and between individuals inside the organization. These interfaces involve transactions, both external and internal, the latter frequently across organizational boundaries. And it is the existence of this perpetual process of transactions or interactions within unstable environments which creates the variety and, indeed, the unpredictability of much managerial work.

Contingency Theory

Contingency theory simply states that the structure and methods of working in an organization are a function of the circumstances in which it exists. In its simplest, deterministic form, the contingency model of an organization looks like Figure 2.

Figure 2
Deterministic contingency model

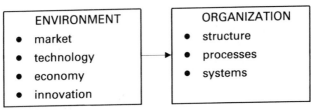

A more sophisticated 'action theory' approach has been developed by Silverman.[2] This suggests a complex and dynamic set of relationships between the contingent factors, which will be both external (market, competitors, economic) and internal (technical, cultural), plus managerial plans and actions.

Again, it is the complexity of this model that demonstrates why managerial jobs can be so different. A sales manager in a fast-moving consumer-goods industry such as photographic equipment, where tastes are changing and new models are being produced continuously, will be living in an unstable environment. This will be completely different from the relatively stable environment of

Figure 3
Action theory contingency model

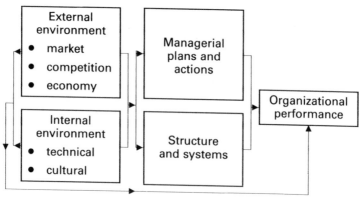

a sales manager in an engineering works manufacturing heavy earth-moving equipment, where customers remain fairly constant and design changes are infrequent. However, even in the latter case, the sales manager may exist in a highly competitive environment and will have to fight hard to retain his or her customers and beat off the opposition. In today's conditions, very few safe and steady jobs exist.

Technology

The managerial task will vary according to the technology of the business. This was demonstrated in a pioneering study by Joan Woodward of a number of Essex firms, from which she concluded that variations in organizational requirements between firms are nearly always linked with differences in their techniques of production. She states that:

> The following features can be traced to the technology of each system of production: a co-ordination of functions and centralisation of authority in unit production; an extensive specialisation and delegation of authority in mass production; and in process industry a specialisation between development,

marketing and production, combined with integration within each function and the co-operative character of decision-making.[3]

As Burns and Stalker found out in another pioneering study of Scottish industry, the type of organizations, the tasks of managers and the way managers managed (management style) were clearly dependent on the technology of the firm. They also emphasized that the rate of change in the firm's environment was a key factor in determining how it could operate.

In a firm processing rayon filament yarn, for example,

> The whole concern can be seen as a three-sided pyramid of power, technical expertise and knowledge of circumstances. At every step down from the top there was less authority, less technical expertise and less information. Each person's task was clearly laid down and defined by his superior. He knew just what he could do in normal circumstances without consulting anyone else; just what point of deviation from the norm he should regard as the limit of his competence; and just what he should do when this limit was reached i.e. report to his superior. The whole system was designed to preserve normality and stability . . . . The outstanding characteristic of the structure was that it was mechanical and authoritarian. And it worked very well.[4]

Burns and Stalker contrast this 'mechanistic' organization with the much more flexible and free-flowing one which had evolved in an electronics firm which was mainly involved in high-technology development. In the volatile environment in which this form of operation exists a rigid system of ranks and routines would inhibit the organization's speed and sensitivity of response. According to Burns and Stalker, the structure and methods of working need to be 'organic' in the sense that they are a function of the situation in which the enterprise finds itself, rather than conforming to any rigid view of how it should operate. Individual managerial responsibilities are less clear-cut and managers must constantly relate what they are doing to their organization's general situation and specific problems.

These and other studies, such as those carried out by Tom Lupton,[5] indicated that the technology or technical system was closely interrelated with the social system – the ways in which work groups were organized and the processes of interaction that took place in the firm. This 'socio-technical' model as evolved by the Tavistock Institute was based on research within industry and it revealed that 'the technological system and the effectiveness of the total production system will depend upon the adequacy with which the social system is able to cope with these requirements.'[6]

The significance of this to managers is that they must be aware that they are managing both the social and the technical systems. And when conditions are unstable and the reactions of individuals are likely to be unpredictable (which is more often than not the case) the task of management becomes correspondingly more complex and difficult. The 'rules of the game', the so-called principles of management, are not very helpful in these circumstances.

Turbulence

Managers have to manage most of their time in turbulent conditions. Turbulence is usually imposed on the organization by its environment, although it can be self-generated on the basis of what entrepreneurial and driving managements think needs to be done. As Rosabeth Moss Kanter says:

> Organizational change is stimulated not by *pressures* from the environment but by the *perceptions* of that environment and the pressures held by key actors. . . . Organizations may not respond to environments so much as 'enact' them – creating them by choosing selectively to define certain things as important.[7]

Perceptions are all-important but they will always be triggered off by some external event or pressure. For example, Book Club Associates (BCA) (a medium-sized direct-mail publishing firm with an £80m turnover and 1,000 employees) had to face over the two-year period 1986–8:

- one 50 per cent partner (Doubleday) being taken over by another partner (Bertelsman) – a change from American to German ownership

- the other partner (W. H. Smith) selling their 50 per cent share to a British publishing firm (Octopus)
- a reference to the Office of Fair Trading for an investigation into the extent to which BCA could be regarded as a monopoly
- rapidly increasing inflation and mortgage rates reducing the amount of disposable income people were prepared to devote to buying books
- the possible imposition of VAT on books
- the possible end of the net book agreement (a form of retail price maintenance)
- increased pressure from the warehouse union, SOGAT, to represent clerical and administrative as well as warehouse staff
- increasing competition from certain sectors of the mail-order business
- increasing pressure from customers for even better service
- concern expressed by some publishers and authors about the level of royalties paid by BCA

These events, together with the appointment of a new chief executive and three new members of the board, put increasing pressure on all levels of management and through them to every member of staff. In one sense, BCA had always been an organization which, in Tom Peters' phrase,[8] thrived on chaos. During these two years this experience was put to the test. Managers had to operate at the leading edge. They had to think and move fast. They had to be innovative and opportunistic. And they had to cope with an almost infinite variety of demands and pressures. Flexibility and resilience were the qualities needed to survive.

Any market-orientated company will face a similar variety of pressures. For example, an electronics firm like Thorn EMI, which is considering launching a new product, may have to face:

- a shift in consumer demand to a substitute product
- the aggressive launch of an almost identical product by a firm based in Taiwan

- a Japanese competitor opening up a factory in the UK
- a European consortium increasing pressure on the UK market as trade develops at an increasing rate within the Community
- problems with suppliers who cannot guarantee delivery in time

As Tom Peters says:

> Violent and accelerating change, now commonplace, will become the grist of the opportunistic winner's mill. The losers will view such confusion as a 'problem' to be 'dealt' with.[8]

Turbulence, however, although often sparked off by external events, can be internally generated. A driving, visionary top management team can impose change, as in ICL, where in 1986 the need was seen for the company to move away from designing clever computers and selling them, to talking to customers and coming up with total solutions to their problems, using the latest technology available. Such a change in philosophy can make a significant difference to the work of managers, and although in a sense a change of this nature is 'imposed', it is also managed with great care, as at ICL, to ensure that managers know what is expected of them and are committed to adopting new modes of behaviour.

Innovation also creates turbulence. New products, new markets, new technology, new organizational structures and systems all require managers to abandon their steady state and learn new ways. And it is happening all the time. Managers have to adopt variety as a way of life.

Ambiguity

As Tom Peters says, 'Predictability is a thing of the past.'

> Nothing is predictable. . . . We don't know from day to day the price of energy or money. We don't know whether protection and default will close borders, making a mess of global sourcing and trade alike, or whether global financing will open up things further. We don't know whether merging or de-merging makes more sense, and we have no idea who will be partners with whom tomorrow or next week, let alone

next month. We don't know who our competitors will be, or where they will come from.[8]

Uncertainty amongst managers about the future, often coupled with uncertainty about exactly what they are supposed to do, adds up to ambiguity. On the whole, people prefer structure. They like to know where they are, where they are going and what is expected of them. But such structured existences are seldom possible in today's conditions.

It is not only turbulence and the difficulty of knowing what is going to happen next which creates this situation. Organizations are becoming more fluid. Layers of management are being removed so that a flatter structure is created. Responsibilities overlap. Information technology means that top management can get instant data on their desk-top screen about anything that is happening anywhere in their organization. They can and do skip layers of management to go straight to the data source to ask what is happening and why. Middle managers feel superfluous. They do not know how they fit into what used to be called the chain of command.

Confusion and ambiguity is also created because of the emphasis on end results. Managers are told what they have to achieve but are often left in the dark about how to achieve it. This is not because they are being deliberately starved of information; it is rather because in turbulent and rapidly changing conditions there are often alternative means available to achieve the ends. One of the modern principles of management to have emerged from the conditions under which managers now have to operate is 'constancy towards ends but flexibility about means'. This is a necessary approach in turbulent times, but managers can often be left asking forlornly, 'Where do I go from here?' And increasingly they will be expected to answer that question themselves.

The days of long, elaborate job descriptions, spelling out in great detail exactly how managers should perform their tasks, have gone. Instead we find at most a one-sentence definition of the overall purpose or objectives of the job, followed by a list of seven or eight 'principal accountabilities', each setting out, again in one sentence, a main area of the job for which the manager will be expected to deliver results. The key words today are performance and delivery, not task or duty. This is appropriate to the prevailing conditions in most organizations, but managers have to learn to cope with ambiguity about means if not about ends. Self-reliance and self-determination are therefore very important qualities in a manager.

Ambiguity can be bad enough in the so-called 'line' jobs – that is, those such as production or sales which are dealing directly with the end product, either making it or selling it. It can be even worse in what used to be termed 'staff' jobs – that is, those jobs which exist to provide support services such as finance, personnel and data processing. (Line and staff are old military terms which are not used so much nowadays, perhaps because the distinction between them has become more blurred.) Be that as it may, there will always be some jobs where it is more difficult to measure the direct contribution of job holders to achieving the objectives of the organization.

Personnel managers in particular may have to become specialists in ambiguity, partly because of the equivocal attitudes of the line managers whom they advise and partly because they are unsure of where they stand. Ambiguity in the role of a manager in a professional function such as personnel can result in confusion between ideals and reality. There may be conflict between their beliefs and the actual conditions of organizational life to which personnel people and other specialists have to conform as 'organiz-ation' men or women.

Williamson and Ouchi[9] distinguish between 'hard' and 'soft' contracting in organizational life. In hard contracting, relationships are formalized, jobs are task-specific and legalistic interpretations are made of the employment contract. A more authoritarian or 'macho' approach to management is likely in these circumstances. In contrast, soft contracting aims to create harmonious units based on tacit understanding and a reciprocal sense of obligation. Any managers who believe in a soft-contracting approach could find themselves in a hard-contracting situation with a feeling of ambi-guity about their role and how they perform it. They may have to choose between going along with it, getting out, or quietly working against the grain (which is not easy).

Ambiguity is created by the often fragmented, variable and diversified nature of managerial work in fluid and rapidly changing organizations. Managers can learn to cope with it simply by recognizing its inevitability on a day-to-day basis and concentrating on clarifying the main goals they are expected to achieve, together with the critical success factors which determine whether these goals have been accomplished. So far as possible, they must take a strategic view of their work, which means defining the broader issues with which they are concerned. Tactics on the things they have to deal with on the spot can be flexed according to the situation, as long as they are conducted within the broad framework of a strategy which provides a sense of direction. In these circumstances, ambiguity is a short-term state and can be managed accordingly.

However, there are two other notable features of organizational life which all managers experience. These are power and politics. Sometimes they arise from ambiguity, sometimes they contribute to it. But they are always present and have to be understood by all managers if they are to cope with organizational life.

Power

Power is linked to position and rank, but in all organizations there are powerful people who are not in the upper levels of the hierarchy. The personal assistant or secretary to the chief executive is often a good example.

Power is a feature of all organizations because organizations exist to get things done, and this means the exercise of authority and authority requires the use of power.

Nietzsche said that 'power has crooked legs', but it is legitimate if it is used to pursue legitimate ends and is wielded in a responsible way by responsible people.

In his analysis of power in industry, Antony Jay comments:

> Power lies in the acceptance of your authority by others, their knowledge that if they try to resist you they will fail and you will succeed. Real power does not lie in documents etc. – it lies in what you can achieve.[10]

Most people say they seek power to achieve objects they believe in but, as Antony Jay says

The real pleasure of power is the pleasure of freedom, and it goes right back to one of man's most primitive needs, the need to control his environment.[10]

Mary Parker Follett writes:

Our task is not to learn where to plan power: it is how to develop power. Genuine power can only be grown, it will slip from every arbitrary hand.[11]

And David McClelland's studies of power in action involving over 500 managers from 25 different American corporations led him to conclude:

Managers must possess a high need for power, that is, a concern for influencing people. However, this need must be disciplined and controlled so that it is directed towards the benefit of the institution as a whole and not toward the manager's personal aggrandizement.[12]

Sources of power

Power can be legitimate, but it can be misused. It is clearly linked to position and rank although to a certain degree it has to be earned. Managers can order their subordinates about but they are going to get more out of them if they obtain their willing co-operation rather than their grudging submission.

The sources of power consist of:

- *Position.* Power is bestowed upon managers because of their position or rank in the organization. The value of the position as a source of power, as Charles Handy points out,[13] depends on the value placed upon that position within the organization.

- *Expertise.* Managers can gain and keep power if they have acknowledged expertise, or can at least convince others that they have it.

- *Control over information.* 'Knowledge is power', or alternatively 'authority goes to the one who knows'. Managers in the know are in a better position to control events. If they are playing politics they can enhance their power by withholding information, or by using the information they have to discredit others.

- *Control over resources.* Managerial power is related to the size of the resources – people, money or equipment – controlled by the job holder.

- *Control over rewards and punishments.* Managers who can influence rewards and punishments will be seen as powerful by those likely to be affected. Rewards include promotions as well as increased pay.

- *Personal power.* Individual managers can acquire and exercise power through sheer force of character. This, as Charles Handy notes, 'is the most elusive form of power, which resides in the person and in his personality, and is fanned by success and self-confidence or can evaporate in defeat'.[13]

- *Identification or persuasive power.* Managers can achieve power over others if they can persuade them to identify with what they (the managers) are doing. This is usually achieved by the exercise of personal power and it is what visionary and charismatic leaders do by enthusiasm, dedication, getting people involved and sheer force of personality.

- *Access to other people with power.* Proximity or a direct line to people with power gives anyone more scope to exert influence. Whether this is actual or only perceived, it is a source of power. This is why secretaries can exert so much influence.

- *Sense of obligation.* Managers who develop a sense of obligation by doing favours for others may be able to exert power over them by creating an expectation that the favour should be returned.

Exercising power

John Kotter[14] interviewed over 20 managers who were in a position to use power. He found that the successful ones had the following characteristics:

- They used their power openly and legitimately. They were

seen as genuine experts in their field and consistently lived up to the leadership image they built for themselves.

- They were sensitive to what types of power are most effective with different types of people. For example, experts respect expertise.

- They developed all their sources of power and did not rely too much on any particular technique.

- They sought jobs and tasks which would give them the opportunity to acquire and use power. They constantly sought ways to invest the power they already had to secure an even higher positive return.

- They used their power in a mature and self-controlled way. They seldom if ever used power impulsively or for their own aggrandizement.

- They derived satisfaction from influencing others.

Politics

Power and politics are inextricably linked. Kissinger referred to power as an aphrodisiac, and in organizations there will inevitably be people who want to achieve their satisfaction by acquiring power, legitimately or illegitimately.

To be politic, according to the Oxford English Dictionary, you can either be sagacious, prudent, judicious, expedient; or you can be scheming or crafty. So political behaviour in an organization can be desirable or undesirable.

Organizations consist of individuals who, while they are ostensibly there to achieve a common purpose, will, at the same time, be driven by their own needs to achieve their own goals. Effective management is the process of harmonizing individual endeavour and ambition to the common good. Some individuals will genuinely believe that using political means to achieve their goals will benefit the organization as well as themselves. Others will rationalize this belief. Yet others will unashamedly pursue their own ends. They may use all their powers of persuasion to legitimize these ends in the eyes of their colleagues, but self-interest remains the primary drive. These are the corporate politicians whom the Oxford

English Dictionary describes as 'shrewd schemers, crafty plotters or intriguers'. Politicians within organizations can be like this. They manoeuvre behind people's backs, blocking proposals they do not like. They advance their own reputation and career at the expense of other people's. They can be envious and jealous and act accordingly. They are bad news.

But it can also be argued that a political approach to management is inevitable and even desirable in any organization where the clarity of goals is not absolute, where the decision-making process is not clear-cut and where the authority to make decisions is not evenly or appropriately distributed. And there can be few organizations where one or more of these conditions do not apply.

Andrew Kakabadse recognises this point when he says, 'Politics is a process, that of influencing individuals and groups of people to your point of view, where you cannot rely on authority.'[15] In this sense, a political approach can be legitimate as long as the ends are justifiable from the view-point of the organization.

Kakabadse identifies seven approaches that organizational politicians adopt.

1 Identify the stakeholders, those who have a commitment to act in a particular way.

2 Keep the stakeholders comfortable, concentrating on behaviour, values, attitudes, fears and drives that the individuals will accept, tolerate and manage (comfort zones).

3 Fit the image – work on the comfort zones and align their image to that of the people with power.

4 Use the network – identify the interest groups and people of influence.

5 Enter the network – identify the gatekeepers, adhere to the norms.

6 Make deals – agree to support other people where this is a mutual benefit.

7 Withhold and withdraw – withhold information as appropriate and withdraw judiciously when the going gets rough.

Some of these precepts are more legitimate than others. Organizational life requires managers to identify the key decision makers when they are involved in developing new approaches and getting things done. Before coming to a final conclusion and launching a fully fledged proposal at a committee or in a memorandum, it makes good sense to test opinion and find out how other people may react. This testing process enables managers to anticipate counter-arguments and modify their proposals either to meet legitimate objections or, when there is no alternative, to accommodate other people's requirements.

Making deals may not appear to be particularly desirable, but it does happen, and managers can always rationalize this type of behaviour by reference to the end result. Withholding information is not legitimate behaviour, but people do indulge in it in recognition of the fact that knowledge is power. Judicious withdrawal may also seem to be questionable, but most managers prefer to live to fight another day rather than launch a doomed crusade.

The danger of politics, however, is that it may be carried to excess, and it can then seriously harm the effectiveness of an organization. The signs of excessive indulgence in political behaviour include:

- back-biting
- buck-passing
- secret meetings and hidden decisions
- feuds between people and departments
- paper wars between armed camps – arguing by memoranda, always a sign of distrust
- a multiplicity of snide comments and criticisms
- excessive and counter-productive lobbying
- the formation of cabals – cliques which spend their time intriguing.

One way to deal with this sort of behaviour is to find out who is doing it and openly confront them with the damage they are doing. They will, of course, deny that they are behaving politically (they wouldn't be politicians if they didn't) but the fact that they have been identified might lead them to modify their approach. It could, of course, only serve to drive them further underground, in which case their behaviour will have to be observed even more closely and corrective action taken as necessary.

A more positive approach to keeping politics operating at an acceptable level is for the organization to manage its operations as openly as possible. The aims would be to ensure that issues are debated fully, that differences of opinion are dealt with frankly and that disagreements are de-personalized, so far as this is possible. Political processes can then be seen as a way of maintaining the momentum of the organization as a complex decision-making and problem-solving entity.

References

1   LAWRENCE Paul and LORSCH Jay. *Developing organizations: diagnosis and action*. Reading, Mass., Addison-Wesley, 1969

2   SILVERMAN D. *The theory of organizations: a sociological framework*. London, Heinemann, 1970

3   WOODWARD Joan. *Management and technology*. London, Her Majesty's Stationery Office, 1958

4   BURNS T. and STALKER G. M. *The management of innovation*. London, Tavistock Publications, 1961

5   LUPTON Tom. 'Best fit in the design of organizations'. *Personnel Review*, vol 4, no 1, 1975

6   TRIST E. L. *Organizational choice*. London, Tavistock Publications, 1963

7   KANTER Rosabeth Moss. *The change masters*. London, Allen and Unwin, 1984

8   PETERS Tom. *Thriving on chaos*. London, Macmillan, 1988

9   WILLIAMSON E. E. and OUCHI W. C. 'The markets and hierarchies programme of research: origins, implications and prospects' *in* FRANCIS A., TURK J. and WILLMAR P. *eds. Power, efficiency and institutions*. London, Heinemann, 1983

10 JAY Antony. *Management and Machiavelli*. London, Hodder & Stoughton, 1967

11 FOLLETT Mary Parker. *Dynamic administration*. London, Pitman, 1941

12 McCLELLAND David and BURNHAM David. 'Power, the great motivator'. *Harvard Business Review*. March–April 1976

13   HANDY Charles. *Understanding organizations.* Harmondsworth, Penguin, 1985
14   KOTTER John. 'Power, dependence and effective management'. *Harvard Business Review.* July–August, 1971
15   KAKABADSE Andrew. *The politics of management.* Aldershot, Gower, 1983

4

Management Processes

As we have seen in the last two chapters, managers carry out their work on a day-to-day basis in conditions of endless variety, turbulence, unpredictability and ambiguity. A single word to describe all these features would be chaos. Tom Peters[1] has suggested that it is possible for managers to thrive on chaos. His prescriptions for a 'world turned upside down' include:

- creating total customer responsiveness
- pursuing fast-paced innovation
- achieving flexibility by empowering people
- learning to love change by a new view of leadership at all levels
- building systems which measure what is important, and decentralise information, authority and strategic planning.

These involve, directly or indirectly, the basic management processes as defined by the classical theorists: planning, organizing, motivating and controlling. To create order out of chaos the classical prescription still has relevance today. Its relevance exists not because it describes how managers actually spend their time but because it indicates the key areas to which they have to give attention as required by future demands or immediate pressures.

The management processes can help to provide a framework within which managers can operate. When looking ahead or dealing with current events they have from time to time to answer questions like these:

- Where do we go from here?
- How do we get there?

- Who does what if we are going to manage the existing situation effectively and make progress?

- How can we get people into action, delivering what the organization requires?

- How should we measure achievements, monitor progress and get ourselves into the situation where we can take swift corrective action wherever necessary?

The answers to these questions are provided by the processes described in this chapter, namely planning, organizing, directing and controlling.

Planning

Winston Churchill once said, 'It is wise to plan ahead but only as far as you can see.' Planning is not a panacea which will eliminate unforeseeable as well as foreseeable problems. The capacity for even large organizations in fairly steady-state conditions to plan more than two or three years in advance for normal operations, as distinct from long-term development or construction projects, is severely limited. The planning horizon for many managers may be restricted to months, weeks or even days.

However, even with a very restricted horizon, it is a useful exercise for managers at the beginning of the week, or the day, to list the things that they have to do and to spend five minutes thinking about actions to be taken, problems to be solved, decisions to be made and the priorities that should be attached to these activities. It doesn't matter that later in the week or day all sorts of things will be thrown at the manager – there is at least a framework within which these activities can be fitted. The plan provides a basis for operations. It may have to be modified constantly but at least the modifications can be made by reference to a defined state so that their significance as deviations can be measured and actions tailored accordingly.

For example, a distribution manager in a large book warehouse will have print-outs in front of him at the start of the day showing the space available for storage and where expected deliveries will be slotted. Because deliveries are not entirely predictable, a massive order may arrive on that same day, one day earlier than anticipated. The initial disposition plan will have to be changed, but the fact that it existed will make the changes easier to implement.

The planning that takes place at corporate level is often called strategic or long-term planning and is dealt with in Chapter 18.

Planning activities

The eight planning activities that managers carry out are

1 Forecasting:

- what sort of work has to be done, how much and by when
- how the workload might change
- the likelihood of the department being called on to undertake specialized or rush jobs
- possible changes within or outside the department which might affect priorities, the activities carried out or the workload

2 Programming – deciding the sequence and time-scale of operations and events required to produce results on time

3 Staffing – deciding how many and what type of staff are needed and considering the feasibility of absorbing peak loads by means of overtime or temporary staff

4 Setting standards and targets – for output, sales, times, quality, costs or any other aspect of the work where performance should be planned, measured and controlled

5 Procedure planning – deciding how the work should be done and planning the actual operations by defining the systems and procedures required

6 Materials planning – deciding what materials, bought-in parts or subcontracted work are required and ensuring that they are made available in the right quantity at the right time

7 Facilities planning – deciding on the plant, equipment, tools and space required

8 Budgeting

Planning techniques

Most of the planning managers do is simply a matter of thinking systematically and using their common sense. Every plan contains five key ingredients:

- objective – the innovation or improvement to be achieved
- financial impact – the effect of the action on sales, turnover, costs, and, ultimately, profit
- action programme – the specific steps required to achieve the right objective
- responsibility – who takes the action
- time-scale and completion date

A production manager, for example, might develop the following plan:

1 *Objective* – to reduce the frequency and cost of faulty castings received from a supplier

2 *Programme, responsibility and time-scale*

Steps	*Action*	*Completion by*
(a) Ensure recognition by supplier of problem with 'hard spots' in castings	Purchasing Manager Production Manager	15 January
(b) Negotiate price concession on all castings received during weeks when more than ten bad castings have to be returned	Purchasing Manager	31 January
(c) Set up storage area to accommodate ruined castings	Facilities Manager	15 February
(d) Establish procedures to record machine downtime and cutter breakage with individual castings	Production Controller	1 March

3 *Financial impact* – cost per unit of output reduced by £x

Organizing

Managers have to develop an organization which effectively gets the work done. This means defining responsibilities, building structures and developing relationships. The essential element is people: what they do and how they work together.

Because fluidity and flexibility are becoming increasingly the norm, organizations are not static things. Most organization manuals and charts are out of date as soon as they have been produced. But the fact that managers are in a constant state of flux does not mean that they should not give continuous attention to who does what.

Many managers will work within a given structure. Apparently they have little scope to organize or reorganize it. But this could be an illusion. There is almost always some room for reallocating responsibilities, and this may be forced on managers by changing circumstances.

Basic approach to organization design

The basic approach to organization design is to:

- define what the organization exists to do – its purpose and objectives
- analyse and identify the activities or tasks required to meet those objectives
- allocate related activities to individual job holders
- group related activities logically into organizational unity
- provide for the management and co-ordination of the activities at each level of responsibility
- establish reporting and communicating relationships

For example, as general manager of a direct-mail publishing company, I was given the responsibility of setting up a new division which would sell books direct to members of the public. Plans were made defining objectives, setting targets and budgets and

allocating responsibility for launching the operation. The next
stage was to decide on the organization. This involved:

- defining the role of the general sales managers
- defining the role of the agents who would carry out the direct
  selling
- deciding on the field management structure – dividing the
  country into regions, areas and districts, and defining the
  responsibilities of managers at each level
- deciding on the headquarters staff required – marketing,
  distribution, buying, finance, personnel – and defining their
  responsibilities
- establishing a basis for co-ordinating and controlling operations
  through regular meetings and reporting systems.

The process of developing an organization as described above and
in more detail in Chapter 15 produces a defined and understandable
framework within which people can operate and the process of
direction as described below can take place. But managers will
still have to cope with the day-to-day turbulence, variety and
stress which cannot be covered by the definitions contained in
organization manuals or job descriptions. Organization charts as
described in Chapter 15 do no more than indicate the main
reporting relationships. They do not convey how communications
and co-ordination actually take place. And job descriptions can
never cover all that managers are expected to do. In fact, they
should not attempt to do so.

Direction

Managers exist to achieve objectives which will contribute to the
attainment of the overall mission and goals of the organization.
To do this they have to direct operations, and therefore people,
towards meeting these requirements. Providing a sense of direction
is a key managerial task, to which must be added ensuring that
people move towards the desired goal – motivation. If managers
know where they are going they are more likely to get there, even

if the route is rough and indistinct and they are plagued with new demands and changing circumstances. This may seem to be a remarkably obvious statement, but it is an equally remarkable fact that a very large proportion of managers when asked what their greatest problem is will reply, 'I don't know where I stand and I don't know where I am going.'

The aim of the directing process is to achieve the results expected by creating order out of chaos. The order consists of a broad understanding amongst the manager's staff of what is expected of them in order to provide a datum line or point of reference for all their activities.

Directing involves exercising leadership, motivating staff, clarifying accountabilities and developing policies and procedures as guidelines for action.

Direction through leadership

Direction involves leadership. Charismatic leaders sweep aside their followers' doubts and problems about their daily tasks by inspiring them with a vision of what is to be achieved. But effective leaders do not necessarily have to be highly charismatic. Non-charismatic leaders who rely on their know-how, their ability to give an impression of quiet confidence and their cool, analytical approach to solving problems can be equally, if not more, effective in some situations. Such leaders can be described as enablers and empowerers. They provide the right sort of guidance, they give people scope to act and they ensure that their staff have the skills and knowledge to achieve their tasks. They encourage their staff to participate and they spend a lot of time generating commitment to achieving objectives. Leadership skills are covered in Chapter 5.

Direction through motivation

Direction also involves motivation, getting people to move in the right direction and to do what they are expected to do, and more. Motivation is dealt with in more detail in Chapter 5.

But direction is also very much about making sure that people know what they are there to do as part of an organization which exists to achieve a defined purpose, and this involves defining accountabilities.

Accountability statements

An accountability statement sets out what the job holder is expected to achieve. It defines objectives and indicates the results for which he or she will be held to account. It is a useful management tool, not only as a means of setting goals and standards of performance, but also as a basis for comparing the results individuals attain with the objectives they have been set. Again, in turbulent times, they can act as a point of reference and can help in developing an orderly approach to problem solving and decision making.

Accountability statements are dynamic affairs, concerned with objectives and goals rather than static definitions of various 'duties' which are contained in traditional job descriptions. Thus an accountability statement for a sales manager would emphasise that he or she is accountable for developing and managing the field sales force to achieve targeted sales figures within the agreed budget and to generate the required contribution to profit and overhead recovery. The statement would not describe how the sales manager deals with key accounts, deploys sales representatives and motivates them. That is up to the individual, within the framework of company policies and procedures on such matters as sales force remuneration.

The process of managing oneself in the changing conditions typical of most managerial jobs is enhanced if you can make sure that you understand your own accountabilities as well as agreeing accountabilities with your subordinates. And there is no excuse for sitting around and bewailing the fact that 'no one tells me what is expected of me'. Good managers do not wait until they are told. They find out for themselves.

Policies

Policies are guidelines for decision making and action. They indicate what people can or cannot do in certain situations. They do not *have* to be written down.

To manage yourself effectively you have to be aware of the policies that affect your work. You have to establish what guidelines exist to help you deal with eventualities. Again, you do not wait to be told – you find them out for yourself. If you are constantly faced with awkward situations in which you are having to make *ad hoc* decisions it is up to you to formulate a policy which will help to smooth over the difficulties and, when necessary, seek approval for your approach from higher authority. You also owe it to your subordinates to guide them on any policies that they can refer to when making decisions in new or changing circumstances.

Procedures

Procedures simply set out the way things should be done. They define activities such as how expense claims should be prepared, the rules for engaging temporary staff, the sequence of actions to be taken when preparing and conducting a market test, the method by which design modifications are incorporated in process plans and operation sequences, or the methods of operating a planned or preventive maintenance programme.

In a process plant or a highly bureaucratic office environment, procedures will be very detailed, even rigid. And this might be appropriate when the circumstances demand that deviations from the norm should be minimized. This would undoubtedly apply in such operations as the manufacture of nuclear fuels or the processing of insurance claims. In contrast, a research laboratory working at the frontiers of knowledge might restrict its written procedures to such purely administrative matters as the procurement of equipment and materials. The scientists would have to be left to get on with their innovative work as free from bureaucratic routines as possible.

In managing yourself, it is up to you to familiarize yourself with relevant procedures which should, if they are good ones, help you to get on with your work by facilitating administrative routines. You can also institute procedures for your staff, always taking care not to inhibit their initiative by hedging them round with bureaucratic regulations.

Controlling

Controlling involves measuring and monitoring performance, comparing results with plans and taking corrective action when required.

Effective control recognizes that a steady progression towards the achievement of a plan is something that seldom happens. In the endemic states of turbulence and change which most managers live in, Murphy's law applies – 'If anything can go wrong, it will.' Deviation from the plan is inevitable and can even be desirable.

Control is relative. It does not deal with absolutes, only with the difference between planned and actual performance.

The basis of control is measurement. It depends on accurate information about what is happening compared with what should be happening. It restores order in chaotic situations by forcing managers to recognize how far they are deviating from the norm. The deviation may be one they have to live with but at least they know what they are doing. If the monitoring process reveals an adverse deviation then corrective action can be taken in good time.

Effective control

To exercise effective control managers need to:

- *Plan* what they aim to achieve
- *Measure* regularly what has been achieved
- *Compare* actual achievements with the plan
- *Take action* to exploit opportunities revealed by this information, or to correct deviations from the plan.

Note that control is not only a matter of putting things right. It also has a positive side – getting more or better things done on the basis of information received.

For example, a retail company launching a new product may well test it in a selected number of stores. Sales will be monitored carefully to assess performance and research will be carried out on customer reactions. This control information will be used to make any adjustments to packaging, pricing policies or merchandising (display) in order to build on successes or to overcome failings. On a continuing basis, when the product is fully launched, the company will monitor sales in each area and store and decide whether or not the product should continue to be sold and, if it is continued, whether or not any changes in marketing methods, such as additional point-of-sale advertising, should be adopted.

As a manager you will be given total responsibility for all that happens within your command. You cannot delegate that responsibility. But you will not have the time to monitor everything that goes on. You are primarily interested in results, not in the detail of how those results have been achieved. This is why you should try to manage by exception as far as possible. This means getting 'exception reports' which emphasise deviations or variances from the plan and therefore alert you to areas where action needs to be taken. Exception reporting, however, does not absolve you from generally monitoring progress towards an objective so that you can either relax (for a moment or two) or initiate action which will anticipate a future problem. The process of delegation and its control is discussed in more detail in Chapter 6.

On an individual basis, you will need to monitor your own performance against objectives or standards that have been set for you or, in their absence, those that you have set for yourself and your team. Any self-set objectives or standards must, of course, be defined within the context of the goals, strategies and plans which affect your work. But, as I have said, good managers are there to use their initiative: in this case, to develop their own performance standards if they have not been given any.

The Orderly Approach to Managing Chaos

The various processes described in this chapter constitute no more and no less than an orderly and disciplined approach to the management of variety, uncertainty, ambiguity and change. They provide the basis for adopting a consistent method of dealing with problems. Alternatively, if events enforce inconsistency, the processes at least identify the extent of the deviation so that managers are fully aware of what they are doing and why, and can justify their actions if they have to.

As I said in Chapter 2, managers spend most of their time dealing with immediate events. They do not consciously divide their day into distinct planning, organizing, directing and controlling segments. They will find that they are carrying out these processes as and when required, and they will often overlap.

But to maintain momentum in the direction they need to go, managers must from time to time deliberately sit back and make or review plans, reconsider the way in which they organize their work, decide what needs to be done to clarify accountabilities or to increase motivation or commitment, and monitor progress towards goals by reference to control information, by talking to people or by directly checking on work in progress.

These processes provide the framework within which managers exercise their skills to deal with the 'here and now' in all its variety, as we shall see in the next chapter.

Reference

1   PETERS Tom. *Thriving on chaos*. London, Macmillan, 1988

5

Managerial Practices and Skills

Managerial skills are the skills that managers need to carry out their day-to-day work of getting things done, either themselves or through other people. They include objective setting, co-ordinating, problem solving, decision making, creative thinking, clear thinking, leadership, and motivation. All these are dealt with in this chapter. They also include time management, delegation, communication and the interpersonal skills of influencing, counselling and assertiveness which are covered in Chapters 6–8.

Management skills depend on personal expertise and are developed by experience and practical training. They cannot be acquired from books. All that I can do here is provide some basic hints which help the process of learning from experience.

Managerial skills should be distinguished from:

- *management techniques*, which are the systematic and analytical methods, such as production control, marketing research, cost-volume-profit analysis, job evaluation and operational research, which are used by managers to assist in decision making, and in planning and control

- *procedures*, which consist of the various administrative tasks, systems and guidelines needed to get work done – for example the way in which sales orders are processed is a procedure

- *activities or functions*, in which various related tasks are carried out using management processes, techniques, procedures and skills in order to achieve a desired result: for example advertising, recruitment and purchasing.

51

Objective Setting

As I said in the previous chapter, making sure that managers know where they are going and convey this sense of direction to their teams is an important method of producing order out of chaos.

Peter Drucker writes, 'Objectives are needed in every area where performance and results directly and vitally affect the management of the business.'[1] Objectives enable management to explain, predict, direct and control activities in ways in which single ideas like profit maximisation do not. More specifically, objectives:

- help managers to explain what they are setting out to do and achieve in a small number of specific statements which emphasise the results or outputs required

- allow the testing of these statements in actual performance

- enable decisions to be examined while they are still being made rather than after they have been implemented

- help to improve future performance by the analysis of past experience

The objectives for individual managers should be set within the context of those for the organization and their department. Organizational objectives are considered in Chapter 18.

Individual objectives

Managers will be in a better position to plan and monitor their work if they have clear objectives which are agreed with their bosses. And, given an overall objective for the organization or unit, they should be capable of determining their own unit, section or individual objectives without detailed guidance from above. These sub-objectives must, of course, be agreed by the manager's superior because they will form the basis for monitoring performance. But they should not be imposed on managers without providing them with the opportunity to work out the objectives for themselves.

The same principle applies between managers and the individual members of their staff. The latter will be more effective if they understand and accept their objectives, and they should be given the maximum opportunity to decide what those objectives are, although some guidance may be necessary.

Setting objectives

The following are guidelines for setting objectives:

- The objective should be attainable, but not too easily. It is important to set 'stretch' objectives which demand higher levels of performance.
- The objective should support the achievement of higher-level objectives and should be translatable into sub-objectives.
- Overall objectives for the job holder should be set, but these may be divided into subsidiary objectives for each key result area.
- It should be possible to measure whether or not the objective has been achieved. As far as possible this should be in quantifiable terms, as long as the figures are realistic and meaningful. An objective can also be defined as a task to be achieved by a certain date. Where objectives cannot be quantified or expressed as a task to be achieved, an attempt should be made to define a standard of performance which will indicate when a job has been well done.
- Managers should encourage their subordinates to set their own objectives for discussion.
- Every attempt should be made to ensure that there is full agreement between the manager and his or her subordinate on what the latter's objectives are.
- Objectives should set out not only what has to be achieved but also:
  - critical success factors
  - performance indicators
  - arrangements for monitoring progress and feedback
  - arrangements for interim and final reviews
- The objective-setting and review system should not generate too much paperwork.

Examples of objective headings

General Manager	*Works Manager*	*Sales Manager*
Profitability	Achievement of factory output targets	Achievement of sales targets
Volume and growth business	Control of costs	Contribution to profits and fixed overheads
Provision and utilization of fixed assets	Utilization of plant and machinery	Development of new accounts
Provision and utilization of current assets	Control of stocks	Extension of existing business
Product innovation	Product quality	Customer satisfaction
Customer satisfaction	Labour productivity	Identification of new products
Operating costs	Industrial relations	Introduction of new products
Management effectiveness	Management effectiveness	Effectiveness of sales force
Employee productivity and attitude	Safety	Control of costs

Example of an objective for a sales manager – development of new accounts

- *Objective*: to acquire x new accounts by y
- *Critical success factors*
  - New accounts must be in outlets with an estimated turnover of not less than £x per annum.
  - The accounts should have potential to achieve within one year sales of at least £y per annum.

- The accounts should be capable of being serviced economically.
- There should be no risk of bad debt (as far as this can be assessed).
- *Performance indicators*
  - number of accounts acquired
  - actual and projected turnover and contribution from these outlets
- *Monitoring arrangements*: progress reports to be submitted monthly.
- *Review arrangements*: formal review to take place quarterly.

Example of a standard of performance for a training manager

Performance is up to standard if training and development programmes are prepared and implemented which satisfy identified and relevant needs within agreed budgets.

Co-ordinating

Co-ordinating is the process of achieving unity of effort. It is necessary because individual actions need to be synchronized and some activities must follow one another in sequence. Others must go on at the same time and in the same direction to finish together and achieve the overall task.

The process of co-ordination

Good co-ordination is primarily a matter of getting individuals to collaborate well with one another. This is more likely to be attained by:

- exercising leadership which emphasises the common task and the need for everyone to work well together. Visionary leaders have the gift of setting what are called super-ordinate goals (those that are greater than the sum of the parts that contribute to them) and gaining commitment and enthusiasm to achieving them.

- team-building activities which help people to work together more effectively. Team building can be developed through training courses which get groups to analyse how well or badly the team functions and practise methods of improving cohesion and co-operation.

- effective communication systems which ensure that both vertical and lateral channels of communication function well.

Co-ordinating techniques

The main co-ordinating techniques are:

- *Planning.* Co-ordination should take place before things are done, rather than afterwards. This means first deciding what should be done and when. It is then a process of dividing the total task into a number of sequenced or related sub-tasks and working out priorities and time-scales. Network systems which analyse the component parts of a project or task and assess the sequential relationships between each event can be used to assist in planning projects or complicated activities.

- *Organizing.* When setting up or amending an organization process, care has to be taken to group related activities together to facilitate co-ordination. It is necessary to avoid dividing tasks which are closely linked together and which cannot be separated clearly from one another.

- *Delegating.* In delegating work it is necessary to ensure that staff are aware of the need to co-ordinate their activities with those carried out in other departments, or by other individuals in the same department. You should delegate not only specific tasks but also the job of working with others.

- *Communicating.* You should make sure that your communication network and systems enable individuals in your team to synchronize, sequence and link their activities properly. You should make an effort to keep in touch with any events and activities elsewhere which impinge on your responsibilities. Managers who fail to find out what they should know cannot plead ignorance – it is no excuse.

- *Controlling.* However carefully co-ordination is planned and organized there will inevitably be times when work becomes unsynchronized or activities are not linked or sequenced. To minimize this risk, it is essential to monitor actions and results continually in order to spot problems and take swift corrective steps as necessary. However, this must be done with a light touch. You should avoid 'breathing down people's necks' and inhibiting initiative and action.

Problem Solving and Decision Making

Effective problem solving and decision making require the following ten stages:

1   *Define the situation.* Establish what is needed, or what has gone wrong or is about to go wrong.

2   *Specify objectives.* Define what you are setting out to achieve now or in the future as you deal with an actual or potential problem or a change in circumstances.

3   *Develop hypotheses.* If you have a problem, develop ideas about the cause.

4   *Get the facts.* In order to provide a basis for testing hypotheses and developing possible courses of action, find out what is happening now and/or what is likely to happen in the future. If different people are involved, get both sides of the story and, where possible, check with a third party. Obtain written evidence wherever relevant. Do not rely on hearsay.

   Define what is supposed to be happening in terms of policies, procedures or results and compare this with what is actually happening. Try to understand the attitudes and motivations of those concerned. Remember that people will see what has happened or is happening in terms of their own position. Obtain information about internal or external constraints affecting the situation.

5   *Analyse the facts.* Determine what is relevant and what is irrelevant. Establish the cause or causes of the problem. Do not be tempted to concentrate on symptoms rather than causes.

6   *List factors.* Establish what factors impinge on the problem and may affect the decision.

7   *Consider possible courses of action.* List the possible courses of action in the light of the factual analysis. Where appropriate, use brainstorming and creative thinking techniques to identify courses of action which may not be immediately evident.

8   *Evaluate possible courses of action.* Consider the possibilities, listing pros and cons and comparing anticipated results with your specified objectives. Evaluate the immediate and future consequences both inside and outside the organization. Compare costs with benefits. Assess how far the needs of those involved will be met and the extent to which your decisions will be acceptable. Consider the risk of creating dangerous precedents. Consider also the implications of any internal or external constraints that might exist.

   Ensure that all concerned participate in the evaluating and decision-making process. Note, however, that the degree of participation will depend on the nature of the problem and the participation procedures and management style of the organization.

9   *Decide and implement.* Decide which, on balance, is the preferred course of action, and discuss it with those concerned. Consider carefully how the decision is likely to affect them. Decide on the method of presentation, giving the reasons for the decision and, so far as possible, allaying any fears. Before implementing the decision ensure that everyone who needs it gets the relevant information.

10 *Monitor implementation.* Check on how effectively the decision is being implemented. Obtain the reactions of those affected. Take corrective action where necessary.

Problem solving as described above is an analytical and logical approach which requires the use of clear thinking. But some problems are so fundamentally new that the normal logical approach may be unproductive. You therefore have to judge whether or not a more creative approach is required when identifying or evaluating alternative courses of action (Step 7). This is where creative or lateral thinking may be required.

Clear Thinking

Clear thinking is logical thinking. It is a process of reasoning whereby one judgement is derived from another and correct conclusions are drawn from the evidence. Clear thinking is analytical: sifting information, selecting what is relevant and establishing and proving relationships. It is sometimes called vertical thinking, following the sequence 'if A, therefore B, if B therefore C' and so on.

Clear thinking is a matter of developing and testing propositions and avoiding the use of fallacious or misleading arguments.

Developing propositions

A proposition which is used as the basis for a decision or argument must be founded on:

- facts that are relevant to the issues
- comparisons of like with like
- trends which are related to an appropriate base date and, when they are being compared, refer to the same base
- fact rather than opinion, unless the latter is supported by reliable evidence
- deep analysis of the situation where appropriate – nothing should be taken for granted
- inferences which are drawn directly from the facts. If there is more than one inference, each one should be tested to establish which most clearly derives from the evidence.

Testing propositions

When testing propositions you should answer the following questions:

- Was the scope of the investigation sufficiently comprehensive?
- Are the instances representative or are they selected to support a point of view?

- Are there contradictory instances that have not been identified?

- Does the proposition or belief in question conflict with other beliefs for which we have equally good grounds?

- If there are any conflicting beliefs or contradictory items of evidence, have they been put to the test against the original proposition?

- Could the evidence or testimony lead to other equally valid conclusions?

- Are there any other factors which have not been taken into account which may have influenced the evidence and, therefore, the conclusion?

Fallacious or misleading arguments

A fallacy is an unusual form of argument leading to a mistake in reasoning. The main fallacies to avoid or to spot in other people's arguments are:

- *Sweeping statements*, based on oversimplification or the selection of favourable instances and the avoidance of unfavourable instances

- *Potted thinking*, which happens when we use slogans and catch-phrases in our arguments or extend a simplistic assertion in an unwarrantable fashion

- *Special pleading*, stressing only one's own case and ignoring any other point of view

- *Oversimplification*, demanding that a sharp line be drawn, when in fact no sharp line can be drawn

- *Reaching false conclusions*, assuming that because *some* are, *all* are. An assertion which may be true of one or two cases is twisted into an assertion which extends it to all cases. False conclusions are drawn when it is forgotten that circumstances can alter cases.

- *Begging the question*. We beg the question when we take for granted what has yet to be proved. Challenging assumptions is a necessary part of clear thinking. Challenge your own assumptions as well as those of other people.

- *Chop logic*, or the use of debating tricks such as:
  - selecting instances favourable to a contention while ignoring those that conflict with it
  - twisting an argument advanced by an opponent to mean something quite different from what was intended – putting words in someone's mouth
  - diverting an opponent by throwing on him the burden of proving something he has not maintained
  - deliberately ignoring the point in dispute
  - introducing irrelevant matter into the argument
  - reiterating what has been denied and ignoring what has been asserted
  - not answering the question as posed.

Creative Thinking

Logical or vertical thinking may result in a good decision but it will not necessarily result in an imaginative decision. Change and turbulence often demand a more creative approach which involves the use of lateral thinking. To break away and generate new ideas you need to:

- identify the ideas, constraints and assumptions that dominate your thinking

- ask yourself if these are valid in the situation you are now in

- keep on asking 'why?'

- challenge assumptions

- keep on asking 'is there another way?'

- reject either/or propositions, and ask if there is really a simple choice between alternatives

- look at the situation differently, exploring all possible angles

- list as many solutions as possible without seeking the 'one best way' – there is no such thing

- arrange discontinuity by setting out to break the mould, using techniques for triggering off new ideas such as:
  - free thinking, allowing your mind to wander over alternative

and in many cases apparently irrelevant, ways of looking at the situation
- deliberately exposing yourself to new influences in the form of people, articles, books, indeed anything which might give you a different insight, even though it might not be immediately relevant
- switching yourself or other people from problem to problem
- arranging for the cross-fertilization of ideas with other people
- using analogies to spark off ideas. The analogy should be suggested by the problem but should then be allowed to exist in its own right to indicate a different way of looking at the problem.

Leadership

The leader's role

Leaders have to do two things. They must:

1 *Achieve the task* – that is why they and their group exist. The role of a leader is to ensure that the group's purpose is fulfilled. If it is not, the result is frustration, disharmony, criticism and, eventually, perhaps, disintegration of the group. This is sometimes called the 'initiating structure' dimension of leadership.

2 *Maintain effective relationships* – between themselves and the group and the people in it, and within the group itself. These relationships are effective if they are conducive to achieving the task. They can be divided into those concerned with the team and its morale and sense of common purpose, and those concerned with the individuals in the team and how they are motivated. This is sometimes referred to as the 'maintenance' function of leadership.

Leadership qualities

John Adair[2] quotes the following ranking of the 12 attributes rated most valuable at the top level of management by successful chief executives:

1   Decisiveness
2   Leadership
3   Integrity
4   Enthusiasm
5   Imagination
6   Willingness to work hard
7   Analytical ability
8   Understanding of others
9   Ability to spot opportunities
10 Ability to meet unpleasant situations
11 Ability to adapt quickly to change
12 Willingness to take risks.

One of the problems with this sort of list is that the qualities are often difficult to define. John Adair points out that another survey of 75 top executives revealed that the definition of dependability included 147 different concepts.

Another difficulty is that the qualities may have to be used in different ways in different circumstances and they need to be deployed judiciously. For example, consistency is a good thing if it means that people know where they stand, don't get unpleasant surprises from your decisions and think that you act fairly. But paying excessive homage to the principle of consistency can lead to inflexibility and being over-predictable.

Types of leaders

Leaders can be classified into the following types:

1   *Charismatic/non-charismatic.* Charismatic leaders rely on their auras, personalities and inspirational qualities. These are natural characteristics, although experience may have taught them how best to project themselves. Non-charismatic leaders rely mainly on their know-how, their ability to give an impression of quiet confidence and their cool, analytical approach to dealing with problems.

2   *Autocratic/democratic.* Autocratic leaders impose their decisions and surround themselves with yes-men. They use their position to force people to do what they are told.

Democratic leaders encourage people to participate and involve themselves in decision making. They will exert their authority to get things done but will rely more on know-how and persuasive ability than the use of position power.

3   *The visionary/enabler and the controller/manipulator.*
Visionary/enablers are the true leaders, inspiring people with their vision of the future and encouraging them to participate and to generate commitment. In contrast, the controller/manipulators are administrators who are concerned essentially with operating the internal system and treating their subordinates with thinly disguised contempt.

Leadership skills

The types of skills leaders use are those required to satisfy the needs of the task, the group and the individuals in the group.
    To satisfy task needs you should:

- Know where you are going. You convey your vision of what you want to do and your enthusiasm for it; you define precisely the objectives of the assignment.

- Know how you are going to get there. You structure your team appropriately and make and communicate clear plans for achieving your objectives.

- Know what you expect each member of your team to achieve. You ensure that work programmes, targets and standards of performance are clearly defined and understood by all concerned.

- Know what you are doing. You deal with problems decisively as they occur, progress the completion of the task in accordance with the programme, adapt the task as necessary, and provide the expertise and guidance the less experienced members of the team need.

To satisfy group needs you should:

- involve the group in agreeing objectives and reviewing results

- ensure that communications flow freely between all members of the team

- encourage informal meetings and contacts between members

- take steps to resolve unnecessary conflict but recognize that differences of opinion, if sensibly discussed, can be productive

- be approachable but maintain sufficient distance from the group to be able to use your authority when the occasion demands it.

To satisfy individual needs you should develop your motivating skills.

Motivating

Managers need motivating skills to be able to persuade individuals to work more effectively and wholeheartedly in achieving the organization's goals as well as their own. Motivating skills are best developed and used against the background of an understanding of the process of motivation and the two theories of motivation which are most relevant to the practice of management – expectancy theory and goal theory.

The process of motivation

Well-motivated people are those who have clearly defined goals which will satisfy their needs and who take the necessary action to achieve the goals. Every individual has his or her own particular needs which, as Maslow[3] suggests, will basically be to survive, and will then progress through the higher orders of safety, social and esteem needs until the ultimate level of self-fulfilment need is reached. As one need is satisfied, another takes its place because, as Maslow says, 'Man is a wanting animal.'

According to Herzberg,[4] some needs such as achievement and recognition are positive motivators, while others, such as pay and working conditions (the 'hygiene' factors), can demotivate if they are not satisfactory, but will not motivate positively for long, even if they are satisfying.

Expectancy theory

Expectancy theory, as developed by Porter and Lawler,[5] suggests that the following factors will influence effective effort and therefore performance:

1   The value of rewards to individuals in so far as they satisfy their needs

2   Their expectations about the extent to which their efforts will produce a worthwhile reward

3   Their ability

4   Their perceptions about their role, which are good from the point of view of the organization if they correspond with what it thinks individuals ought to be doing. They are poor if the views of individuals and the organization do not coincide.

Figure 4
Expectancy theory model

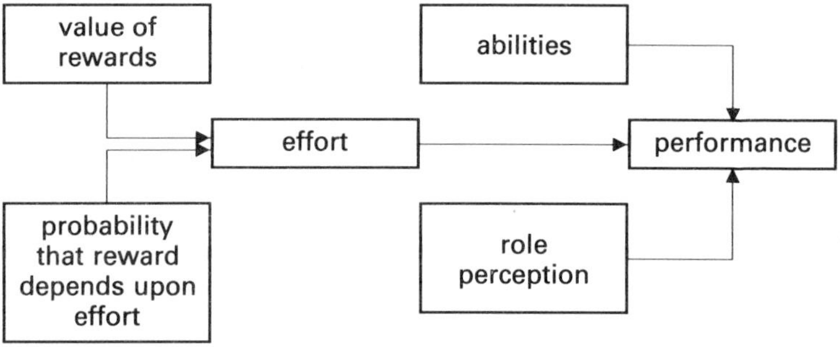

Goal theory

Goal theory, as developed by Locke,[6] states that motivation and performance will be higher when:

●   individuals are set specific goals

●   goals are difficult but accepted

- participation between managers and subordinates takes place as a means of getting agreement to the setting of higher goals

- the agreement of difficult goals is reinforced by guidance and advice

- there is feedback on performance to maintain motivation, particularly towards reaching even higher goals.

Motivating skills

Motivating skills are based on the combined messages of expectancy and goal theory. The following approaches should be used:

1 Set and agree demanding goals.

2 Provide feedback on performance.

3 Create expectations that certain behaviours and outputs will produce worthwhile rewards when they succeed but will result in penalties if they fail.

4 Design jobs which enable people to feel a sense of accomplishment, to express and use their abilities and to exercise their own decision-making powers.

5 Provide appropriate tangible rewards for achievement (pay for performance).

6 Provide intangible rewards such as praise for work well done.

7 Communicate to individuals and publicize generally the link between performance and reward, thus enhancing expectations.

8 Select and train managers and supervisors who will exercise effective leadership and have the required motivating skills.

9 Give people the guidance and training which will develop the knowledge, skills and understanding they need to improve their performance.

10 Show individuals what they have to do to satisfy their aspirations through career progression.

References

1   DRUCKER Peter. *The practice of management.* London, Heinemann, 1955
2   ADAIR John. *Effective leadership.* Aldershot, Gower, 1983
3   MASLOW A. H. *Motivation and personality.* New York, Harper & Row, 1954
4   HERZBERG F. W. *The motivation to work.* New York, Wiley, 1957
5   PORTER L. W. and LAWLER E. E. *Managerial attitudes and performance.* Homewood, Illinois, Irwin-Dorsey, 1968
6   LATHAM G. P. and LOCKE F. A. 'Goal setting – a motivation technique that works'. *Organizational Dynamics.* vol. 8, 1979

6

The Management of Time

Managers have to work under constant pressure: problems pile up, priorities conflict, deadlines loom, several balls have to be kept in the air at once. And the manager's day, as we saw in Chapter 2, is full of interruptions, interminable meetings, new requests or demands for action and an incessant flow of paperwork. The processes of planning, organizing, diverting and controlling described in Chapter 4 may provide a raft of certainty in a sea of troubles but they do not eliminate the constant succession of waves that threaten to swamp the craft. Something else must be done to cope with the pressures.

What is required is:

- a systematic approach to the management of time
- carefully controlled delegation
- clear allocation of tasks to subordinates

Time Management

The positive approach

The positive approach to time management means you should do each of the following:

- *Analyse your job* – the objectives you have to achieve and the tasks you have to carry out. Try to establish orders of priority among your objectives and between your tasks.

- *Analyse how you spend your time* – identify time-consuming activities by keeping a diary. Divide the day into 15-minute sections, note what you did in each period and summarize how you spent your time by giving a VDU rating: V for valuable,

D for doubtful and U for useless. Sum up at the end of the week by analysing the VDU ratings under the following headings:

- reading
- writing
- dictating
- telephoning
- dealing with people
- attending meetings
- travelling
- other (specify)

The analysis provides the information needed to spot any weaknesses in the way in which you manage time.

- *Use your diary* to free at least one day a week from appointments, if at all possible, and leave blocks of unallocated time during each day for planning, thinking, reading, writing and dealing with the unexpected.

- *Organize yourself weekly* by planning at the beginning of the week how you are going to spend your time, assessing priorities and leaving blocks of time free wherever possible.

- *Organize yourself daily* by writing down 'things to do' at the beginning of the day by reference to yesterday's organizer to see what is outstanding in your diary and your pending tray. Establish priorities and decide when you are going to fit each task in around any fixed meetings. Classify your tasks under three headings:

  - must be done today, if so, in what order and when
  - ideally should be done today but could be left for tomorrow
  - can be dealt with later (specify a date for completion).

  Refer to this organizer regularly during the day to check progress and, as necessary, reallocate priorities.

- *Organize other people*:
  - your secretary, who can be a great help in sorting mail into priority sections, dealing with correspondence (the more you can delegate the better), organizing papers to achieve easy access, keeping unwanted callers at bay
  - your boss, by doing your best to prevent him or her wasting

your time with over-long meetings, needless interruptions, trivial requests and general nit-picking
- your colleagues, by trying to educate them to avoid unnecessary interruptions
- your subordinates, by systematically delegating work to them and giving them clear instructions not only on what you expect them to do but also the arrangements for feedback. An open-door policy of letting anyone breeze in when they like is fine in theory but time-wasting in practice. Say no to subordinates when you are engaged in important business. Give them a time (not too distant) when they can see you and stick to it
- outside contacts, by only seeing them if they have made an appointment

Cutting back time-consuming activities

The following is a list of possible remedies for typical time-consuming activities:

- *Getting involved in too much detail.* Delegate more.

- *Trying to do too much at once.* Set priorities, learn to say no to yourself as well as to other people.

- *Postponing unpleasant tasks.* Set a timetable and stick to it, get unpleasant tasks over with quickly; you will feel better afterwards.

- *Constant interruptions from people.* Use your secretary to keep unwanted visitors out, make appointments and see that people stick to them; reserve block times when you are not to be interrupted.

- *Constant telephone interruptions.* Get your secretary to intercept and, where possible, divert calls. State firmly that you will call back later.

- *Too much time spent in conversation* (face-to-face or on the telephone). Decide in advance what you want to say and achieve, and keep pleasantries and social chit-chat to a minimum at the beginning and end of the conversation. Concentrate on keeping to the point and avoid diversions. Learn how to end conversations quickly but not too brusquely.

- *Flooded with incoming paper*
  - Get your secretary to sort it into two folders, action and information, also get him or her to intercept pointless circulars.
  - Take yourself off the circulation list for useless information.
  - Only ask for or send written memos (which generate written replies) when you really need to; use the telephone or electronic mail.
  - Encourage people to present information clearly and succinctly and to provide summaries for their lengthier reports.
  - Take a course in rapid reading.
- *Too much time spent in meetings*
  - Avoid holding or, if possible, attending meetings which do not serve a continuing useful purpose.
  - When in the chair, set limits for the duration of meetings and stick to them, cut out waffle and repetition, allow discussion but insist on making progress, have a logical agenda and stick to it.
  - Don't waffle, don't talk for the sake of talking.
- *Too much time spent on travelling.* Use the phone, fax or post, or send someone else.

Delegating

Delegation is the process of allocating work which is within your area of responsibility to subordinates for them to carry out to your satisfaction. You continue to be responsible for whatever they do – you 'carry the can' because you cannot delegate your responsibility – but they are accountable to you for getting the work done properly and on time.

Advantages of delegation

- It relieves you of routine and less critical tasks.
- It frees you for more important work – planning, organizing, motivating and controlling.

- It extends your capacity to manage.

- It reduces delay in decision making – as long as authority is delegated close to the point of action.

- It allows decisions to be taken at the level where the details are known.

- It develops the capacity of staff to make decisions, get things done and take responsibility.

When to delegate

You should delegate when:

- you have more work than you can effectively carry out yourself

- you cannot allocate sufficient time to your priority tasks

- you want to develop your subordinate

- the job can be done adequately by your subordinate

What to delegate

You delegate:

- work you do not need to do yourself (but not just difficult, tedious or unrewarding tasks)

- routine and repetitive tasks that you cannot reasonably be expected to do yourself

- specialist tasks to those who have the skills and know-how to do them. You cannot be expected to do everything yourself, nor can you know all about how to do it yourself. Your job is to know what you want done – and if you cannot do it yourself, find someone who can, and let him or her do it in their own way. You must, however, know what the expert is capable of doing and know enough about the subject to understand whether or not what is produced is worthwhile.

Choosing who does the work

You delegate to people who:

- so far as you can judge, have the knowledge, skills, motivation and time needed to get the work done to your satisfaction. If they are not available you have to estimate how much of your time and attention will have to be given to supervising, bearing in mind that it is one of the prime responsibilities of managers to develop their subordinates and that guided and controlled delegation is the best way to do this.

- are trustworthy, again so far as you can judge. When you first delegate to someone you are taking a risk, but a controlled risk, because you will need to monitor his or her actions and decisions fairly closely at first. But as they develop you can learn to trust them more and more. The art of delegation is to bring people to this state as quickly as possible.

Controlled delegation

Delegation must not result in loss of control. You are still responsible for whatever your subordinate does. If something goes wrong you 'carry the can'. You can *never* say, 'It was his or her fault.' It is *always* your fault, because you delegated to the wrong person, or delegated the wrong task, or failed to make your expectations clear, or failed to monitor actions and results adequately. This principle of total responsibility is the reason why management is such a demanding task. And this is why effective control is always necessary.

As I said in Chapter 4, control is exercised by specifying objectives, standards and time-scales, monitoring performance through reports and personal contacts and initiating any corrective action if required.

As far as possible you should 'manage by exception'. In other words, you should only be interested in reports or information on variations from the expected results, which can then prompt an investigation of what is going on. This approach reduces the danger of 'breathing down people's necks', which is a recipe for inhibiting initiative and stultifying personal development.

Control by exception requires you to identify the critical areas and ensure either that any deviations outside defined limits are reported to you or that you check personally that everything is going according to plan.

In exercising control you have to achieve a delicate balance between over- and under-controlling. This is a matter of judgement based on experience, knowledge and understanding of the individual concerned. To develop that understanding it may be necessary to adopt a reasonably light-handed approach to monitoring performance by informal conversations, using 'How's it going' or some such phrase as the starting point. In the case of longer-term projects regular review or 'milestone' meetings are useful when individuals can report progress to you and the other members of the team. This assists in controlling as well as in co-ordinating the project. Control is concerned not only with seeing that things get done but also with pre-empting any tendency, such as poor co-operation, which will prevent things from being done.

Allocating Tasks

Allocating tasks to staff means giving them instructions on what they have to accomplish. Instructions, however, implies that the manager dictates what people do. This may sometimes have to be the case, but in many situations managers can obtain more commitment from their staff if they involve them in the process of decision making which determines what happens next.

Following Tannenbaum and Schmidt,[1] a continuum of managerial behaviour in giving instructions can be developed (as in Figure 5), in which the manager can choose between 'telling' people what to do, 'selling' the need to do something or 'joining with' staff in deciding on the task.

This continuum may be termed the 'tell-sell-join' style of giving instructions. But no one style is better than another. Managers must be prepared to adjust the style according to the circumstances. Although there will be many occasions when they should fully involve their subordinates in agreeing any actions the latter should take, there will be other times when the manager has to say, in effect, 'Get on with it.'

Figure 5

Continuum of managerial behaviour in giving instructions

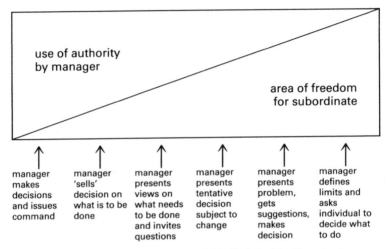

| manager makes decisions and issues command | manager 'sells' decision on what is to be done | manager presents views on what needs to be done and invites questions | manager presents tentative decision subject to change | manager presents problem, gets suggestions, makes decision | manager defines limits and asks individual to decide what to do |

Source: Based on R. Tannenbaum and W. H. Schmidt, 'How to choose a leadership pattern', *Harvard Business Review*, May–June 1973

Giving out the work

When you give out work you should ensure that those involved know:

- why the work needs to be done
- what they are expected to do
- the date by which they are expected to do it
- what authority they have to make decisions
- what problems they must refer back
- what progress or completion reports they should submit
- how you propose to guide and monitor them
- what resources and help they will have to get the work done

Your subordinates may need guidance on how the work should

be done. The extent to which you spell it out will clearly depend on how much they already know about how to do the work. You don't want to give directions in such laborious detail that you run the risk of stifling their initiative. As long as you are sure they will get the job done without breaking the law, exceeding the budget, embarrassing you or seriously upsetting people, let them get on with it.

Reference

1 TANNENBAUM R. and SCHMIDT W. H. 'How to choose a leadership pattern'. *Harvard Business Review*, May–June 1973

7

The Management of Performance

The Concept of Performance

Performance is the process of carrying into effect policies, programmes and plans in order to achieve defined and measurable results. Performance in profit-making organizations can be measured in such terms as:

- net profit (the 'bottom line')
- return on capital employed
- productivity – performance achieved in relation to resources consumed
- cost – cost per unit of output
- stockturn – ratio of sales to stock in trade.

In non-profit-making organizations, performance is measured by the results received in relation to the resources used, i.e. the ratio between outputs and inputs. In such organizations, cost-effectiveness will be a key performance measure, although ultimately they will be judged on whether or not they are achieving their purpose efficiently.

Individual performance is assessed by comparing achievements with targets, budgets and standards. Managers are accountable for the attainment of certain defined results and are measured accordingly.

Efficiency and effectiveness

When assessing performance it is important to distinguish between efficiency and effectiveness. Peter Drucker has pointed out forcibly that to concentrate on efficiency rather than effectiveness can be limiting and therefore dangerous. He writes:

Management, we are usually told, should concern itself with efficiency, that is with doing better what is already being done. It should therefore focus on costs. But the entrepreneurial approach focuses on effectiveness, that is, on the decision what to do. It focuses on opportunities to produce revenue, to create markets and to change the economic characteristics of existing products and markets. It asks not: how do we do this or that? It asks: which of the products really produce extraordinary economic results or are capable of producing them? Which of the markets and/or uses are capable of producing extraordinary results? It then asks: to what results should therefore the resources and efforts of the business be allocated so as to produce extraordinary results rather than the 'ordinary' ones which is all efficiency possibly can produce.[1]

Developing this theme, Bill Reddin[2] suggests that the manager who concentrates on efficiency instead of effectiveness tends to:

- do things right rather than do right things
- solve problems rather than produce creative alternatives
- safeguard resources rather than optimize resource utilization
- lower costs rather than increase profit

The danger of placing too much emphasis on efficiency is that the object of the exercise becomes obscured by the bureaucratic machinery set up to achieve it. You should aim – in Drucker's phrase again – to manage for results. Clearly you adopt the most efficient way of getting there but never forget that it is the end that counts, not the means. This applies to organizations as well as individuals. Costs must be controlled and, if they are excessive, cost-cutting exercises may be necessary, even drastic ones like a 10 per cent cut 'across the board'. But money is not made by cutting costs. Organizations have to go for growth, they must invest in success and they often have to spend money to make money.

The Basis of Performance Management

Performance management is about increasing organizational effectiveness by getting better results from people. It starts with the concept of accountability. To achieve the results required, managers must:

1   Set objectives, targets and standards of performance for themselves and their teams
2   Monitor progress
3   Evaluate results
4   Take corrective action as necessary

Managers also use, as appropriate, analytical and other techniques such as:

* SWOT analysis
* problem solving and decision theory using operational research techniques
* budgetary control
* output budgeting
* zero-base budgeting
* operational auditing

These techniques are discussed later in this chapter (pages 91 to 104).

The Concept of Accountable Management

An accountable manager, as defined by John Garrett,[3] is one to whom specific authority over part of an organization's resources has been delegated, and who is required to answer for the results he or she has obtained from the use of those resources. Accountability involves the delegation to managers of authority over money and human resources. It implies:

* a form of organization in which managers can be made responsible for the activities of sub-units
* a strategic planning framework in which the objectives of those managers can be related to corporate objectives
* an arrangement of control information so that progress towards the attainment of the objectives can be monitored

- a procedural system for securing managerial commitment to unit objectives and for reviewing results

Accountable management as a method of operation was developed by Alfred P. Sloan in the 1920s in order to weld a number of separate and competing motor companies into one firm – General Motors. His book, *My years with General Motors*,[4] is a classic in management literature and is still worth reading today.

Accountability has been described by Peter Drucker as 'the development of the maximum of independent command at the lowest possible level and the development of an objective yardstick to measure performance in these commands'.[5]

Within the British civil service, the concept of accountable management was introduced by the Fulton Committee of 1966–8 which defined accountability as 'holding individuals and units responsible for performance measured as objectively as possible'.[6]

The principle of accountability is important to individual managers because it defines precisely their managerial role. They have full *responsibility* for what they and their department or unit does. They are delegated *authority* to make decisions within certain parameters. And they are *accountable* to their superiors for the results they have obtained.

The concept of accountable management contains within it the principle of management by objectives, a technique in which subordinates agree with their managers their objectives, which are aligned with those of the unit and the organization. So far as possible, these objectives are quantified. Performance is reviewed jointly by the manager and subordinate by reference to the objectives. They then agree a 'job improvement plan' to achieve better results and, as necessary, redefine objectives.

Management by objectives, or M by O, became very popular in the 1960s but it has been criticized because it overemphasized short-term goals at the expense of long-term results. Attempts to quantify the unquantifiable have also led managers to reject M by O as unrealistic. This rejection was accelerated by the volume of paperwork generated by some schemes, which was perceived by managers as placing an extra and unproductive burden on them.

But the principle of management by objectives remains a good one. It helps to ensure that managers know where they stand and where they are going. It eliminates the ineffectiveness and misdirection that result from management by 'crisis' and 'drives'. Finally, and most importantly, it enables managers to control their own performance.

Setting Objectives, Targets and Standards

Definitions

- An *objective* is a broadly defined statement of what the business or individual is expected to achieve on a continuing and progressive basis. An objective may be defined for the whole of an individual's job. Thus the overall objective of a production manager could be described as being: 'to achieve targets and standards of throughput, cost per unit of output, productivity, quality and employee relations'. Objectives can also be defined for each individual accountability. For example, an objective for a production manager in respect of cost control could be expressed as: 'to maintain a constant attack on costs in order to control them within budgets and achieve agreed cost-reduction targets'.

- A *target* is a specified result to be attained. It is usually expressed in quantified terms, for example: 'Reduce the cost per unit of output to £*x* by . . . ' But it can be defined as a task to be achieved, for example: 'Introduce a system of group technology, according to specification, in plant A by . . .'

- A *standard of performance* describes the observable behaviour that will indicate whether the task has been well or badly done, for example: 'Performance is up to standard with regard to employee relations if all grievances are settled within the department without any interruption to work.'

Objectives

Setting objectives as a management skill was described fully in Chapter 5. Briefly, it is the process of defining overall and key accountabilities. Each of these can be expressed in a sentence beginning with an active verb which defines outputs in terms such as:

- 'Prepare financial plans and budgets for approval by the Board.'
- 'Set pricing levels for catalogue items to maximize revenues and gross margin.'
- 'Schedule the provision of component parts and sub-assemblies so that the customer's final requirement is satisfied on time.'

Objectives should initially be prepared by managers for agreement with their superior. This 'bottom-up' process ensures that managers think for themselves. A 'top-down' approach in which objectives are handed down by senior managers to their subordinates is far less likely to obtain the latter's commitment.

Targets

Targets are best defined for each main accountability area by adopting a combined 'top-down' and 'bottom-up' approach. The top-down element consists of overall guidelines on the results to be achieved by the organization: for instance, an increase in sales turnover in real terms (i.e. allowing for inflation) of x per cent in the 12-month period of the budget. This overall target may be subdivided at each level in the organizational hierarchy by a bottom-up process of target setting. For example, the general sales manager may say to each of his or her regional sales managers that an x per cent overall increase in sales is required for the company. They will be asked to indicate the contribution their region can make to achieving the company target. If the individual proposals fall short of the total required, an iterative process ensues in which the general sales manager goes back and forth between his or her regional sales managers (individually or collectively) until a realistic and acceptable target for each region is agreed. If the regional sales manager is certain on the basis of this process that the company target is unachievable, it is up to him or her to make a case to the marketing director, and the latter must take it up with the board. The iterative process may then continue, but not for long. The aim will be to achieve agreement at all levels; but in the last analysis it may be necessary for the board to instruct the marketing director on the target that has to be achieved.

The same process will be carried on between the regional sales managers and their area sales managers, and between the latter and their sales representatives.

Target setting in a key area such as sales can be a lengthy process and sometimes it is necessary to lay down a tight timetable which allows for some iteration but prevents endless discussions and revisions.

In other areas the process may not be so prolonged. If, for example, it has been agreed as part of the capital expenditure budget of a company that an integrated CAM (computer-aided manufacture) system should be installed in a new plant, then the operations director can undertake to achieve an installation, testing and training programme which will enable the plant to become fully operational by a certain date. A project plan can then be prepared by the project manager which allocates a series of targets for completing different sections of the project. Each target, however, would be discussed and agreed with the individual concerned.

The essential requirements of an effective target-setting process are that:

1   The individual target should support the achievement of a higher-level target.

2   Wherever possible individual targets should be agreed between the parties directly concerned. Individuals should be given the maximum opportunity to develop their own targets (a bottom-up process) but these must be congruent with the overall target, as long as that is realistic.

3   While targets must be attainable they do not have to be attainable too easily. In other words, it is perfectly legitimate for management to insist that the targets should 'stretch' the managers who have to meet them. The setting of 'stretch targets', however, implies that managers will be rewarded appropriately if they achieve them.

4   Performance indicators or measures should be available for each target which will enable progress towards them to be monitored and the final result to be evaluated. The performance indicators can include a number of different sorts of measures of effectiveness. For instance:

- positive measurements, i.e. a hoped-for event, result or other outcome should occur
- negative measurements, i.e. an undesirable event or other outcome should not occur
- measurements in terms of quantity
- measurements in terms of cost
- measurements in terms of time
- measurements that can be compared against a standard item or specification

5 Critical success factors should be worked out by the managers involved for each target. These may be agreed with the managers' superiors, but this is not always necessary. Effective managers should be capable of working out for themselves their critical success factors.

The following is an example of a target-setting process in a machine tool manufacturing concern. A contract has been agreed to develop a range of special-purpose machine tools for a firm in the aerospace industry. The initial target for the chief project engineer might be to develop by a certain date a solution which meets the customer's requirements for an optimum machining sequence, using appropriate machine tools as set out in the specification. This will involve the development of alternative solutions which will be analysed and evaluated to establish their relative technical and economic merits, so that the optimum solution can be selected. The agreed performance criterion would be that an acceptable solution is provided to the customer by the agreed date. The critical success factors could include:

- making the right choice between general and special-purpose machines
- devising a logical and efficient flow path down the line
- the appropriate grouping of similar operations (for example, surfaces to be flat milled)
- flexible response to design changes
- capital investment required

Standards of performance

A standard of performance provides a qualitative basis for judgement where a quantified target or a set date for completing a task cannot be established. When determining a standard of performance you should always ask yourself: 'How will I and any other people involved know when this task has been well done?' It is hard work defining good standards. You have to visualize a performance review session when you and your boss are looking at a particular work area. You will both need to think of examples and ask yourselves, 'How can we judge that the job had been done well?' For example, a financial director and a newly appointed management accountant might get together. One of the latter's responsibilities is to produce for the monthly board meeting a set of management accounts which provides details of performance against budget and highlights any variances. Thinking of examples where things have gone wrong in the past, the financial director will suggest the following performance standards or criteria:

Performance is up to standard when:

a)   a complete set of management accounts is in the hands of board members at least two working days before the board meeting;

b)   the accounts are complete and contain no inaccuracies;

c)   key variances are highlighted; and

d)   valid explanations are provided as to why variations have taken place.

The new management accountant should agree these standards but can seek further explanation as to what is involved. He might, for example, ask how much authority he has to require explanations for variances from operational managers, and what he must do if he thinks that the explanation is unsatisfactory. In this way, the process of standard setting becomes a useful method of clarifying responsibilities and authorities, thus reducing ambiguity.

A system of accountable management

The process of setting objectives, targets and standards can be built into a system of accountable management as illustrated in Figure 6.

Figure 6
A system of accountable management

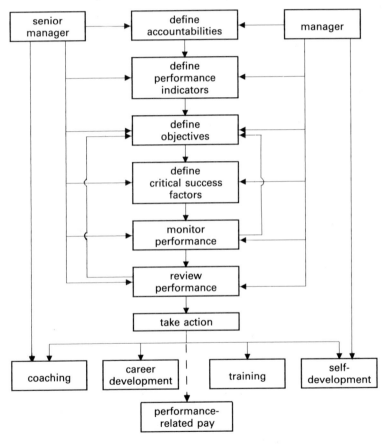

This system involves managers and their superiors in jointly defining accountabilities, performance indicators, objectives, targets and standards and critical success factors. They each monitor and evaluate results against objectives, targets or standards using the performance indicators. They then meet periodically to review performance jointly, exploring the reasons for any variances and, as necessary, discussing any problems concerning the critical success factors and how they may be overcome in the future. They also agree on any action to be taken and any necessary changes or updates to objectives, targets or standards.

The action that can be taken following the review can be operational, which might mean positive action to exploit an opportunity, or corrective action to overcome a problem or deal with a short-fall. Alternatively, the action can be directed to improving the manager's performance.

Monitoring and Evaluation

The process of monitoring and evaluation is carried out by exercising controlling skills, as we saw in Chapter 5. Managers clearly have to monitor and evaluate the work of their subordinates by comparing achievements or output with requirements as recorded in control documents, received in the form of written or oral reports or observed during the course of inspections. The emphasis is on information, not just data because, as Peter Drucker has said, 'Information is data endowed with relevance and purpose.'[7] The data must be relevant to the task or result area under review, and it must be purposeful in that it points the way clearly to action. Managers receive a lot of data, and it is up to them to ensure that it contains the information they need to monitor and control their own activities and those of their staff. If it does not, they must either generate it themselves or persuade someone else to generate it for them.

Monitoring and evaluating systems should be regarded as positive processes which help to get things done properly, not sticks with which to beat people. If the data is used in a threatening manner it can inhibit achievement by forcing people on the defensive. If an adverse variance occurs, managers should not descend on their staff too heavily. Rather they should find out why the variance has happened and ask for proposals on what to do about it. If you are asked to account for a variance you should follow the principle of 'never explain (in the sense of explain away), never excuse'. You should simply describe what has happened and why, and indicate how you are proposing to remedy the problem. The aim, of course, is to anticipate questions of this nature. You should aim always to be the first to hear any bad or, indeed, good news, relating to your activities so that you can pre-empt any actions or reactions from other people.

Taking Action

The whole purpose of monitoring results against objectives, targets and standards is to enable swift and appropriate action to be taken.

Operationally it will alert all concerned to the need for corrective action, which should itself be expressed in terms of the results to be attained and the critical success factors relating to their achievement. Individually, the action that can result from the accountable management process as shown in Figure 6 consists of:

- *Self-development.* This is the most important direction in which action should take place. The most successful managers are those who can absorb the messages coming from feedback information, analyse them in terms of why their performance has or has not been satisfactory (having set high performance standards in the first place) and decide for themselves what they need to do to improve performance, to correct a shortfall or mistake, or to avoid making the same mistake again. Effective managers are also good at seeking advice from their bosses and their colleagues, but this is always on the basis of checking their own plans or getting a second opinion. They control their own destinies.

- *Coaching.* Managers can help their subordinates by providing guidance in the form of coaching. This is a key responsibility for all managers, whose performance is or ought to be judged as much on their ability to improve the performance of their staff as on any other accountability. Coaching is best carried out informally as part of the normal process of management. It consists of:
  – making staff aware of how they are managing; for example,

by asking them questions on how well they have thought through what they are doing
- controlled delegation
- using situations of all kinds as teaching opportunities
- setting individual projects and assignments
- spending time in looking at higher-level problems as well as looking at the immediate job

- *Career development and training.* Managers should provide additional experience to develop potential and broaden knowledge and skills, and encourage staff to attend in-company and external courses dealing with specific areas of knowledge and management techniques.

- *Motivating.* It is important to provide additional motivation by enriching the job (giving the individual wider responsibilities), recognizing achievement, accelerating promotion and providing performance-related rewards.

Performance Management Techniques

The overall approach to accountable management, including setting objectives, measuring performance and taking action, requires the deployment of a number of skills in the management of other people and oneself. These skills are best used with the help of various analytical techniques which assist in setting targets and standards and in reviewing performance and results. The main techniques discussed here are:

- SWOT analysis

- problem solving

- budgetary control

- responsibility accounting

- output budgeting

- zero-base budgeting

- operational auditing

SWOT Analysis

SWOT stands for strengths, weaknesses, opportunities and threats. These are often used as the headings in a corporate planning appraisal exercise. For example, a small management consultancy specializing in human resource management and operating in a particular market segment or 'niche' may analyse its situation as follows:

- *Strengths*
  - reputation established in the market
  - expertise at partner level in human resource management consultancy
  - track record of successful assignments

- *Weaknesses*
  - shortage of good consultants at operating rather than partner level
  - inability because of size and lack of expertise in certain areas to deal with large multi-disciplinary assignments
  - inadequate administrative back-up

- *Opportunities*
  - a well-established position in a well-defined market niche in the UK
  - an identified market for consultancy in areas other than human resource management in this sector
  - scope for extending consultancy into Europe

- *Threats*
  - the large consultancies, which are at present operating in this market in a small way, and may get more heavily involved
  - other small consultancies, which may recognize and seize the opportunity to invade the market
  - the limited financial resources of the many small businesses in the market, which may mean that they will turn for advice to the various government agencies and voluntary bodies from which it is available at low or nil cost

The discipline of proceeding through each stage of this analysis is a good way of ensuring that every eventuality is recognized. A

SWOT analysis at corporate level is best carried out by a group of people, e.g. the board, who can 'brain-storm' their way through each heading.

This approach can be used equally effectively by departmental managers in relation to their area of responsibility and by managers generally about their own performance and future. A personnel department, for example could carry out a SWOT analysis with the following outcome:

- *Strengths* – well developed techniques for dealing with the major areas of personnel management such as job evaluation, psychometric testing and basic training

- *Weaknesses* – tendency to be reactive rather than pro-active; to want to be asked to do things rather than coming up with bright unsolicited ideas.

- *Opportunity* – a new and vigorous team at the top, providing the department with a greater chance of helping to improve overall organizational effectiveness through organization development and culture management programmes.

- *Threat* – top management may underestimate the contribution the personnel department can make and by-pass it by seeking the direct aid of management consultants in such areas as those described above.

As an individual manager, it is useful from time to time to take a long hard look at yourself, with particular emphasis on your strengths and weaknesses, but also considering your opportunities for advancement and the threats that might exist to prevent you from realizing your ambitions. A SWOT analysis for an individual could look like this:

- *Strengths* – enthusiasm, energy, imagination, expertise in my particular subject, a good track record so far in my specialized area

- *Weaknesses* – not always good at directing and controlling my energies to achieve the results required by my superiors; not so good at expressing myself orally or on paper – the ideas are there but they tend to tumble out incoherently; expertise and experience in management somewhat limited

- *Opportunities* – the company needs to develop specialist managers like myself to take on more general management responsibilities arising from its policy of decentralization into small profit centres.

- *Threats* – the policy of decentralization is accompanied by a policy of slimming down support departments like mine and eliminating layers of middle management, such as the area I am in.

This type of analysis usefully indicates areas where strengths can be developed and weaknesses overcome in order to make the best use of opportunities and minimize threats. Clearly in this sort of situation individuals have to demonstrate that they can use their talents more positively and get results in areas such as a decentralized unit where the accountability for results is clear cut. They have to broaden their knowledge and skills in aspects of management other than their speciality. And, if they are going to make a noticeable impact, they must polish their communicating skills. The threat of redundancy should be countered by demonstrating their likely value in other functions and their potential for promotion.

Problem Solving

The basic problem-solving and decision-making skills were described in Chapter 5 but managers should be aware of a number of operational or management science techniques which assist in dealing with complex problems. These include decision theory, modelling, simulation and sensitivity analysis, and are described briefly below. For a fuller description you could refer to my book, *A handbook of management techniques*.[8]

Operational research

Operational research (OR) has been defined by the Operational Research Society as follows:

> Operational research is the application of the methods of science to complex problems arising in the direction and management of large systems of men, machines, materials

and money in industry, business, government and defence. The distinctive approach is to develop a scientific model of the system, incorporating measurement of factors such as chance and risk, with which to predict and compare the outcomes of alternative decisions, strategies or controls. The purpose is to help management determine its policy and actions scientifically.

Operational research methods essentially conform to the basic problem-solving approaches described in Chapter 5, but the maximum use is made of statistical techniques and computer technology. The three key tasks are as follows:

1   Gain an understanding of the system and the relevant factors affecting it, including uncertainty and risk, so that the problem can be defined in useful terms for analysis by means of a mathematical model that represents the system.

2   Collect and analyse relevant data using appropriate statistical and other quantitative techniques and, often with the help of a computer, formulate and test a practical solution. This frequently requires a degree of optimization, i.e. obtaining the best answer *in the circumstances* by balancing the parameters and variables.

3   Evaluate alternative proposals and present them for decision.

Decision theory

In a sense, all operational research is about decisions. It is concerned with decision rules, evaluating alternative decisions, optimizing decisions, predicting the outcome of decisions, helping to cope with uncertainty and risk and sorting out the complexity of the typical situations managers face, which contain many interacting variables and conditions of uncertainty.

The decision theory techniques available are:

●   the clarification of decision rules; pessimistic, optimistic, opportunity cost (i.e. the income you will lose by rejecting alternatives) or expected value (the likelihood of a particular situation occurring and the estimated benefits accruing from that situation)

- means-ends analysis to establish a chain of objectives and identify a series of decision points
- decision-matrix analysis to model relatively simple decisions under uncertainty and make explicit the options open to the decision maker
- decision trees to assist in making decisions in uncertainty when there is a series of either/or choices
- algorithms which set out the logical sequence of deductions required for problem solving
- subjective probability techniques which aim to systematize the process of making intuitive decisions or decisions based largely on personal experience.

Modelling

Modelling is a representation of a real situation. It depicts interrelationships between the relevant factors in that situation and, by structuring and formalizing any information about those factors, presents reality in a simplified form. Models can help managers to:

- increase the decision maker's understanding of the situation in which a decision has to be made and the possible outcomes of that decision
- evaluate alternative courses of action

For example, a financial model developed in Book Club Associates to forecast profit 'out turns' over a five-year period has built-in parameters which define the relationships between various inputs such as sales, investments and marketing costs, and outputs in terms of profit. Alternative investment plans can then be tested to establish which are likely to yield the most profitable result.

Simulation

Simulation is the construction of mathematical models to represent the operation of real-life processes or situations. The objects are to explore the effect of different solutions and to discuss what might happen in practice, without going to the risk of trial and error in the real environment. For example, it is possible to simulate a stock-control system where the inputs are daily demand and delivery lead times. The operational effects of different stocking policies can then be explored.

Sensitivity analysis

Sensitivity analysis is the study of the key assumptions or calculations upon which a management decision is based in order to predict alternative outcomes of that decision if different assumptions are made. It is a 'what if' technique that measures how the expected values in a decision model will be affected by changes in the data. For example, the likely level of profits in a business is forecast at £33m and the effect on this figure is calculated for a change of 1 per cent in a number of factors:

A difference of 1% in	Will change profits by
Market growth rate	£1m
Market share	£1.25
Selling price	£1.9
Direct labour costs	£ .2
Direct material costs	£ .45

Budgetary Control

Budgetary control compares actual costs, revenues and performances with the budget so that, if necessary, corrective action can be taken or revisions made to the original budgets.

It has been said that budgets don't win friends but they do influence people.[8] They can be painful to create and agonizing to manage. But they do translate policy into financial terms and, whether we like it or not, that is the way in which plans must be expressed, and ultimately performance controlled.

The process of budgetary control consists of the following five steps:

1　A *budget* is prepared for each budget or cost centre controlled by a manager, which sets out the budgeted expenditure allowed against whatever activity levels have been built into the budget. These will be expressed as budget guidelines so that, for instance, a manufacturing department would be told that it has to base its budget on the sales forecast for the next twelve months.

2   A system of *measurement* or recording is created which allocates expenditure to the cost centre and records the activity levels achieved.

3   A system for *comparison* or reporting is established which shows actuals against budgets and indicates any positive and negative variances which have occurred. This system of comparison must ensure that performance reports are made available quickly to the right person and are presented in such a way that variances are immediately identifiable.

4   A procedure is laid down for *acting* on the control information received. This requires reports to higher management on what is being done to deal with variances.

5   A procedure is established for *feeding back* changes in activity or performance levels so that the budget guidelines can be amended and budgets updated.

This process of budgetary control is illustrated in Figure 7.

The role of managers in budgetary control

Individual managers play a key role in making the budgetary control system effective as a means of controlling and, more importantly, improving performance. They must prepare realistic budgets with targets that are not so high as to be unattainable but not so low as to be meaningless. When drawing up budgets, they can use output and zero-base budgeting techniques, described later in this chapter, to ensure that proper consideration has been given to every relevant factor.

Managers should also use the information created by the budgetary control system. Budgets are not just voluminous printouts produced by accounts departments as historical records. Their only value is if they highlight for managers the things they must do.

Figure 7
Budgetary control

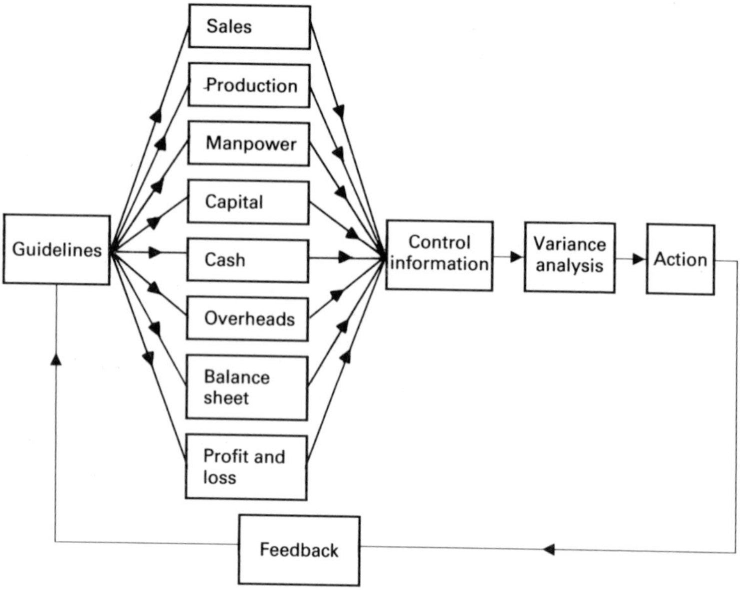

Responsibility Accounting

Responsibility accounting is a development of budgetary control which involves defining responsibility centres throughout the organization. The managers of each of these centres are held responsible for the costs and revenues assigned to them.

The three main areas of responsibility covered are:

1 *Cost centres*, where only costs are reported formally. Typically, cost centres are departments, but a department may contain several cost centres.

2 *Profit centres*, where both costs and revenues are reported formally. They are usually segments of a business responsible for the sales and profits of a product line.

3 *Investment centres*, where there is a formal reporting of reven-

ues, expenses and related investments. Their success is measured not only by their income but also by relating that income to their invested capital. Typically, a whole business or subsidiary can be treated as an investment centre.

Method

The steps taken to develop and implement a responsibility accounting system are as follows:

1 The organization is divided and subdivided into responsibility centres for return on investment, profit, contribution to profit and overheads, revenues or controllable costs.

2 Managers are identified who will be accountable for the results achieved in each responsibility centre.

3 Objectives, standards, targets and budgets are agreed for the organization as a whole and for each responsibility centre.

4 An information system is set up which reports actuals, targets or budgets and highlights variances.

5 Procedures are instituted for the analysis of control reports, for taking any action required and for providing information on outcomes.

Responsibility accounting combines the merits of accountable management and budgetary control. It places individual managers firmly in areas of defined responsibility and facilitates the delegation of decision making. Responsibility centre managers can be given an appropriate and controlled degree of authority over their units knowing what they are expected to achieve and what they are allowed to do.

Individuals in a responsibility accounting system have to rely on their own resources to a very large extent to manage their affairs. They cannot depend on accountants to do their budgeting for them or to provide all the central information needed. Managers must decide how they are going to direct and control their activities in a way which suits their circumstances and ensures that their accountabilities are fulfilled. If they approach their budgeting by using output budgeting and zero-base budget techniques, they are more likely to be successful in running their responsibility centre.

Output Budgeting

Output budgeting, also known as programme budgeting, is the integration of a number of planning, budgeting and control techniques for:

- establishing priorities and strategies for major developments or operational programmes
- identifying, allocating and costing the resources required
- planning the work to be done to achieve the expected outputs
- monitoring performance and controlling results

The process of output budgeting is illustrated in Figure 8.

Output budgeting is an organizational approach to the preparation, implementation and control of plans to achieve goals and improve performance. The role of individual managers in output budgeting is to contribute their skills and expertise at each stage. Its value for their purposes is that it provides a framework of action and it can be used as a model of the processes of management they need to follow in planning and controlling their work.

Zero-base Budgeting

Zero-base budgeting is a technique that requires budget managers to re-evaluate systematically all their activities and programmes in order to decide whether they should be eliminated, or funded at a reduced, similar, or increased level. Appropriate funding levels will be determined by the priorities established by top management and the overall availability of funds.

Each activity is broken down into defined decision units, and each unit is analysed to establish:

- its objectives
- the activities carried out
- the present costs of these activities

Figure 8
The process of output budgeting

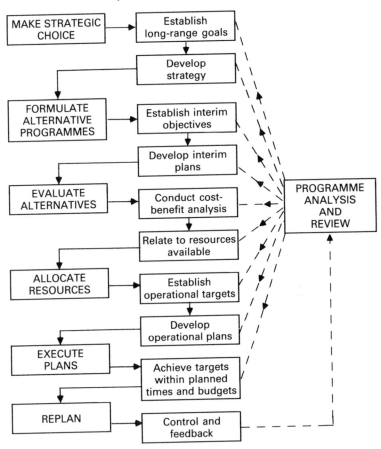

- the benefits resulting from each activity
- the standards and other performance measures that exist
- alternative ways of achieving objectives
- priorities among the objectives
- the advantages and disadvantages of incurring different levels of expenditure

Zero-base budgeting techniques should be used by managers to develop an attitude of mind in which they examine and control all their activities. The techniques should not be used in a threatening way. The emphasis should be on their value in getting priorities right and ensuring that costs and benefits are thoroughly reviewed to the advantage of all concerned.

Operational Auditing

An operational audit is a systematic examination of the systems, procedures and management processes of an organization, function or department to determine the extent to which it is operating effectively and to indicate where improvements are required.

Areas covered

At organizational level, an operational audit will cover the following areas:

- *Top management vision* – the extent to which top management has a realistic vision of the future of the organization
- *Top management concept of function* – the extent to which top management has a clear view of its role and carries it out effectively
- *Objectives* – whether or not they are appropriate, clearly defined and understood
- *Strategic plans* – the extent to which they are considered, comprehensive, realistic, adventurous and acted upon
- *Organization* – the appropriateness of the organization structure
- *Management* – the strengths and weaknesses of the management team
- *Finance* – the strength of the financial base of the company; the extent to which financial targets are achieved; the inferences that can be obtained in studying trends in the key management ratios, especially those dealing with return on capital, liquidity, inventory control and overheads; the control of cash and

working capital, and the effectiveness of investment appraisal and capital, revenue and overhead budgeting procedures

- *Innovation* – the amount of innovation that takes place and its effectiveness in preventing stagnation and in encouraging growth
- *Marketing* – the degree to which the company is marketing orientated, i.e. understands and acts on the principle that the purpose of the business is to create and keep customers
- *Operations* – the efficiency with which manufacturing and distribution operations are planned and controlled and inventory is managed; the extent to which higher levels of productivity are being achieved and the incidence of wasteful practices and inefficiencies
- *Customer care* – the amount of attention paid to achieving high levels of customer service
- *Quality* – the importance attached to total quality improvement and the results achieved
- *Human resource management* – the ability of the organization to attract, retain and motivate the quality and quantity of people it needs; the extent to which employees are committed to the organization and a sense of common purpose exists
- *Management information* – the quality of management information systems
- *Control* – the effectiveness of control procedures

Individual managers should generally cover the same areas in so far as they are relevant to their department and themselves.

Operational audit techniques

The main operational audit techniques are:

- *Checklists* which ensure that a systematic approach is adopted to the identification of weaknesses
- *Trailing* – tracing from start to finish a sequence of events such as customer order processing to ensure that each activity or operation is sequenced logically and carried out properly

- *Procedure or flow charts* representing 'trails' diagrammatically providing a visual representation of the sequence of events and their interrelationships thus revealing any logical weaknesses

- *Critical examination* – challenging an existing procedure or system by answering these questions:
  - What is done? Why do it?
  - How is it done? Why do it that way?
  - Where is it done? Why do it there?
  - When is it done? Why do it then?
  - Who does it? Why that person?

- *Quality assurance* reviewing quality levels, using codes of quality assurance standards either developed specially for the company or those published by the British Standards Institute to verify that the levels of quality required are being achieved or indicate areas of weakness

- *Ratio analysis* – analysing performance as revealed by management ratios to assess trends and to compare results with those achieved by similar companies or other divisions in the same company.

These techniques can be used systematically in a formal operational audit conducted by a management team or by external consultants. But they can and should be used by individual managers continuously as a means of monitoring their own performance and that of their department so that corrective action can be taken when required.

References

1   DRUCKER Peter. *Managing for results*. London, Heinemann, 1963
2   REDDIN Bill. *Management effectiveness*. London, McGraw-Hill, 1970
3   GARRETT John. *The management of government*. Harmondsworth, Penguin, 1972
4   SLOAN Alfred P. *My years with General Motors*. London, Sidgwick & Jackson, 1986

5   DRUCKER Peter. *The concept of the corporation.* Boston, Beacon Press, 1960

6   *Committee on the Civil Service.* Report, June 1968, Cmnd. 3636 Vol. 1 para. 150

7   DRUCKER Peter. 'The coming of the new organization'. *Harvard Business Review.* January–February 1988, pp. 45–51

8   ARMSTRONG Michael. *A handbook of management techniques.* London, Kogan Page, 1986

8

The Management of Stress

What is Stress?

Stress refers to any demands which unduly tax the psychological or physiological system of a human being, and the response of that system. This reaction, according to R. S. Lazarus, 'depends on how a person interprets or appraises (consciously or unconsciously) the significance of a harmful, threatening or challenging event'.[1]

Stress can be physical or emotional. Physically induced stress comes from a direct disturbance to the body by the immediate environment. Bodily fatigue suffered by a door-to-door sales representative working excessively long hours is an obvious example. Emotionally induced stress is caused by a person's own conscious or unconscious thought processes, without any physical stress factors directly affecting the body. It may be triggered off by pressure but it is often self-induced.

Physical stress is more easily controllable than emotional stress and it is the latter variety which can have the most impact on the effectiveness and mental health of managers. This chapter therefore concentrates on emotional stress.

Varieties of emotional stress

Emotionally induced stress can be classified into four general categories, as follows:

1 *Time stress*. This is an anxiety reaction, either to the feeling that something, or a number of things, must be done before a deadline, or to the general feeling that time is running out and something terrible will happen when it does.

2 *Anticipatory stress*. Commonly known as 'worry', this is a

106

feeling of anxiety about an impending event. It is often a generalized anxiety, with little or no specific basis.

3   *Situational stress.* This is anxiety as a result of finding oneself excessively pressurized by events or people, and occurs in situations which are threatening and wholly or partially beyond one's control. It can also happen when there is conflict or distrust between people.

4   *Encounter stress.* This is anxiety about dealing with individuals or groups of people who are perceived as potentially unpleasant or unpredictable.

Stress and pressure

Stress and pressure are not the same. Some pressure is normal and desirable as a motivating force. It is only when the pressure becomes excessive that it can turn into stress, which will then have a de-motivating effect.

Causes of Stress

The main causes of stress are:

- *Working conditions* – unpleasant work conditions such as the need to work fast and expend a lot of physical effort, or excessive or inconvenient hours

- *Work overload* – either having too much or too many things to do, or carrying out work that is beyond one's capacity

- *Role ambiguity* – when one is unclear about the scope and responsibilities of one's jobs or the authority one has to make decisions

- *Role conflict* – where one has conflicting job demands, is doing things one does not want to do or is having to do things which are outside the specification of one's job

- *Responsibility* – increased responsibility for people, being involved more in interacting with others, attending meetings and meeting deadline pressures and schedules. Such people may also worry about 'carrying the can' for the mistakes or inadequacies of their staff

- *Accountability* – accountability for results, which can increase stress because of the pressure on meeting targets and improving standards of performance, especially in conditions where the future is uncertain

- *Change* – coping with rapid technological change, the acquisition of new skills, different responsibilities in the job and the variety of tasks to be undertaken in turbulent conditions

- *Relationships with subordinates* – inability to delegate, critical or unco-operative staff, difficulties in exercising authority

- *Relationships with colleagues* – office politics, rivalry, competitiveness, lack of support, difficulties in achieving co-operation on joint projects

- *Job security* – fears of redundancy, obsolescence or early retirement

- *Lack of status*, actual or perceived

- *Feelings about job or career* – frustration at reaching career ceiling, lack of prospects, under- or over-promotion

- *Impact of the organization* – pressurized or tense climate, autocratic management style, restrictions on behaviour, lack of information and involvement

- *External pressures* – clash between demands made by the organization and those made by the family or other external interests; domestic problems created by excessive hours; priority being given to work rather than spouse and family; travelling away from home, company transfers

These causes can combine in many ways. They are probably most acute for middle managers who are pressurized from above and below, are busy making their mark and advancing their career, are having to travel and move with the company, yet may be married with growing home responsibilities. But older managers may also be subject to stress either because of the extra weight of responsibility or because their careers have 'plateaued' and their ambitions are not being realized.

The Impact of Stress

The pressures listed above are concerned with the work, the job, the working environment, personal relationships, personal ambitions and the home. These are mainly imposed on people, but the extent to which pressure becomes stress depends very much on the individuals themselves.

Some people seem to be able to withstand stress more than others. This is because we speak of stress factors as those aspects of the environment which we consider as grounds for being anxious. Clearly, these psychological factors will vary from person to person because we all have our own characteristic pattern of reactivity. A highly reactive person finds more of life's experience stressful than does a less reactive person. A well-adjusted person is someone who has learned to cope with pressure. Adaptive and flexible people can deal with pressure better than those whose approach to life is relatively rigid and inflexible. We each have our own threshold where pressure turns into stress.

Stress can have one or more of the following effects as identified by Cooper and Marshall:[2]

- *Poor physical health*
  - increased pulse rate
  - high blood pressure
  - high cholesterol levels
  - excessive smoking
  - ulcers
  - cardiovascular heart disease
- *Poor mental health*
  - low motivation
  - lowered self-esteem
  - job dissatisfaction
  - job-related tension
  - neurotic behaviour
  - escapist drinking
- *Organizational symptoms*
  - low productivity
  - absenteeism
  - high staff turnover

Coping with Stress

As I have said, how people deal with stress will depend on their personality, tolerance for ambiguity and ability to live with change. Motivation also comes into it. Motivation is a form of pressure. People can be too highly motivated and pressure becomes stress when they cannot achieve what they are setting out to do or what is expected of them.

Stress can be managed by adaptive behaviour. An overworked manager may adapt successfully by delegating more work and spending more time in managing time. But someone else may accept the overload, with the result that pressure and stress increase and performance deteriorates. And as Torrington and Cooper[3] point out, managers who adapt successfully to role ambiguity will seek clarification from superiors and colleagues, but managers who cannot adapt will withdraw from some aspect of their work role.

Managing Stress – What the Organization Can Do

There are two main reasons why organizations should take account of stress and do something about it; first, because they have the social responsibility to provide a reasonable quality of working life and, secondly, because excessive stress amongst managers and other staff can reduce organizational effectiveness.

The ways in which stress can be managed by an organization include:

- *Job design* – clarifying roles, reducing the danger of role ambiguity and conflict and giving people more autonomy within a defined structure to manage their responsibilities

- *Placement* – taking care to place people in jobs which are within their capabilities

- *Career development* – planning careers and promoting staff in accordance with their capabilities; taking care not to over- or under-promote

- *Performance and potential reviews*, which allow a dialogue to take place between managers and their subordinates about the latters' problems and ambitions

- *Counselling* – giving individuals the opportunity to talk about their problems with a member of the personnel department or the company medical officer
- *Management training* in performance review and counselling techniques and in what managers can do to alleviate their own stress and reduce it in others
- *Motivation* – encouraging methods of leadership and motivation which do not place excessive demands on people

In addition, Cooper[4] suggests the following ways of alleviating stress:

- stress awareness training which focuses on the physical, emotional and behavioural problems which may be stress related
- sabbaticals
- keep-fit programmes
- a conscious policy of recognizing and alleviating domestic problems

Managing Stress – What you can do

The following are various ways in which you can manage stress.

1 Build rewarding, pleasant, supportive relationships with your superior, colleagues and subordinates.

2 If in any doubt about your role, seek clarification from your superior.

3 If there are interface problems between you and other managers, bring the issues out into the open and discuss them in a frank but friendly way.

4 Take steps to clarify your objectives and get them agreed with your superior.

5   However much you may wish to present yourself as the willing horse, don't take on extra work and make promises you will have great difficulty in keeping. Don't refuse outright, or you will get the reputation of being uncooperative. Don't plead overwork or you may be regarded as a shirker. Simply say that you have a set of priorities which you have to keep to and that, while you will be glad to help, you will have to give this job a lower priority unless your other priorities can be changed. If the task is completely beyond your capabilities, say so, but offer to help in finding someone who has the required skills and knowledge.

6   Appraise your own strengths and weaknesses. If your problems are the result of an identifiable weakness, do something about it or seek help.

7   Determine an aiming point in your career which is realistic in relation to your own self-appraisal. Check on the competences and qualifications required to move to where you want to be. If you are confident that you have them, pursue your ambition vigorously. If you do not have the qualities required, decide whether or not you can build them. If so, go ahead. If not, think of an alternative aiming point and career path which is within your capabilities.

8   If you are under pressure to meet deadlines or have too many balls in the air at once, plan your priorities to fit the time available, and delegate as much work as possible.

9   If you are facing a crisis take time to decide how to tackle it. Don't run in all directions at once.

10 If you are under extreme pressure, deliberately allow yourself time to relax for a few minutes.

11 Use the time-management techniques described in Chapter 6 to plan your working day, always allowing some time – even if only ten minutes – for complete privacy and freedom from pressure.

12 Try to make sure that you are placed in a job suitable to your characteristics and talents.

13 Face up realistically to what you can do and achieve.

14 Do whatever you can to achieve an acceptable balance between yourself, your work and your family.

15 Foster relationships which help you cope with work pressure, and enable you to admit, and take steps to remedy, work-related stress.

References

1 LAZARUS R. S. 'The concepts of stress and disease' *in* LEVI L. *ed. Society, stress and disease.* Vol. 1. Oxford, Oxford University Press, 1971

2 COOPER C. L. and MARSHALL J. *Understanding executive stress.* London, Macmillan, 1978

3 TORRINGTON D. P. and COOPER C. L. 'The management of stress in organizations and the personnel initiative'. *Personnel Review.* Summer, 1977

4 COOPER C. L. 'What's new in stress'. *Personnel Management.* June, 1984

9

Managing One's Career

To manage your career effectively you need to do five things:

1 Know yourself
2 Assess your abilities
3 Know what you want
4 Develop yourself
5 Plan your career progression

Knowing Yourself

Carlyle once described the saying 'know thyself' as an impossible precept. He felt that to 'know what thou canst work at' would be better advice. Therefore the starting point in career management is what you can do – your strengths and your weaknesses. This means developing self-awareness by analysing your achievements, skills and knowledge and by assessing your own performance.

Achievement, skills and knowledge

The questions to ask yourself are:

1 *What have I achieved so far?* Answer this question by looking back on your life and listing the key events, incidents and turning points. Whenever you have succeeded in doing something new or better than ever before, analyse the factors which contributed to that success. Was it initiative, hard work, determination, the correct application of skills and knowledge based upon a searching analysis of the situation, the ability to work in a team, the exercise of leadership, the capacity to seize

an opportunity (another and better word for luck) and exploit it, the ability to articulate a need and get into action to satisfy it, the ability to make things happen – or any other factor you can think of.

2   *When have I failed to achieve what I wanted?* You do not want to dwell too much on failure but it can be treated positively as long as you analyse dispassionately where you went wrong and assess what you might have been able to do to put it right.

3   *What am I good or bad at doing?* What are my distinctive competences? Consider these in terms of professional, technical or managerial know-how as well as the exercise of such skills as communicating, decision making, problem solving, teamwork, exercising leadership, delegating, co-ordinating, meeting deadlines, managing time, planning, organizing and controlling work, or dealing with crises.

4   *How well do I know my chosen area of expertise?* Have I got the right qualifications? Have I acquired the right know-how through study, training and relevant experience?

5   *What sort of person am I?* (the most difficult question of all to answer truthfully). The following is a checklist of the points you should consider, based on Cattell's[1] classification of primary personality factors. In each case, assess the extent to which either of the paired descriptions applies to you.

- *Outgoing* – warmhearted, easygoing, participating, extroverted; or
  Reserved – detached, critical, cool, introverted

- *Intellectual* – good at abstract thinking; or
  Non-intellectual – better at concrete thinking

- *Emotionally stable* – calm, can face reality; or
  Affected by feelings – emotionally unstable, easily upset

- *Assertive* – independent, aggressive, stubborn; or
  Submissive – mild, obedient, conforming

- *Enthusiastic* – lively, happy-go-lucky, heedless, talkative; or
  Sober – prudent, serious, taciturn

- *Conscientious* – persevering, staid, rule-bound; or
  Expedient – a law to yourself, by-passing obligations

- *Venturesome* – bold, uninhibited, spontaneous; or
  Shy – restrained, diffident, timid

- *Tender-minded* – dependent, over-protected, sensitive; or
  Tough-minded – self-reliant, realistic, with a no-nonsense approach

- *Suspicious* – self-opinionated, distrustful, hard to fool; or
  Trusting – free of suspicion or jealousy, adaptable, easy to get on with

- *Imaginative* – speculative, careless of practical matters, wrapped up in inner urgencies; or
  Practical – inclined to action rather than speculation, regulated by external realities, careful, conventional

- *Shrewd* – calculating, penetrating, worldly; or
  Artless – guileless, ingenuous, natural

- *Apprehensive* – worrying, depressive, troubled; or
  Confident – self-assured, serene, placid

- *Experimenting* – critical, liberal, analytical, free-thinking; or
  Conservative – respectful of established ideas, tolerant of traditional practices

- *Self-sufficient* – resilient, resourceful, preferring to make your own decisions; or
  Group-dependent – a 'joiner', happiest in a group, reliant on the support of others

- *Controlled* – socially precise, self-disciplined, compulsive; or
  Casual – careless of protocol, untidy, following your own inclinations

- *Tense* – driven, overwrought, fretful; or
  Relaxed – tranquil, unfrustrated, calm.

A self-administered questionnaire such as the one in Pedlar, Burgoyne and Boydell's book *A manager's guide to self-development*,[2] pages 38–45 may be helpful in increasing self-awareness.

Assess your Managerial Abilities

While self-awareness is the basis for a more specific assessment of your strengths and weaknesses as a manager, you need also to consider your basic managerial qualities and the competences required to operate effectively. A selection of checklists you can use for this purpose is set out below.

Managerial qualities

Pedlar, Burgoyne and Boydell[2] suggest on the basis of their extensive research that there are 11 qualities or attributes which are possessed by successful managers.

1   *Command of basic facts.* Successful managers 'know what's what in their organization'. They know where the organization is going and the part they can play in getting it there. If they don't have this knowledge they know where to find it.

2   *Relevant professional knowledge.* They have a good knowledge of their own discipline (e.g. finance, marketing, personnel) and of the principles and practice of management.

3   *Continuing sensitivity to events.* They know what is going on and why, and thus are able to react fast to situations as they arise.

4   *Analytical, problem-solving and decision/judgement-making skills.* They have the ability to analyse data and draw conclusions leading to relevant action. They are decisive. They can weigh all the factors in the light of their experience and an intuitive 'feel' for the situation, and draw the right conclusions or at least, the best conclusions in the circumstances (i.e. optimize decisions by taking a balanced view).

5   *Social skills and abilities.* Successful managers have good interpersonal skills such as communicating, delegating, persuading, negotiating, delegating, resolving conflict and using and responding to authority and power.

6   *Emotional resilience.* They can cope with pressure in meeting targets and deadlines and resolving conflict in conditions of uncertainty and ambiguity.

7 *Proactivity.* They anticipate rather than simply respond to events. Where events force a reactive response, this is related to longer-term goals and plans rather than an expedient short-term solution.

8 *Creativity.* They can develop new responses to situations and initiate different approaches.

9 *Mental agility.* They can grasp things quickly and switch rapidly from one problem or situation to another.

10 *Balanced learning habits and skills.* Successful managers learn independently, find things out for themselves and are capable of abstract thinking as well as concrete, practical thought. They are able to relate concrete ideas to abstract ones (and vice versa) relatively quickly.

11 *Self-knowledge.* Successful managers know their strengths and weaknesses and exploit the former while doing what they can to manage the latter.

Managerial competences

In analysing your effectiveness as a manager it is useful not only to look at the qualities listed above, but also the criteria used by major organizations in measuring the competence of their managers at their assessment or development centres (two- or three-day affairs where managers are subjected to a number of tests and undertake various exercises to demonstrate their skills). The headings used by two organizations in their assessment centres are set out below.

1 *A large international group in the finance sector*
Effective managers:

- are *achievement orientated.* They are strongly motivated by achievement, recognition and reward and possess internal drive that continually urges them forward to higher levels.

- have a *positive outlook.* They are energetic, enthusiastic and want to make a unique personal contribution to every job they do.

- are *reliable.* They are noted for always doing a job properly with attention to relevant detail.

- are *adaptable*. They are flexible, self-organized and self-monitoring.

- are *good organizers*. They are able to organize themselves and those around them to meet targets effectively and on time.

- have a *natural affinity with people*. They possess well-developed leadership skills and a high degree of maturity in dealing with others.

- are *good team builders*. They understand that their progress can be enhanced by building up the performance of their teams. They are therefore keen to advance the interests of others as well as themselves.

- are *good communicators*. They can communicate both face to face and on paper.

2 *W. H. Smith*
The performance areas used in W. H. Smith's general management assessment centre are:

- *Self management* – the ability to organize, plan and manage time

- *Interaction management and leadership* – the ability to work constructively with peers and seniors and to interface with other functions

- *Financial management* – financial knowledge and ability to make sound financial judgements

- *Marketing management* – the ability to consider and approve strategic marketing issues, recognizing and responding to strengths and opportunities

- *Strategic planning* – the ability to think and act at a strategic level and to define clear longer-range business-related objectives

- *Situation assessment* – the ability to make an analysis of a business situation, to identify its key variables and to generate appropriate objectives and courses of action

- *Staff management* – the ability to work successfully with subordinates and experts to obtain information and understanding of unfamiliar subjects

- *Manpower planning* – the ability to determine future requirements against available resources, identifying training and development needs

- *Oral communications* – the ability to speak clearly and present or argue a situation in a logical and positive manner which gains commitment and support

- *Written communications* – the ability to create businesslike correspondence and, where appropriate, present well-argued proposals supported by relevant data

Using the checklists

There is some overlap between these checklists. The first one, however, concentrates on basic skills and abilities while the others are more biased towards applied managerial skills. In the case of the W. H. Smith list, this is directed mainly at the skills of general management.

Because of the different focus of each list, and in spite of the overlaps, it is helpful to go through them all and assess your own performance against the relevant headings. If you wish, you can give yourself marks of 1–10 for each item corresponding to a classification along these lines:

A = outstanding   (9–10 points)

B = very effective   (7–8 points)

C = satisfactory   (5–6 points)

D = barely satisfactory   (3–4 points)

E = unsatisfactory   (0–2 points)

On completing this assessment, note the particularly high and low scores in each list and draw up a schedule of your strengths and weaknesses as a manager.

Knowing What You Want

Knowing what you want means analysing your self-assessment to find out what you are good at and then doing it. It involves the following actions:

1 Refer to the analysis of your strengths in terms of achievements, personality, and distinctive competences, and decide how best you can use, indeed exploit, them. Note particularly the factors that contributed to any successes.

2 Refer to the analysis of your weaknesses in terms of any failures and those aspects of your personality which you believe could hinder you in your future career. List these as areas for self-development.

3 Find out what the requirements are for success and promotion in your profession or occupation and in your firm. You need to know what competences in terms of skills and knowledge are required at each stage in the promotion ladder so that you can devise an 'aiming point' over a period of time. You should establish what the critical success factors are and the criteria used for judging performance.

It is unlikely that this information will be readily available in most organizations. You can ask your superior, but his or her knowledge may be limited. You can seek advice from the personnel department and, in a reasonably large organization, there should be someone there who is responsible for career development and knows the answers. If you cannot get direct answers you will have to find out for yourself, by observation and by asking around. Every organization has its own culture which determines the values and behavioural norms that lead to high ratings for performance and potential. They will not always be put down on paper, but they will be there. It is up to you to find out what they are and react accordingly. But you will have to decide whether or not these values and norms are those which you can live with and thrive on. If not, it is best to go elsewhere.

4 Set demanding targets and deadlines for yourself. As Peter Drucker says, 'People grow according to the demands they make on themselves.'[3] But don't over-commit yourself. Be

realistic about what you can achieve. It is a mistake to be unambitious but over-ambition based on an unrealistic analysis of your strengths and potential can be even more disastrous. It can lead to over-promotion or tackling jobs in which you are bound to fail. Be aware always of the Peter Principle: 'Managers tend to rise to the level of their own incompetence.'[4]

5   Focus on what you believe *you* can contribute: 'To ask "what can I contribute?" is to look for the unused potential in a job.' (Peter Drucker)[3]

6   Get your priorities right. As Drucker says:[3]

  ● Pick the future as against the past.

  ● Focus on opportunities rather than on problems.

  ● Choose your own direction, rather than climb on the bandwagon.

  ● Aim high: aim for something that will make a difference rather than something that is safe and easy to do.

7   Learn to adapt to changing demands. 'The executive who keeps on doing what he has done successfully before is almost bound to fail.' (Peter Drucker)[3]

8   Challenge your assumptions about what you can do and what you want to do. Try to develop a conceptual framework for these assumptions which, as Charles Handy[5] suggests, can:

  ● help one to *explain* the past, which in turn

  ● helps one to *understand* the present, and thus

  ● to *predict* the future which leads to

  ● more *influence* over future events and

  ● less *disturbance* from the unexpected.

Developing Yourself

Peter Drucker says that:

> Development is always self-development. Nothing could be more absurd than for the enterprise to assume the responsi-

bility for the development of people. The responsibility rests with individuals, their abilities, their efforts.[6]

Self-development involves a constant search for excellence. As Robert Townsend says:

> If you can't do it excellently, don't do it at all. Because if it is not excellent it will not be profitable or fun and if you're not in business for fun or profit, what the hell are you doing there?[7]

A self-development programme starts from the analysis of your strengths and weaknesses and your conclusions on where you are going. Self-development activities include:

- learning from experience
- learning from your boss
- learning from your colleagues
- learning from your subordinates
- reading
- acquiring extra qualifications
- attending conferences, meetings and training courses

Learning from experience

'Experience is the best teacher' may be a truism, but it is none the less valid for being so. It can be said that 'managers learn to manage by managing' – but experience alone is not enough. We have all come across highly successful managers who treat every new problem as a challenging opportunity to develop existing skills and add new ones to their repertoire. We also know managers who claim that they have had ten years' experience but in fact have only had one year repeated ten times!

Learning from experience means learning from your mistakes as well as your successes. As Robert Townsend says, 'Admit your own mistakes openly, even joyfully.'[7] But learn from them by analysing what went wrong and what you need to do to avoid making the same mistakes again. A reasonable boss will tolerate one mistake as part of the learning process. But he or she has every right to be intolerant if the mistake is repeated.

People only learn from experience if they analyse what that experience is and how well or badly they tackled the opportunity or problem. Every time something goes right or wrong for you it is necessary to sit back and answer the following questions:

1   What was the situation?

2   What did I do – or not do?

3   What was the outcome?

4   To what extent did my behaviour contribute to success or lack of success?

5   What, therefore, should I do next time to repeat my success or eliminate the possibility of failure?

6   What knowledge and skills must I develop or acquire to achieve this success?

7   How do I develop the knowledge and skills I require? Can I do it myself, or do I need help? If the latter, where do I get it from?

Learning from your boss

You do not simply learn to manage by managing. You learn even more effectively by both managing *and* by being managed by a good boss. All successful managers will recall the experiences they have had in the past when they have learned from the behaviour or wisdom of their superior at the time. They take care not to copy them slavishly, but extract what is good and relevant and put the rest to one side.

One can also learn, of course, from the mistakes or weaknesses of a superior. But this is negative learning and the positive approach is much more likely to lead to beneficial results.

You can learn not only by observing your boss in action, but also from his or her appraisal of your performance. As long as this is results orientated, i.e. it concentrates on achievements against objectives rather than dwelling on abstract personality assessments, it should provide an ideal opportunity to get an objective view of how well you are doing. The appraisal should concentrate on facts and observable behaviours. It should not only assess what went right or wrong but also why it happened that way and what you *and* your boss are going to do about it. Although the emphasis should be on self-development, all managers have the responsibility to develop their subordinates by guidance and coaching.

Learning from your colleagues

Interpersonal skills are important items in the manager's repertoire. You can learn something about your effectiveness in practising them by observing and analysing other people's reaction to your proposals and behaviour. This requires the exercise of sensitivity, as we will see in Chapter 14.

If you can establish really good relationships with your colleagues you can get them to give you feedback on their reactions to what you are saying and doing. You can ask them questions like, 'Did it make sense?' 'Was what I said quite clear?' 'Were you convinced by my argument?' 'Are you happy that I am setting about this in the right way?' 'Could you suggest any improvements to what I am proposing?' 'How can we improve the ways in which we work together for our mutual benefit?' Note that these are all matters of fact. You do not ask for personal comments based on opinion.

Learning from your subordinates

Some organizations have performance review schemes in which subordinates appraise their bosses. This is a high-risk area, but it can be very revealing if it highlights matters of fact like an absence of clear objectives or inadequate delegation. Without going as far as that, however, you can learn from your subordinates by studying their reactions to your requests or behaviour and, on occasion, asking them outright to comment on a particular point. Asking for generalized views is more difficult and, unless an extraordinarily good relationship exists, it can lead to embarrassment.

Reading

To extend your knowledge and understanding it is essential to read in and around your area of expertise. You must broaden your knowledge and keep up to date with the latest thinking and the new techniques. You have to be able to speak the language of innovation and demonstrate that you are living for the future rather than existing in the past. Beware, however, of leaping too fast onto the latest bandwagon. You must be careful to relate a new idea to the practical realities of your organization and your job.

You can keep up to date quite easily by reading professional or trade journals and the management pages of the quality newspapers, including book reviews. There is a plethora of books on management, so you will benefit from the guidance provided by reviewers and commentators on which ones are most likely to be helpful. A bibliography of selected titles is given at the end of this book.

It is useful to cultivate the art of skimming through articles and books to find really relevant parts, and then concentrating on those.

Qualifications

Clearly, you should obtain relevant qualifications or memberships to show that you have achieved a certain level of professional knowledge and status. Beyond that you must consider whether an additional qualification such as an MBA will help your career. Educationally it will extend your knowledge and skills considerably and, of course, it will look good on your CV. But you have to avoid falling into the trap of assuming that this sort of qualification automatically advances a career. By itself it doesn't. You have to add it to your other abilities, skills and achievements and use it to enhance them.

Conferences, meetings and training

Conferences and meetings of your professional association are a good way of updating yourself and keeping in touch with other people's ideas and experiences. It is often said at such affairs that people learn more from one another than from the contributors to the conference.

Clearly, formal training – in-house or an external course – can be an invaluable adjunct to a developing career. It can fill in any knowledge or enhance managerial skills. But it has to be relevant to your needs and it can only supplement your experience, which cannot be replaced by formal training.

When analysing your strengths and weaknesses and assessing your career prospects it is up to you to decide in which areas training might be able to help. You should discuss this with your boss and get his or her support. An effective training department in your organization will be able to advise you.

At the same time a formal performance review system can be used to identify training and development needs which may be suggested by your boss. But this process will be most beneficial if it is based on a joint analysis of these needs.

Planning your career progression

When you assess your abilities and potential you may set your sights at the top or near the top, but you must still work out a series of aiming points which you believe you can realistically achieve within a certain time-scale. If you are starting from the bottom it may be advisable to graduate your plan so that it can establish:

1   A firm aiming point for the next stage in your career. You can attach a time-scale of, say, two or three years to this achievement and map out a specific programme of what you need to do and learn to get there. If you believe you can get further, then you proceed to planning stage 2.

2   A broader aiming point for the second stage. This will indicate where you hope to be in 3–5 years' time. If you are starting from scratch you may well aim to extend your experience during this stage into other areas of management as a preparation to getting into general management. Again, you can decide now whether you want to pursue your ambitions to the next stage.

3   A longer-term aim of 5–10 years which will move you into general management or the upper echelons of your profession

or occupation. This should be treated as an achievable strategic objective which will be met by progressive development in stages one and two.

4   A final and overriding aim, if you believe it to be advisable, of rising to the top. You are most unlikely to be able to set a realistic time-scale for achieving this ambition, which can only take the form of a scenario of what might be accomplished if your career at earlier stages goes according to plan.

A career development plan is never fixed. It can only evolve with your career and it will be necessary constantly to review and amend your aiming points. How far you look ahead will also depend on where you have got so far, and your ability to project your future progress on the basis of an understanding of your capacity for growth, and of the scope provided within your organization or elsewhere to satisfy your ambitions.

In a realistic career plan you may have to settle for an ultimate aiming point somewhere below the top of the tree. Career progression curves tend to follow the pattern shown in Figure 9.

Figure 9
Career progression curves

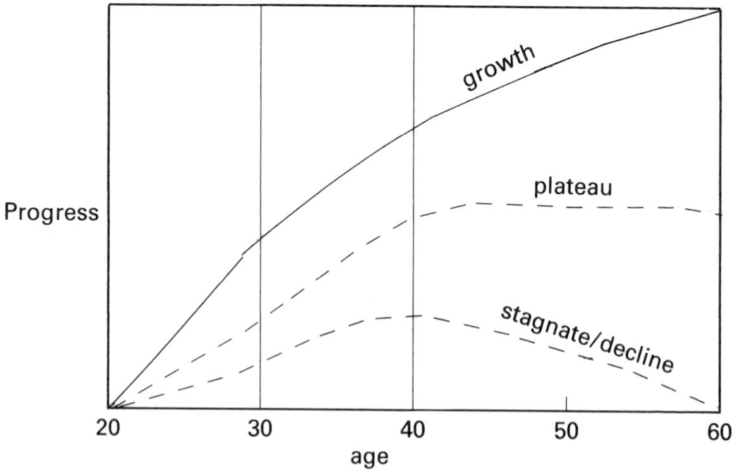

You may be confident enough to project steady growth for yourself through the expanding, establishing and maturing parts of your career. Or you might have to accept that at some stage you could 'plateau out', in which case you have to decide whether you are prepared to accept that situation (many people do) or whether you need to plan a new direction for your career. You may even have to accept the prospect of stagnation or decline unless you do something about it, which might have to be a drastic change in career plans, unless you are content to soldier on.

The important thing is to do your best to project your career so that you can select realistic aiming points or decide on alternative action in good time. Career planning is not about sitting around and waiting for something to happen. It is a pro-active process. You have to do it for yourself.

References

1 CATTELL R. B. *The scientific analysis of personality*. Harmondsworth, Penguin Books, 1965
2 PEDLAR Mike, BURGOYNE John and BOYDELL Tom. *A manager's guide to self-development*. Maidenhead, McGraw-Hill, 1986
3 DRUCKER Peter. *The effective executive*. London, Heinemann, 1962
4 PETER Lawrence. *The Peter principle*. London, Allen & Unwin, 1972
5 HANDY Charles. *Understanding organizations*. Harmondsworth, Penguin Books, 1985
6 DRUCKER Peter. *The practice of management*. London, Heinemann, 1955
7 TOWNSEND Robert. *Up the organization*. London, Michael Joseph, 1970

10

Working for Other People

Working for other people involves:

- responding to objectives
- achieving standards of performance
- meeting deadlines
- completed staff work
- managing your boss.

Responding to Objectives

In earlier discussions on setting objectives (Chapters 5 and 7) I emphasised that you and your manager will be in a better position to plan your work and monitor your progress if you have agreed objectives. The key word is 'agree'. Nobody can respond properly to objectives unless they feel that these are within the scope of their job and are attainable. In objective-setting sessions your response should be to obtain answers to the following questions:

- Is the achievement of this particular objective going to help with the attainment of overall corporate and departmental objectives?

- Does this objective fit into my role as presently defined? If it does not, you should not, of course, decline to discuss it. What you should do in these circumstances is to clarify that this is an extension of your job, which, if it is reasonable, you can welcome as an enrichment of your experience.

- What are the critical success factors in achieving this objective? It is vital that you get an answer to this question because only by knowing what these factors are will you be able to monitor progress and to evaluate the outcome.

- What resources do I need? These will include people, money, equipment and materials. Importantly, it also includes your own time. If there are shortages in any of these areas *except your own time*, you should seek to remedy them now. What you must not do is to complain that this is an extra burden on *you* – unless it is totally beyond your competence. It is your job to manage your time, establish priorities and delegate in order to free yourself to accept additional responsibilities. This is how people progress in organizations.

- What are the targets, budgets, standards of performance and time-scales I have to work to. If any of these are unreasonable or inadequate, the time to make this point is at the beginning of the project when you have been able to assess the resources required, rather than halfway through.

Meeting Standards of Performance

Meeting standards of performance, achieving results, getting things done, making things happen, is what management is all about.

David McClelland[1] carried out extensive research on what motivates managers and what makes them successful in getting things done. He identified three needs which he believes are the key factors:

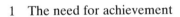

1 The need for achievement
2 The need for power (having control and influence over people)
3 The need for affiliation (to be accepted by others)

All effective managers have these needs to a certain degree, but by far the most important one is achievement. Achievement is what counts and achievers, according to McClelland, have these characteristics:

- They set themselves realistic but achievable goals with some 'stretch' built in.

- They prefer situations which they themselves can influence rather than those in which chance plays a large part.

- They are more concerned with knowing they have done well than with the rewards that success brings.

- They get their rewards from their accomplishment rather than from money or praise. This does not mean that high achievers reject money, which does in fact motivate them as long as it is seen as a realistic measure of their performance.

- They are most effective in situations where they are allowed to get ahead by their own efforts.

What do achievers do?

High achievers do some, if not all, of these things:

- They define to themselves precisely what they want to do.

- They set demanding but not unattainable time-scales in which to do it.

- They convey clearly what they want done and by when.

- They are prepared to discuss how things should be done and will listen to and take advice. But once the course of action has been agreed they stick to it unless events dictate a change of direction.

- They are single-minded about getting where they want to go, showing perseverance and determination in the face of adversity.

- They demand high performance from themselves and are somewhat callous in expecting equally high performance from everyone else.

- They work hard and work well under pressure; in fact, it brings out the best in them.

- They tend to be dissatisfied with the status quo.

- They are never completely satisfied with their own performance and continually question themselves.

- They will take calculated risks.

- They snap out of setbacks without being personally shattered and quickly regroup their forces and their ideas.

- They are enthusiastic about the task and convey their enthusiasm to others.

- They are decisive in the sense that they are able quickly to sum up situations, define alternative courses of action, determine the preferred course, and convey to their subordinates what needs to be done.

- They continually monitor their own and their subordinates' performance so that any deviation can be corrected in good time.

Meeting Deadlines

Getting things done on time can be the most stressful activity that managers engage in (see Chapter 8). But it is certainly the area where the performance of managers is most 'on the line' and where they have to be able to satisfy the stringent requirements of their superiors, who undoubtedly are under pressure to meet deadlines themselves.

Some people do not worry about planning to meet deadlines because they are happy to leave everything to the last minute and, with the adrenalin flowing, so they say, deliver a better result than if they had phased their activities over a longer period. Lesser mortals, which means most of us, will achieve more within their time-scale if they:

- programme individual task or projects by:
  - listing the major operations in sequence
  - breaking down each major operation into major and subsidiary tasks
  - estimate the time required to complete each operation
  - add up the operation times to obtain a total time. In a complex project where there are a number of interrelated activities, network planning techniques can be used which estimate activity durations, identify the key activities and deduce from this analysis the critical path, which is defined as that unbroken sequence of events and activities through

the network from the first to the last event which add up to the total duration time required.

- prioritize separate tasks or projects by an assessment of the order in which they should be completed. This assessment could be related to an evaluation of the contribution the task could make to achieving the overall programme, which might be determined by how the task fits into this programme or, if it is a separate activity, by an assessment of its relative importance. The assessment could be based on the expressed views of higher management or a more subjective review of the task's relative importance in the scheme of things. In really complex situations, the operational research technique of queuing theory can be used. This applies mathematical techniques to describe the characteristics of queues of people, material, work-in-progress etc. The aim is to find the best way to plan and time the sequence of events so that bottlenecks can be avoided and the task can be completed on time.

- Set up information systems which will monitor work-in-progress against the programme and deadlines. Network planning systems use computers to generate precise control information on progress in relation to plan along the critical path. A simpler control system uses a Gantt chart to plot in bars the period of time which each operation should take, as illustrated in Figure 10.

Figure 10
A Gantt chart

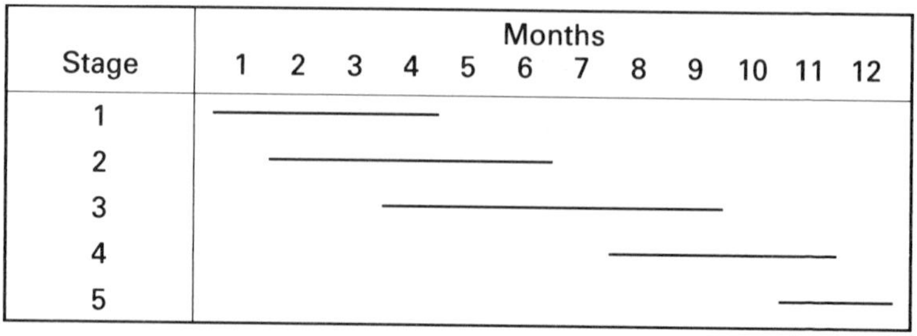

Stage	Months											
	1	2	3	4	5	6	7	8	9	10	11	12
1	————————											
2		————————										
3				————————								
4						————————						
5									————			

- Monitor progress against the programme and deadlines and,

as necessary, add extra resources to complete the task on time or adjust priorities so that deadlines are met.

Completed Staff Work

Completed staff work is a military phrase which is equally applicable to the management task of working for other people. It means that if you are asked to do something you should do it thoroughly and come up with solutions, not problems. Test your ideas in draft form if you like, but having done so, present a complete proposal with whatever supporting arguments or evidence you need. Avoid half-baked suggestions. Your boss wants answers, not questions. When you have finished your report and studied your conclusions and recommendations, ask yourself the question: 'If I were my boss would I stake my reputation on this piece of work and put my name to it?' If the answer is 'no', tear up your report and do it again. It's not completed staff work.

Managing Your Boss

Bosses need managing as much as anyone else. Managers exist to get results. They are not there simply to please their superiors. But they are more likely to get things done and progress in the organization if they can:

- get agreement from their superiors on what they, the managers, are expected to do
- deal with them effectively when problems arise
- impress them generally with their efficiency and effectiveness

Getting agreement

Getting agreement from superiors involves:

- finding out what they expect – their likes and dislikes, their quirks and prejudices, how they like things presented to them, how they like things to be done

- establishing the best ways, times and places to tackle them with a proposal, request or problem

- avoiding open confrontation. If you can't get your own way at first, return later at a more propitious moment. If you get into an argument, leave an escape route – a way open for them to consent without having to climb down

- not trying to achieve too much at once. It is often better to tackle one or two things at a time. Bosses have many other preoccupations and their boredom thresholds are often low. Avoid overwhelming them with detail. They will always prefer a clear-cut proposition supported by arguments which are compelling but limited in number and complexity.

Dealing with problems

If things are going wrong managers should adopt the following approach with their superiors.

- Keep them informed. Never let them be taken by surprise. Prepare them in advance for any bad news.

- If something has gone wrong explain what has happened and why (no excuses) and what you propose to do about it.

- Emphasise that you would like their views on what you propose as well as their agreement – everyone likes to be consulted.

Impressing your boss

Your boss needs to trust you, to rely upon you and to believe in your capacity to come up with good ideas and to make things happen. He doesn't want to wet-nurse you or to spend his time correcting your mistakes or covering up.

To succeed in impressing your boss without really trying (it is fatal to push too much), you should:

- always be frank and open. Admit mistakes. Never lie or even be economical with the truth. If there is the faintest suspicion that you are not perfectly straightforward, your boss will never trust you again.

- aim to help your boss to be right. This does not mean being subservient or time-serving. Recognize, however, that you exist to give support – in the right direction.

- respond fast to requests on a can do/will do basis.

- not trouble him or her unnecessarily with your problems

- provide protection where required. Loyalty is an old-fashioned virtue, but you owe it to your boss. If you cannot be loyal then you should get out from under as quickly as you can.

Reference

1   McCLELLAND David. *Power, the inner experience*. New York, Irvington, 1975

11

Working in a Group

Organizations consist of groups of people working together. Managers spend much of their time leading teams and dealing with people collectively. Getting people to work well together is as important as motivating individuals. And, as an executive, you will have to play your part in one or more groups.

To become an effective team leader or member of a group it is necessary to understand:

- the nature of groups
- the processes which take place within groups
- the roles people play in groups
- the factors which make for group effectiveness
- how best to lead a group
- how best to work in a group

The Nature of Groups

The Hawthorne experiment

An understanding of the nature of groups in organizations first emerged in the 1920s, especially in the so-called Hawthorne experiment as described by Elton Mayo.[1] Although this research took place a long time ago its findings are still relevant today and it has certainly been the foundation for most of the current views on how groups operate.

In the first stage of the experiment a study was made of a specially selected group assembling telephone relays in the Hawthorne plant of GEC. A series of changes was made to their work involving improvements in rest-pause arrangements and working hours. Each improvement resulted in increased productivity. The improvements were then taken away, and productivity continued to increase. This became known as the Hawthorne effect. The explanation given was that by asking their help and co-operation, the investigators had made the women feel important. Their whole attitude had changed from being separate cogs in a machine to being a cohesive and congenial group trying to help solve a problem. They had found stability, a place where they belonged, and work whose purpose they could clearly see. And so they worked faster and better than they ever had in their lives.

This aspect of the experiment was therefore the foundation for our current belief, that groups will be most effective when they are cohesive and when their members are fully involved in planning and controlling how they operate.

The second stage of the experiment looked more carefully at how cohesive groups function. The group studied was a team engaged on bank-wiring. The investigation showed that the group had developed spontaneously into a team with natural leaders who had risen to the top with the active consent of the group. These natural leaders, as has been found in numerous similar investigations since the Hawthorne studies, do not necessarily coincide with those put in authority by management. Within the group, however, they may have greater power than the official leader.

It was also established that an informal organization existed which had its own social norms, some expressed orally, others implicit in actions. For example, the daily output represented a standard of what the group considered to be a fair day's work, but this was never expressed explicitly.

The second stage established the distinction between formal and informal groups. It also led to further investigations into group processes.

Formal groups

Formal groups are set up by organizations to achieve a defined purpose. They include organizational units, project teams, working parties and committees. People are brought together with the necessary skills to carry out the task and a system exists for directing, co-ordinating and controlling the group's activities. The structure, composition and size of the group will depend largely on the nature of the task, although tradition, technology and the organization's behavioural norms and management style (how managers exercise authority) may exert considerable influence.

The more routine or clearly defined the task is the more structured the group will be. In a highly structured group the leader will have a positive role and may well adopt an authoritarian style. The role of each member of the group will be precise and a hierarchy of authority is likely to exist.

The more varied or ambiguous the task the more difficult it will be to structure the group. The leader's role is more likely to be supportive, he or she will tend to concentrate on encouragement and co-ordination rather than on issuing orders. The group will operate in a more democratic way, and individual roles will be fluid and less clearly defined.

Informal groups

Informal groups are set up by people in organizations who have some affinity with each other. It could be said that formal groups satisfy the needs of the organization while informal groups satisfy the needs of their members. The aims of the organization should be to set up and manage groups which will satisfy both these needs. Cohesive groups can work for the organization but, as the Hawthorne studies showed, they can work against the organization by regulating their own behaviour and output levels irrespective of what management wants.

Work types

Recent research by Seth Allcorn[2] has identified four types of work groups.

1 *The homogenized group.* Homogenization, in psychological terms, is what occurs when an individual fails to satisfy his or her need to feel valued by others. This happens in homogenized groups where members behave as though the group lacked effective leadership and a clear agenda or task, even though these may be present to some degree. Members are uncertain

as to what to do and how to act, and they feel isolated from their work and from one another. Participation in the group is unrewarding, since individuals feel neither secure nor good about the group and themselves. Under these circumstances the group is ineffective and members of it are dissatisfied with their lot.

2   *The institutionalized group.* This is a highly structured group which controls its members' actions by creating rigid routines. This sort of group can fail over the long term when feelings of oppression and alienation may emerge, threatening its security.

3   *The autocratic group.* This is a group which is dominated by a powerful charismatic leader who provides direction, rewards and punishments and who maintains as much control as possible to minimize members' anxiety. Such groups are often successful but members can feel frustrated. This reveals itself in aggression against the leader which may result in his or her removal, probably to be replaced by another autocratic leader. The group can rapidly move to take advantage of sudden opportunities but it is also likely to follow a leader in any direction, even down a wrong path.

4   *The intentional group.* This type of group encourages group members to work on their task by facilitating open discussion of the needs of the task and of the group members. Group members are encouraged to be responsible for their own actions. Strong leadership is only supplied when it is needed.

Characteristics of established groups

To summarize, the main characteristics of a well-established group (formal or informal) are as follows:

1   It is cohesive – the members of the group put up a united front to outsiders (who may include their boss or the management).

2   The members are interdependent – they rely upon each other for support in achieving both work and social goals.

3   It develops its own norms so that members of the group act in ways which are not in accordance with their own needs, or those of the organization, or those of the group leader.

4   The members will tend to share beliefs and values (the group develops its own ideology) which may or may not be in accord with those of the organization or their boss.

5   The whole is greater than the sum of the parts, i.e. a well-knit group may exert greater influence when working as a whole than the total influence of each of its members if they were working separately.

Group Processes

Group processes are the dynamics of how groups operate and the study of each process is often referred to as group dynamics. It is necessary to know something about these processes in order to understand what is happening in groups, and thereby to increase your effectiveness as a leader or member of a team.

The main processes described below are concerned with interaction, key functions, norms and identification, but these need first to be considered against the background of the size and structural factors which affect the working of groups.

Size

The way in which groups function will be affected by the nature of the task and by the behavioural norms of the organization. An additional factor will be size. There will be a greater diversity of talent, skills and knowledge in a large group, but individuals will find it more difficult to make their presence felt. In general, the larger the group the greater are the unseen pressures for conformity.

Meredith Belbin[3] suggests on the basis of his extensive research into the workings of groups that about six members is a fair compromise figure for a group, coming as it does between eight, which is too big and four, which is too small. According to Charles Handy,[4] to achieve maximum participation and the highest all-round involvement, the optimum size is between five and seven. But to achieve the requisite breadth of knowledge the group may have to be larger, and this makes greater demands on the skills of the leader in getting participation.

Structure

Behaviour within a group is heavily influenced by its structure. In strong, formal structures and autocratic groups, people are more likely to be expected to do as they are told. They will not be encouraged to show initiative and as Belbin[3] says, 'There is less tolerance for dissenters or any form of deviant expression.' In informal structures there will be more discussion and tolerance of individuality or dissent. But unstructured groups may not be so effective at getting the work done than the formal groups. There may be less open dissent and argument in a structured group because everyone does as they are told, although resentful feelings may be simmering away to boil over in a crisis. In an informal group the team members can work together cohesively on a voluntary basis. But conflict can arise easily and could be more acute in a highly cohesive group simply because people are working so closely together. Strong leadership or a very powerful group culture which can manage conflict may be necessary in these circumstances. (Conflict management is discussed in Chapter 15.)

Interaction

Within any group various interactive processes take place which involve interrelationships between the leader (if there is one) and the group members; between the group members and the leader; and amongst the group members themselves. These processes will include agreement or disagreement, co-operation or conflict, friendliness or hostility, openness or reticence, involvement or withdrawal, taking the group forward or holding it back.

The channels of communication within which these interactions take place form three basic patterns as defined by H. J. Leavitt[5] and illustrated in Figure 11, where A is the group leader and B–E are group members.

The following are the characteristic processes that take place in these three types of groups.

- Wheel groups tend to deal with straightforward tasks and the members work faster, need fewer messages to solve problems and make fewer errors than circle or all-channel (star) groups. But they are inflexible if the task changes.

Figure 11
The three basic channels of group communication

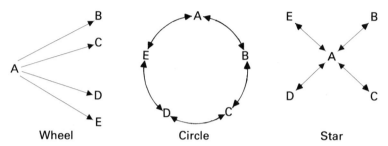

Wheel   Circle   Star

Source: Based on H. J. Leavitt, 'Some effects of certain communication patterns on group performance'. *Journal of Abnormal Psychology*, 1951.

- Circle groups are faster than wheel groups at solving complex problems.
- Star or all-channel groups are the most flexible and function best in complex open-ended situations.

The level of satisfaction for individuals is lowest in the circle (where contact between the leader and its members is incomplete), fairly high in the star or all channel group and mixed in the wheel, where the leader is more satisfied than the outlying members.

Functions of groups

As identified by Ed Schein[6] groups will only operate effectively if they carry out what he terms task and maintenance functions.

- *Task functions* are carried out to achieve the purpose of the group and comprise:
  - initiating – someone has to state the objective or the problem, make proposals as to how to work on it and set targets and time limits.
  - opinion seeking and giving – there has to be a free and forthright exchange of opinions.
  - information seeking and giving – time has to be allowed for

the right questions to be asked and answered by members of the group.

– clarifying – someone has to be able to clarify the issues of a group in tackling a complex problem, otherwise the discussion can drift.

– elaborating – groups can be simplistic in looking at situations or solutions; someone has to be ready to elaborate on a basic idea to ensure that it is practical.

– summarizing – someone must be capable of summarizing a discussion by reviewing the points the group has covered and by listing the different ideas that have emerged. This prevents ideas being lost and means that the group is operating on full information.

– consensus taking – groups need a person who will periodically test whether they are nearing a decision or should continue to discuss the issue.

In formal groups the leaders will be expected to make sure that these task functions are carried out. But they do not have to do it all themselves. One of their key jobs is to identify people in the group who have skills in one or more of these areas and use them. Effective group leaders are people who make the best use of the skills and resources available in their teams. (Team roles are discussed in the next section of this chapter.)

● *Maintenance functions* exist to establish good relations within the group, a sense of common purpose and group cohesion in achieving the task. They include:

– harmonizing and compromising to reduce destructive types of disagreement between individuals. It should be noted, however, that the aim should not be to smooth over differences at all times. There is such a thing as creative conflict in which the group confronts and works through tough disagreements to some genuine integrative solution which does not involve any compromising (obtaining bland and superficial agreement).

– gatekeeping, providing opportunities for members of the group to make a contribution.

– encouraging, helping people to make their point, partly to ensure that the group has the benefit of the suggestion, but also to make sure that the group climate is one of acceptance rather than hostility to suggestions and ideas. Nothing can wreck team spirit more effectively than people who spend their time scoring points off each other or cutting each other down to size. If this destructive behaviour exists it has to be stopped, by the other members of the group as well as by the leader.

– diagnosing the effectiveness with which the group is operating to establish remedial measures when relationships have to some degree broken down. Ideally, the group should suspend task operations to look at the way in which interactive processes are taking place, check on how people are feeling about the groups' method of working and air any problems and conflicts that have arisen. This is, however, a difficult task for a group to undertake and a 'process' consultant can help as a facilitator of the joint analysis required to understand how the group's processes are functioning.

Group norms

Group norms are sets of assumptions held by members of the group on what kind of behaviour is right or wrong, good or bad, appropriate or inappropriate, allowed or not allowed. Norms may be stated or unstated and could include such beliefs as: 'We must be informal with one another', 'Everyone must be allowed to have his or her say', 'We must always stick to the issues and never get involved in personality conflicts', 'We should reach consensus and not fall back on voting'.

Long-standing groups can develop an ideology over time which affects the attitudes and actions of their members and the degree of satisfaction which they feel. Well-established norms and ideologies may be difficult to change in the short term. Strong leaders can try and will often succeed, but sometimes at the expense of the team spirit built up by the group.

Identification

Individuals will identify with their group if they like the group leader and other members, approve of the purpose and work of the group and wish to be associated with the standing of the group in the organization. Identification will be more complete if the standing is good.

Group Roles

The basic roles and behaviours that people adopt in groups can be classified under the following headings:

- Agree
- Attack
- Clarify
- Distract
- Build
- Cross-talk

A more detailed list of roles which can be used to analyse behaviour at meetings consists of:

- Proposing
- Building
- Supporting
- Disagreeing
- Defending
- Attacking
- Blocking
- Open
- Testing
- Summarizing
- Seeking information
- Bringing in

Belbin's classification of roles

Meredith Belbin's classification of roles[3] identifies eight categories:

1 *Chairmen* – control the way in which a team moves towards the group objectives by making the best use of team resources,

recognizing where the team's strengths and weaknesses lie and ensuring that the best use is made of each team member's role

2   *Shapers* – specify the ways in which team effort is applied, directing attention generally to the setting of objectives and priorities and seeking to impose some shape or pattern on group discussion and on the outcome of group activities

3   *Company workers* – turn concepts and plans into practical working procedures and carry out agreed plans systematically and efficiently

4   *Plants* – specify new ideas and strategies with special attention to major issues, and look for possible breaks in approaches to the problems with which the group is confronted

5   *Resource investigators* – explore and report on ideas, developments and resources outside the group, creating external contacts that might be useful to the team and conducting any subsequent negotiations

6   *Monitor-evaluators* – analyse problems and evaluate ideas and suggestions so that the team is better placed to take better decisions

7   *Team workers* – support members in their strengths (i.e. building on their suggestions), underpin members in their shortcomings, improve communications between members and foster team spirit generously

8   *Completer-finishers* – ensure that the team is protected from mistakes, actively search for work which needs more than a usual degree of attention, and maintain a sense of urgency in the team

Belbin suggests that although the main roles of team members can be slotted into one or other of these categories, most people have an alternative back-up role which they use as necessary.

Group Effectiveness

An effective team is cohesive, self-supportive and knows where it is going. Douglas McGregor[7] describes the main features which indicate such a team.

1   The atmosphere tends to be informal, comfortable, relaxed.

2   There is a lot of discussion in which initially everyone participates, but it remains pertinent to the task of the group.

3   The task or objective of the group is well understood and accepted by the members. There will have been discussion of the objective at some point until it was formulated in such a way that the members of the group could commit themselves to it.

4   The members listen to each other. Every idea is given a hearing. People do not appear to be afraid of looking foolish by putting forward a creative thought, even if it seems fairly extreme.

5   There is disagreement. It is not suppressed or overridden by premature group action. The reasons are carefully examined, and the group seeks to resolve them rather than to dominate the dissenter.

6   Most decisions are reached by consensus in which it is clear that everybody is in general agreement and willing to go along.

7   Criticism is frequent, frank, and relatively comfortable. There is little evidence of personal attack, either openly or in a hidden fashion.

8   People are free in expressing their feelings as well as their ideas both on the problem and on the group's operation.

9   When action is taken, clear assignments are made and accepted.

10 The leader of the group does not dominate it, nor does the group defer unduly to him or her.

These characteristics present an ideal which you might strive for but will seldom attain. There will be times when you have to do away with some of the more time-consuming ones, such as 2, 6 and 8 and concentrate on 3 and 9. 'The task or objective of the group is well understood and accepted by the members . . . when action is taken, clear assignments are made and accepted.'

Belbin's research into winning teams[3] indicated that the following factors were important:

1   A leader who is a patient but commanding figure and who generates trust. Good leaders know how to find and use ability and, although they do not dominate proceedings, they know how to pull things together if a critical decision has to be reached.

2   The existence of one strong 'plant' i.e. one very creative and clever member

3   A fair spread in mental abilities, which means that people with slightly lower abilities look for other ways of fulfilling themselves apart from the sheer application of intelligence

4   A spread in personal attributes covering, ideally, all the team roles either as a main role or in a back-up capacity

5   A good match between the attributes of the members and their responsibilities in the team

6   An ability to adjust to the realization of imbalance in the team, i.e. the capacity to understand weaknesses in the composition of the team and compensate for them

Leading Groups

John Adair[8] suggests that working groups have three basic needs which the leader must satisfy.

1   The need to achieve the common task

2   The need to be held together and maintain themselves as cohesive unities

3   The needs which individuals bring with them to the group

To build an effective team it is necessary to satisfy these needs and ensure, so far as possible, that you have people who can carry out the various roles described earlier. If the team is ineffective you have to ask yourself why. Is it because you are ineffective as a leader or do the members of the team need more guidance and help in working together?

To be effective as a group leader you must demonstrate to your team that:

- you know where you want them to go

- you know how they are going to get there

- you know what you expect each member of the team to achieve

- you know what you are doing

- you know their strengths and weaknesses and can capitalize on the former and help to overcome the latter.

To do this you have to be equally concerned with your task and maintenance functions. You can then concentrate on doing the following things:

- encouraging participation in agreeing objectives and targets

- grouping related tasks together so that group members know that they can make their jobs easier by co-operating with others

- rotating jobs within groups so that group members identify with the team as a whole rather than with their own jobs

- ensuring that communications flow freely within and between groups

- encouraging informal meetings between groups to resolve problems

You can also consider whether your team could benefit from specific training with the objectives of:

- increasing awareness of the social pressures taking place within groups

- developing the interactive or interpersonal skills which enable individuals to function effectively as team members

- increasing the overall effectiveness with which groups operate in the organization

How Best to Work in a Group

To work effectively in a group you need to:

- understand the purpose of the group

- find out what you are expected to contribute

- analyse the other members of the group, especially the leader, to decide who plays which role

- observe the behaviour of the group to identify group norms so that you can conform or consciously deviate from them if necessary

- analyse your own skills and competences to establish how you might best contribute, referring to the lists of roles for guidance on how you might use your talents most effectively

- prepare yourself well before meetings – get your facts and arguments at your fingertips

- not talk too much. It is often best to 'keep your powder dry' and not rush in too quickly. The art of being a good team member is to know when and how to intervene

- assess your own performance as a team member. Ask yourself what you are good and not so good at doing by reference to your successes and failures, and take appropriate action.

References

1 MAYO Elton. *The human problems of an industrial civilisation*. London, Macmillan, 1933
2 ALLCORN Seth. 'Understanding groups at work'. *Personnel*. August 1989, pp 28–36
3 BELBIN Meredith. *Management teams: why they succeed or fail*. London, Heinemann, 1981
4 HANDY Charles. *Understanding organizations*. Harmondsworth, Penguin, 1985

5 LEAVITT H. J. 'Some effects of certain communication patterns on group performance'. *Journal of Abnormal Psychology*, 1951
6 SCHEIN Edgar. *Process consultation: its role in organization development*. Reading, Massachusetts, Addison-Wesley, 1969
7 McGREGOR Douglas. *The human side of enterprise*. New York, McGraw-Hill, 1966.
8 ADAIR John. *Effective leadership*. Aldershot, Gower, 1983

12

Managing Change

All organizations are, to a greater or lesser extent, in a perpetual state of change. To survive and thrive, businesses have to grow. They must innovate, develop new products, expand into new markets, reorganize, introduce new technology, and change working methods and practices. Even if this does not happen voluntarily, change may be forced upon them by competition and changes in the business, political and social environment. And, because of political, economic and social pressures, this pressure for change is as great in the public and voluntary sectors as in the private sector.

Managers have to be able to introduce and to manage change and gain the commitment of their teams. They must become, in the words of Rosabeth Moss Kanter, 'Change masters, helping and guiding the organization, its management and all who work in it to manage and, indeed, to exploit and triumph over change'.[1]

To manage change it is necessary to understand:

- the impact of change

- why people resist change

- introducing change

- the approaches that can be used to overcome resistance and obtain commitment to change

- the steps that can be taken to accelerate change

The Impact of Change

Change can create instability and ambiguity and replace order and predictability with disharmony and surprise. As we will see in Chapter 16, the corporate culture can create solidarity and meaning and can inspire commitment and productivity. But the culture can actively and forcefully work against an organization when change becomes necessary.

Some people welcome change as a challenge and because it brings variety to their lives. But most people resist it to a greater or lesser degree, and therefore we must explore why this resistance exists before we can discuss what can be done about it.

Resistance to Change

Resistance to change takes place when the expected goals, norms and values of management are in conflict with those of employees. The change is then perceived as a threat to familiar patterns of behaviour. If it is also perceived as a threat to the security, income, status, authority or personal circumstances of an individual it can be regarded with suspicion, fear or even open hostility. These reactions may well occur if people feel that in any way they are going to be worse off, even if their fears are without foundation.

Change often takes place in conditions of uncertainty and can itself create feelings of uncertainty. Fear of the unknown is likely when the situation creates ambiguities in:

- goals – employees not being clear about what they are supposed to achieve
- data – information about the situation and its likely effects is absent, unclear, changing or confused
- roles – lack of clarity about authority and responsibility and how the individual fits into the new set-up
- methods – lack of clarity about the means required to achieve the ends
- criteria – no means of judging whether or not the change has been introduced successfully and the objectives of the change programme have been achieved.

What management in general and individual managers in particular should always remember is that resistance to change is a natural, not an unnatural, process. Change is a threat to familiar patterns of behaviour as well as to security, status and financial rewards. Joan Woodward makes this point clearly.

> When we talk about resistance to change we tend to imply that management is always rational in changing its direction, and that employees are stupid, emotional or irrational in not responding in the way they should. But if an individual is going to be worse off, explicitly or implicitly, when the proposed changes have been made, any resistance is entirely rational in terms of his best interests. The interests of the organization and the individual do not always coincide.[2]

If not properly managed, change can decrease morale, motivation and commitment and create conditions of conflict within an organization.

Change Management

Basic mechanisms

The basic mechanisms for managing change as suggested by Lewin[3] are:

1 *Unfreezing* – altering the present stable equilibrium which supports existing behaviours and attitudes. This process must take account of the inherent threats change presents to people and the need to motivate those affected to attain the natural state of equilibrium by accepting change.

2 *Changing* – developing new responses based on new information.

3 *Refreezing* – stabilizing the change by introducing the new responses into the personalities of those concerned

Programming change

A change programme should incorporate the following processes as suggested by Richard Beckhard:[4]

1 Setting goals and defining the future state or organizational conditions desired after the change
2 Diagnosing the present condition in relation to these goals
3 Defining the transition state activities and commitments required to meet the future state
4 Developing strategies and action plans for managing this transition in the light of an analysis of the factors likely to affect the introduction of change

Analysis

Those wanting change should be constant about the ends but they may have to be flexible about the means. This requires them to come to an understanding of the forces likely to resist change as well as those creating the need for change.

Lewin[3] called this process 'field force analysis', and it involves:

1 Analysing the restraining or driving forces which will affect the transition to the future state. These restraining forces will include the reactions of those who see change as unnecessary or constituting a threat.
2 Assessing which of the driving or restraining forces are critical
3 Taking steps both to increase the critical driving forces and to decrease the critical restraining forces

When analysing the potential impact of change in one part of the organization, it is necessary not only to consider how it directly affects the people in that area but also to take a helicopter view of how the proposed changes will affect the organization as a whole.

In making this analysis the individual introducing the change, who is often called the 'change agent' should recognize that new ideas are likely to be misunderstood and make ample provision for the discussion of reactions to proposals to ensure complete understanding of them. It is also necessary to try to gain an understanding of the feelings and fears of those affected so that unnecessary worries can be relieved and, so far as possible, ambiguities can be resolved.

Overcoming Resistance to Change

Resistance to change is likely to be less if:

- the change is perceived as being consistent with the norms of the organization and in accordance with its existing values

- the programme for change offers the kind of new experience which interests participants

- the change is seen as reducing rather than increasing present burdens

- those affected feel that their autonomy and security are not threatened, so far as this is possible

- it can be demonstrated that the change meets the needs of those affected, i.e. 'there is something in it for them'

- the outcome of change is reasonably certain

- there is a compelling and fully understood reason for change

- the organization is familiar with change

- it can be demonstrated that the organization will take steps to reduce, if not eliminate, any potentially detrimental results of change. These steps could include retraining, guarantees of employment elsewhere in the organization, protection of existing status and pay (if this is possible) or comprehensive outplacement programmes for those who, unavoidably, have to be made redundant.

Gaining Commitment to Change

'People support what they help create.' Commitment to change will be greater if those affected are allowed to participate as fully as possible in planning and implementing it. The aim should be to get them to 'own' the change as something they want and will be glad to live with.

Getting involvement in the introduction of change will only be effective in gaining commitment when management is prepared to listen and to change its plans if there is a clear message that they are unworkable, or if the plans could be made more acceptable without prejudicing the achievement of the objectives of the change programme.

Accelerating Change

The steps outlined above are an essential part of a change management programme. If they are carried out properly the further actions required to accelerate the pace of change are as follows:

1 Agree firm objectives, i.e. an 'agenda for change'.

2 Determine success criteria and define methods of measuring performance and progress towards achieving the objectives, both short and long term.

3 Provide, in Rosabeth Moss Kanter's words, 'an environment of support in which recognition of achievements to date will reinforce confidence to do more'.[1]

4 Deliver visionary leadership which encourages people to be bold and innovative and harnesses the ideas and talents of employees in the search for better ways of doing things.

5 Ensure the full collaboration and partnership of all resources in the business.

6 Generate a widespread attitude amongst all employees that encourages commitment to innovation and change by:

- Conducting personal briefings on the proposed changes cascading down through each level in the organization to cover all employees. This is better than simply issuing pieces of paper which may only generate a 'so what' reaction.

- Conducting workshops in which groups get together to discuss, analyse and interpret the proposed changes. These should be treated as opportunities for employees to get involved in planning change as well as implementing it.

- Introducing educational and training programmes which allow plenty of time to get the various messages across and to discuss their meaning and application fully.

References

1 KANTER Rosabeth Moss. *The change masters.* London, Allen & Unwin, 1984
2 WOODWARD Joan. 'Resistance to change'. *Management international review.* Vol. 8. 1968
3 LEWIN K. *Field theory in social science.* New York, Harper & Row, 1951
4 BECKHARD Richard. *Organization development: strategy and models.* Reading, Massachusetts, Addison-Wesley, 1969

13

Communicating Skills

The ability to express oneself clearly on paper and by the use of the spoken word is one of a manager's most important skills. It is through the medium of reports that managers often convey their thoughts and recommendations to their superiors and colleagues and inform them of the progress they are making. Managers may be called on to make presentations to their board, at a meeting or at a conference. They must therefore develop effective speaking skills. In addition, managers have to spend much of their time in meetings engaged in intercommunications with their colleagues. Managers not only transmit information, they also have to receive it. Listening skills are the most neglected of all the skills that managers practice, but if you do not hear messages 'loud and clear' how can you understand what is happening or what you are expected to do?

Communicating skills are best developed through experience and, wherever possible, by means of feedback from recipients. There are certain basic approaches which are described in this chapter but it would be well to remember the words of Ernst Gombrich:[1] 'We must not confuse response with understanding, expression with communication.'

This chapter deals with the following aspects of communicating:

- report writing
- effective speaking
- meetings
- listening

Report Writing

A good report has the following characteristics:

- a logical structure
- the use of plain words to convey meaning
- messages presented lucidly, persuasively and, above all, succinctly

Structure

The report should be structured to include:

- A *beginning*, which explains why the report has been written, its aims, its terms of reference, and why it should be read. If the report is divided into sections the readers should be given an indication of the logic of the structure as a signpost to direct them through the report.

- A *middle*, which contains the facts you have assembled and your analysis of those facts. If you are identifying different courses of action, list the pros and cons of each but make it clear which one you favour. This analysis should lead clearly and logically to the conclusions and recommendations contained in the last section of the report.

- An *end*, in which conclusions and recommendations are set out. The benefits and costs of any proposals should be described and a clear indication should be given of what sort of action should be taken, who should be responsible for it and the time-scale for starting and completing the programme of work.

- A *summary* of conclusions and recommendations, if the report is at all lengthy or complex. This concentrates the reader's mind and can serve as an agenda for discussion. Always remember that some people will only read the summary so make it as compelling as you can – you can refer them to the main text or to appendices if they want further detail.

- *Appendices* – complex tables and lengthy supporting material should be relegated to an appendix and suitably cross-referenced.

- *Contents* – only necessary for a long report, but potentially very helpful to the reader.

The use of language – some quotations

- Have something to say and say it as clearly as you can. This is the only secret of style.
  Walter Bagehot. *Shakespeare – the individual.*

- I looked out for what the metropolitan reviewers would have to say. They seemed to fall into two categories: those who had little to say and those who had nothing.
  Max Beerbohm. *Seven Men*

- Personally, I like short words and vulgar fractions.
  Winston Churchill.
  Speech in Margate, 1953

- If language is not correct, then what is said is not meant; if what is said is not meant, then what ought to be done remains undone.
  Confucius. *Sayings*

- Prefer the familiar to the far fetched.
  Prefer the concrete word to the abstract.
  Prefer the short word to the long.
  H. W. Fowler. *Modern English Usage*

- Let's have some new clichés.
  Sam Goldwyn (attributed)

- He draweth out the thread of his verbosity
  finer than the staple of his argument.
  William Shakespeare. *Love's Labours Lost*

- If anything can be said at all it can be said simply.
  Ludwig Wittgenstein.
  Tractatus Logico Philosophicus

Plain words

These quotations, plus the heading of this section, tell you most of what you need to know about writing. The rest can be gained from Sir Ernest Gower's *The complete plain words*.[2] This book is required reading for anyone interested in report writing. Gower's recommendations on how best to convey meaning without ambiguity, and without giving unnecessary trouble to the reader are:

1   Use no more words than are necessary to express your meaning, for if you use more you are likely to obscure it and to tire your reader. In particular do not use superfluous adjectives and adverbs, and do not use roundabout phrases where single words would serve.

2   Use familiar words rather than the far-fetched if they express your meaning equally well; for the familiar are more likely to be understood.

3   Use words with a precise meaning rather than those that are vague, for they will obviously serve better to make your meaning clear; and in particular, prefer concrete words to abstract for they are more likely to have a precise meaning.

You will not go far wrong if you follow these precepts.

Presentation

The way in which you present your report affects its impact and value. The reader should be able to follow your argument easily and not get bogged down in too much detail.

Paragraphs should be short and each one should be restricted to a single topic. If you want to list or highlight a series of points, tabulate them.

In long reports paragraphs should be numbered for ease of reference. Some people prefer the system which numbers main sections 1, 2, etc. subsections 1.1, 1.2, etc. and sub-subsections 1.1.1, 1.1.2, etc. However, this can be clumsy and distracting. A simpler system, which eases cross-referencing, is to number each paragraph, not the headings, 1, 2, 3 etc; sub-paragraphs or tabulations can be indicated as 'bullet points'.

Use headings to guide people on what they are about to read and to help them find their way about the report. Main headings should be in capitals and subheadings in lower case.

Your report will make most impact if it is brief and to the point.

Read and reread your draft to cut out any superfluous material or flabby writing.

Effective Speaking

The three keys to effective speaking are:

- overcoming nervousness
- thorough preparation
- good delivery

Overcoming nervousness

Some nervousness is a good thing. It makes you prepare, makes you think and makes the adrenalin flow, thus raising performance. But excessive nervousness ruins your effectiveness and must be controlled.

The common reasons for excessive nervousness are: fear of failure, fear of looking foolish, fear of breakdown, a sense of inferiority and dread of the isolation of the speaker. To overcome nervousness you should:

- *practise.* Take every opportunity you can get to speak in public. The more you do it, the more confident you will become. Solicit constructive criticism and act on it.

- *know your subject.* Get the facts, examples and illustrations which you need to put across.

- *know your audience.* Who is going to be there? What are they expecting to hear? What will they want to get out of listening to you?

- *know your objective.* Make sure that you know what you want to achieve. Visualize, if you can, each member of your audience going away having learned something new which he or she is going to put into practical use.

- *prepare*
- *rehearse*

Thorough preparation

Allow yourself ample time for preparation. You will probably need at least ten times as much as the duration of your talk. The main stages are:

1 *Get informed.* Collect and assemble all the facts and arguments you can get hold of.

2 *Decide what to say.* Define the main messages you want to get across. Limit the number to three or four – few people can absorb more than this number of new ideas at any one time. Select the facts, arguments and examples which support your message.

3 *Structure your talk* into the classic beginning, middle and end. Start with the middle first, with your main messages and the supporting facts, arguments and illustrations. Arrange your points so that a cumulative impact and a logical flow of ideas is achieved. Then turn to the opening of your talk. Your objectives should be to create attention, arouse interest and inspire confidence. Give your audience a trailer to what you are going to say. Underline the objective of your presentation – what *they* will get out of it. Finally, think about how you are going to close your talk. First and last impressions are very important. End on a high note.

Think carefully about length, reinforcement and continuity. Never talk for more than 40 minutes at a time. Twenty or 30 minutes is better. Very few speakers can keep people's attention for long. An audience is usually very interested to begin with (unless you make a mess of your opening) but interest declines steadily until people realize that you are approaching the end. Then they perk up. Hence the importance of your conclusion.

To keep their attention throughout, give interim summaries which reinforce what you are saying and, above all, hammer home your key points at intervals throughout your talk.

Continuity is equally important. You should build your argument progressively until you come to a positive and overwhelming conclusion. Provide signposts, interim summaries and bridging sections which lead your audience naturally from one point to the next.

4   *Prepare your notes.* In the first place write out your introductory and concluding remarks in full and set out in some detail the main text of your talk. It is not usually necessary to write everything down.

You should then boil down your text to the key headings to which you will refer in your talk. Your aim should be to avoid reading your speech if you possibly can as this can completely remove any life from what you have to say. So as not to be pinned down behind a lectern it is better to write your summarised points on lined index cards to which you can refer easily as you go along.

5   *Prepare visual aids.* As your audience will only absorb one-third of what you say, if that, reinforce your message with visual aids. Appeal to more than one sense at a time. Flip charts, slides and so on all provide good back-up, but don't overdo them and keep them simple. Too many visuals can be distracting and too many words, or an over-elaborate presentation, will divert, bore and confuse your audience.

6   *Rehearse.* Rehearsal is vital. It instils confidence, helps you to get your timing right, and enables you to polish your opening and closing remarks and coordinate your talk and visual aids.

Rehearse the talk to yourself several times and note how long each section takes. Get used to expanding your notes without waffling.

Practise giving your talk out loud – standing up, if that is the way you are going to present it. Some people like to tape record themselves but that can be off-putting. It is better to get someone to hear you and provide constructive criticism. It may be hard to take but it could do you a world of good.

7   *Check arrangements in the room.* Ensure that your overhead or slide projector works and you know how to operate it. Check also on focus and visibility. Before you begin your talk, check that your notes and visual aids are in the right order and to hand.

Delivery

- Talk audibly and check that you can be heard at the back.

- Vary the pace (not too fast, not too slow), pitch and emphasis of your delivery. Use pauses to make a point.

- Try to be conversational and informal. Avoid a stilted delivery. That is why you must not read your talk. If you are your natural self people are more likely to be on your side. They will forgive the occasional pause to find the right word.

- Light relief is a good thing but don't drag in irrelevant jokes or, indeed, make jokes at all if you are not good at telling them.

- Use short words and sentences.

- Keep your eyes on the audience, moving from person to person to demonstrate that you are addressing them all, and also to gauge their reactions to what you are saying.

- Use hands for gesture and emphasis in moderation. Don't fidget.

- Stand naturally and upright. Do not be too casual.

- You can move around the platform a little to add variety but avoid pacing up and down like a caged lion.

Meetings

For many managers, meetings can become almost a way of life. A good meeting will:

- ensure that important matters get proper consideration from all involved

- clarify thinking in that members have to justify their positions before the others present

- ensure that different viewpoints are aired

- act as a medium for the exchange of information

- save time by getting a number of people together

- promote co-ordination
- create something as a group which the individuals could not have achieved working separately – this is the process of synergy, where the whole is greater than the parts

Effective meetings

The effectiveness of a meeting depends on three things:

1 The existence of a clear purpose or terms of reference
2 An agenda which clearly sets out what the committee is going to discuss – all of which must be relevant to the committee's purpose
3 A chariman who:
   - plans the agenda to provide for a structured meeting covering all the points in a logical order
   - ensures that briefing papers and reports are sent out to members in good time with clear indications of what they will be expected to do prior to the meeting
   - starts the meeting with a definition of its purpose and how long it will take
   - goes through each item of the agenda in turn ensuring that a firm decision is reached and recorded
   - initiates the discussion on each item by setting the scene and posing the questions to be answered
   - ensures that there is a full discussion, inviting contributions from all members of the meeting
   - does not allow members to dominate the meeting or drift from the point
   - encourages different points of view, not allowing reasonable expressions of opinion to be suppressed
   - allows disagreement as long as it does not become contentious
   - intervenes as necessary to summarize where the committee is making progress and to ensure that it continues towards a conclusion

- summarizes the decision made on each item of the agenda for the minutes

- summarizes the final conclusions of the meeting, defining who has to do what by when

On being a member of a meeting

If you are a member of a meeting you can contribute effectively if you:

- prepare thoroughly – have all the facts at your fingertips, with any supporting data you need

- make your points clearly, succinctly and positively – try to resist the temptation of talking too much

- remain silent if you have nothing to say

- keep your powder dry if you are not leading the discussion or if it is a subject you are not knowledgeable about. Listen, observe and save your arguments until you can make a really telling point. Don't plunge in too quickly or comprehensively – there may be other compelling arguments.

- avoid making statements such as 'I think we must do this' if you are not sure of your ground. Instead, pose a question to the chairman or other members of the meeting such as 'Do you think there is a case for doing this?'

- are prepared to argue your case firmly, but don't persist in fighting for a lost cause. Don't retire in a sulk because you cannot get your own way: accept defeat gracefully.

- remember that if you are defeated in committee there may still be a chance for you to fight another day in a different setting.

Listening

There are many good writers and speakers but few good listeners. Listening is an art which not many people cultivate. But it is a very necessary one, because a good listener will absorb more information and achieve better rapport with the other person. And both these results of good listening are essential to good communications.

Why people don't listen effectively

People don't listen effectively because they are:

- unable to concentrate, for whatever reason
- too preoccupied with themselves
- over-concerned with what they are going to say next
- uncertain about what they are listening to or why they are listening to it
- unable to follow the points or arguments made by the speaker
- simply not interested in what is being said

Effective listeners:

- concentrate on the speaker, following not only words but also body language, which through the use of eyes or gestures often underlines meaning and gives life to the message
- respond quickly to points made by the speaker, if only in the shape of encouraging grunts
- ask questions frequently to elucidate meaning and to give the speaker an opportunity to rephrase or underline a point
- comment on the points made by the speaker, without interrupting the flow, in order to test understanding and demonstrate that the speaker and listener are still on the same wavelength. These comments may reflect back or summarize something the speaker has said, thus giving an opportunity for him or her to reconsider or elucidate the point made
- make notes on the key points – even if the notes are not referred to later, they will help to concentrate the mind
- are continuously evaluating the messages being delivered to check that they are understood and relevant to the purpose of the meeting

- are alert at all times to the nuances of what the speaker is saying

- do not slump in their chairs – they lean forward, show interest and maintain contact through their oral responses and by means of body language

- are prepared to let the speaker go on with the minimum of interruption

References

1   GOMBRICH Ernst. *Meditations on a hobby horse.* London, Phaidon, 1963
2   GOWER Sir Ernest. *The complete plain words.* London, HMSO, 1977

14

Interpersonal Skills

Interpersonal skills are the skills people use when they interact with one another. Anyone working in an organization as a member of a group or team will spend a considerable amount of time relating to other people. This will involve using powers of persuasion to influence others, being assertive as necessary to make a point or carry conviction, and counselling people to help them improve their performance or overcome problems.

The effective use of such interpersonal or, as they are sometimes termed, interactive skills depends on sensitivity to the needs of other people and one's own impact on them. Before dealing with influencing, assertiveness and counselling skills it is necessary to consider in broad terms the issue of sensitivity.

Sensitivity

Sensitivity in managerial terms is about perceiving how people react to one's own behaviour and using that knowledge to continue with productive behaviour or to modify unproductive behaviour. It is *not* about being soft with people.

When, for example, we try to influence other people we adopt an approach that we believe is going to be effective. But what we believe is appropriate behaviour may be regarded by others as unacceptable. And what is all right for one person may be all wrong for another. If we can develop sensitivity to how people, as individuals or in groups, react to what we say or do we will be much better placed to play our parts as members of a team or to persuade others – our bosses, colleagues or subordinates – to accept our point of view.

Sensitive people are alert to the nuances of other people's reaction to what they say or do. They not only listen but also observe. This is not easy. We may receive evidence that we are

not achieving what we want. For example, we may get an outright
rejection of something we say or we may be faced with a more
subtle indifference which could take the form of paying lip-service
to our views but doing nothing about them. But we seldom get
reliable feedback on why we have created these reactions.

A form of training called sensitivity or T-Group training was
developed in the 1950s in an attempt to help managers become
more sensitive about their own and other's behaviour. Chris
Argyris[1] defined the process as follows:

> Basically it [the T-Group] is a group experience designed to
> provide maximum possible opportunity for individuals to
> expose their own behaviour, give and receive feedback,
> experiment with new behaviour and develop everlasting
> awareness and acceptance of self and others. The T-Group,
> when effective, also provides individuals with the opportunity
> to learn the nature of effective group functioning. They are
> able to learn how to develop a group that achieves specific
> goals with minimum possible human cost . . . . It is in the T-
> Group that one learns how to diagnose one's own behaviour,
> to develop effective leadership behaviour and norms for
> decision making.

During a T-Group members spend much of their time giving
feedback or expressing their reactions to one another. With the
help of the tutor they analyse and interpret these actions and,
supposedly, understand more about aspects of their behaviour
previously hidden from them. They then develop for themselves
alternative ways of behaviour and test them on others. This is why
they have been referred to as T-Group laboratories.

The problem with T-Groups is that they require highly skilled
inputs from tutors, who have to exercise careful control to avoid
detrimental effects on those involved. Many people find it difficult
to take negative feedback. A further problem is that it has not
been proved that they produce lasting changes in behaviour. What
works well in the contrived atmosphere of a T-Group may not be
effective back at the workplace.

For these reasons, T-Groups have not been accepted as a valid
means of sensitivity training although some of their concepts (e.g.
the use of controlled and guided feedback) have been adopted in
interpersonal or interactive skills training. A typical interpersonal
skills course will include three stages.

1 The *diagnostic stage*, in which the groups undertake a wide range of activities. These are designed to provide reliable examples of behaviour which the trainer records and analyses.

2 The *formal feedback stage*, in which the trainer gives groups and individuals feedback on their interactive performance during the diagnostic phase.

3 The *practice and monitoring stage*, in which the group undertakes further activities to develop and practise new behaviour patterns and receives feedback from the trainer to gauge the success of attempts at behaviour change.

Group training experiences like this are probably the best way to develop increased sensitivity but, if you are unable to attend such a course, you can try some or all of the following approaches:

• Observe as carefully as you can reactions to what you say or do. If you get a hostile reaction try to find out why and modify accordingly the way in which you present your argument, comment or request. Analyse successful or unsuccessful behaviour on your part and ask yourself why it produced a particular result. Use those approaches which appear to be more effective on the next occasion and be prepared to analyse and, as necessary, modify them again. This is a continuous process. You will not get it right first time. You can only hope that you will develop sensitivity progressively – but be prepared for setbacks.

• Listen not only to what other people say but also to how they say it. Develop alertness to a negative or indifferent tone of voice even if the words apparently express agreement.

• Observe body language. If the other person's attention is wandering or if they show withdrawal or disagreement by facial expressions or bodily movements, take note and modify your approach.

• Don't assume that verbal assent or even apparently encouraging nods or gestures really mean that you are getting your message across. People will often go along with you on the surface while rejecting you internally. They don't respond negatively because they prefer an easy life. If you only get superficial and misleading responses like these you will never know the true impact you are making. A sensitive approach may involve probing, as subtly as possible, to find out what people are really thinking. If you can get a true indication of how people are reacting to you you will be better placed to take appropriate action.

- Bear in mind that although sensitivity to other people's reactions to your words or behaviour may often suggest that you need to modify what you are saying or doing, it may also indicate that you should persist with your existing behaviour if you want to achieve your objective. Sensitivity is about understanding reactions in order to take the right action, which may be the same or a modified version of your original approach.

- Try to get feedback from others about how they react to your behaviour. This may be extremely difficult because it depends on the existence of an open and trusting relationship. But this is the relationship you should try to cultivate with your boss, colleagues and subordinates. If you succeed, you will be better placed to get their frank but helpful views about your impact on them.

- Even if you cannot get direct feedback, try to test reactions as you go along. If, for example, you feel that your approach is not being received sympathetically, check the response by asking such questions as: 'Are you happy about this suggestion?' 'Do you see any problems in going this route?' 'How do you feel this will affect you?' 'Is there anything I have not made clear?' 'Would you like me to elaborate a little?' 'You've heard my views, now I'd like to hear yours – what do you think we should do?'

    You can, if appropriate, be more direct than this. For example, you could say things like: 'I don't think you're with me yet – could you tell me why?' or 'I am getting the impression that you are not really happy with this, what's the problem?' These questions are not challenging the other person, instead, they are opening up the conversation to provide opportunities to express points of view and, by so doing, reveal feelings which give you an indication of the effect you are having on them.

Influencing Skills

It has been said that the manager's job is '60 per cent getting it right and 40 per cent putting it across'.[2] Managers spend a lot of time in meetings, in face-to-face contacts, in writing reports and memoranda and in making presentations influencing people – persuading them to accept new ideas and suggestions. The development of influencing skills is essential to the effective manager.

People are influenced by arguments or proposals which are logical and practical, which indicate solutions to pressing problems, which suggest ways of making progress towards a desired objective and which are generally in accord with their own views, although they may provide a new perspective or add an extra dimension to their thoughts on the subject. They are much more likely to agree to a proposal suggesting change if they feel that they will benefit from it. However objective they may try to be, people tend to allow subjective beliefs to sway their judgement. This is often an entirely unconscious process. Some people are, of course overtly prejudiced and, although persuading them to take a different point of view may appear to be difficult, it is sometimes easier to confront the issue openly rather than contend with unexpressed opinions.

It follows that if you want to influence others you must not only present powerful, well-balanced and fully backed-up arguments convincingly, you must also take pains to understand the other person's point of view, whether or not it is openly expressed, and take account of it in presenting your proposal or idea.

Persuading skills

The key influencing skill is persuasion – using facts, logic and reason to present your own case, emphasizing its strong points, anticipating objections to any apparent weaknesses and appealing to reason.

The ten rules for persuading others are:

1   *Define your objective.*
2   *Get the facts.* Assemble as much data as possible. Even if you do not use it all it may come in useful later as supporting material.

3   *Marshal your argument.* Your aim should be to ensure that you devise a powerful argument which clearly addresses the problem and which is developed logically and inexorably from the facts. You should assemble the supporting data in a way which clearly supports your conclusion.

4   *Anticipate objections.* When marshalling your arguments and developing your proposition, anticipate any objections that may be raised. You can then either deal with them in your proposition – putting them up and then knocking them down – or you can prepare yourself for dealing with them if they crop up in discussion. It is often useful to suggest different patterns of action; list the pros and cons for each and come down firmly in favour of one. There is no harm in admitting that you have made this judgement 'on balance'. You accept that points can be made against your proposal, 'but the points for significantly outweigh those against for the following reasons . . .'

    Remember that there are at least twelve ways of saying no:

    ● It won't work.

    ● It's good in theory but not in practice.

    ● It will cost too much.

    ● We've tried it before and it didn't work.

    ● This is not addressing the real problem.

    ● The benefits won't be realized until it is too late.

    ● This is not the right time.

    ● It will set a dangerous precedent.

    ● We haven't got the resources to implement it.

    ● Our shareholders, managing director, sponsors, trustees, shop stewards, workers, customers, clients, suppliers, sales outlets, sales representatives, agents won't like it.

    ● We need to consult with . . . etc. before we go any further.

    ● We must spend more time considering the implications of this proposal.

5   *Find out what the other person or people want.* Never underestimate a person's natural resistance to change. But bear in mind

that such resistance is proportional, not to the total extent of the change, but to the extent to which it affects that person. When asked to accept a proposition, the first questions people ask themselves are: 'How does this affect me?' 'What do I stand to lose?' 'What do I stand to gain?' These questions must be answered before persuasion can start. The key to all persuasion is empathy – seeing your proposition from the other person's point of view. If you can really put yourself into their shoes you will be able to foresee objections and present your ideas in the way most attractive to them. You must find out how they look at things and what they want. Listen to what they have to say. Don't talk too much. Ask questions. If they ask you a question reply with another question. Find out what they are after, then present your case in a way that highlights its benefits to them, or at least reduces their objections or fears.

6 *Look for the 'hidden agenda'.* A meeting may be called for a particular purpose but behind this there may be different and more significant things people want to achieve. Some people, for example, may be more interested in improving their status or extending their authority than in achieving something which benefits the organization.

7 *Prepare a simple and attractive presentation.* Your presentation should be as simple and straightforward as possible. Emphasize the benefits. Don't bury the selling points. Lead them in gently so there are no surprises. Anticipate objections.

8 *Make them party to your idea.* Get them to contribute, if at all possible. Find some common ground in order to start off with agreement. Don't antagonize them. Avoid defeating them in arguments. Help to preserve self-esteem. Always leave a way out for them.

9 *Sell the benefits positively.* Show conviction. You are not going to influence anyone if you don't believe in what you are proposing and communicate that belief. To persuade effectively you must spell out the benefits of what you are proposing. What you are proposing may be of less interest to the individuals concerned than the effects of that proposal on them.

10 *Clinch and take action.* Choose the right moment to clinch the proposal. Make sure that you are not pushing too hard, but when you reach your objective don't stay and risk losing it. Take prompt follow-up action. There is no point in going to all the trouble of getting agreement if you let things slide afterwards.

Other influencing skills

Influencing skills involve more than persuasion. They also consist of:

- *asserting* – making your views clear (as described below).
- *bridging* – drawing out other people's points of view, demonstrating that you understand what they are getting at, giving credit and praise in response to their good ideas and suggestions and joining your views with theirs
- *attracting* – conveying your enthusiasm for your ideas, getting people to feel that they are all part of an exciting project.

Assertiveness

Assertiveness is the process of expressing your opinions and beliefs in direct ways, and standing up for your rights in a manner which does not violate other people's rights. Assertive behaviour is not the same as aggressive behaviour. Aggression involves violating other people's rights in order to get your own way. Aggression can breed aggression and this is always counter-productive.

Behaving assertively puts you into the position of being able to influence people properly and react to them positively. Assertive statements:

- are brief and to the point
- indicate clearly that you are not hiding behind something or someone and are speaking for yourself by using words such as 'I think that . . .', 'I believe that . . .', 'I feel that . . .' – *your* beliefs and views are important

- are not overweighted with advice
- use questions to find out the views of others and to test their reactions to your behaviour
- distinguish between fact and opinion
- are expressed positively but not dogmatically
- indicate that you are aware that other people have different points of view
- express, when necessary, negative feelings about the effects of other people's behaviour on you – pointing out in dispassionate and factual terms the feelings aroused in you, and suggesting the behaviour you would prefer
- point out to people politely but firmly the consequences of their behaviour

Counselling

Managers are constantly being faced with people's problems. They may find themselves frequently involved in counselling their subordinates on how they can overcome a personal difficulty. There may be occasions when you have to be directive and tell people what they must do but there will be many others when a different approach is required.

Approaches to dealing with people problems

The four styles that can be adopted in dealing with people problems are:

1 *Tell.* You adopt an authoritarian approach and solve the problem for them, telling them what to do.

2 *Manipulate.* You do not adopt the direct 'tell' approach but instead steer people in the way in which *you* want them to go, irrespective of their real needs.

3 *Advise.* You advise individuals on how to solve their problems by analysing the situation jointly against the background of their needs, expectations, hopes and fears. If, however,

someone with authority or expertise *gives* advice, the weight of opinion they bring to bear on the problem will give the recipient little choice but to go along with the offered solution, at the time. But if they are over-persuaded and are not truly involved they may react later against the advice because they were never entirely convinced. Deep inside they took a different view, one which suited them.

4 *Counsel.* This means being more concerned with the individual than the problem. Good counsellors seek involvement in solving the problem. They do discuss the problems presented for consideration, but prefer to get individuals to decide, with the counsellor's help, what the best solution would be for them. The strength of the counselling approach over the others is that people will become more truly committed to doing something if they can 'own' the problem and its solution. And they will only do this if they have made up their own minds and personally believe it is the right thing to do. Telling, manipulating, even advising, can put undue pressure on people, to which they can react negatively.

Counselling skills

Counselling involves the use of certain skills. You need to be able to do the following to counsel effectively.

- *Listen actively.* Show interest and attention so that the individual thinks that only he or she matters.

- *Observe.* Take note of body language (gestures, manner, tone and expression), as well as listening to the words.

- *Question.* Help people to understand their situation and define their problem by asking questions such as:
  - What do *you* think is happening?
  - How does this problem affect *you*?
  - When did *you* first become aware of this difficulty?
  - Where have *you* come across this problem?
  - Who *else* is involved?
  - Why do *you* think the problem has arisen?
  - What do *you* feel should be done about it?

- *Recognize feelings.* Listen sympathetically and allow feelings to be expressed without comment, except possibly 'reflecting' what is being said by feeding back a remark in your own words, such as 'So you feel that . . .', which either demonstrates that you understand or gives the other person a chance to restate his or her case.

- *Define the problem.* Help people to define the problem for themselves with the aid of sympathetic listening and brief, well-directed questions. Ask a summarizing question at the right time such as 'Is this what you mean . . . ?' Do not pass any moral judgement. You will be forming a hypothesis of the real problem as the counselling session proceeds. Do not reveal your hypothesis but instead test it by exploring views, opinions, reactions and feelings. This hypothesis will then indicate how you can help the person to revise his or her initial description of the problem following mature analysis. The emphasis is, however, on helping people to help themselves. Your hypothesis is only a guide on the approach you adopt to get people to develop their own hypotheses. It does no more than indicate the direction that is most likely to lead to a resolution of the problem.

- *Explore solutions.* Start from the hypothesis on why the problem exists, as defined by the person, who should then be encouraged to suggest alternative ways of dealing with it. You should neither approve nor disapprove any solutions, only indicating that further consideration is required when a possible solution fundamentally contravenes company policy or when you are convinced that it will have a detrimental effect.

- *Implement.* Let the person implement his or her own solution but, as necessary, provide help.

References

1 ARGYRIS Chris. 'T-Groups for organizational effectiveness'. *Harvard Business Review*. March–April, 1964, pp 60–74
2 ARMSTRONG Michael. *How to be an even better manager*. London, Kogan Page, 1988

15

Organization Structure and Development

Purpose of Organization

Organizations exist to get work done and their structures provide the framework for the planning, operational and controlling activities that take place within them.

The purpose of organization is to design, develop and maintain a system of co-ordinated activities in which individuals and groups of people work co-operatively under authority and leadership towards commonly understood and accepted goals.

In this chapter, organization will be dealt with under the following headings:

- Basic considerations affecting the design of organizations, including formal and informal organizations, the organization as a system and contingency theory

- The different types of organization and functional roles within them

- Organization design, including the guidelines affecting the shape of the structure

- Defining and describing the organization

- Job design

- Introducing organizational change

- The features of an effective organization

- Methods of developing effective organizations

Basic Considerations

Factors affecting the structure

Organizations vary in complexity, but in every case it is necessary to divide the overall management task into a variety of activities and to establish means of co-ordinating those activities.

The structure of an organization consists of positions and units between which there are relationships involving the exercise of authority and exchange of information. The structure must be appropriate to the organizational purpose and to the situation in which it exists. As Tom Lupton says:

> Organizations are patterns of human tasks and relationships, shaped so as to allow at least survival, at most growth and development in environments which constrain but also offer opportunities.[1]

Formal and informal organizations

The formal organization consists of defined relationships and roles which are described in organization charts and manuals and in job descriptions. Traditionally, the design of organizations has conformed to the bureaucratic model as defined by Max Weber,[2] writing in the late nineteenth century, which has the following features:

- maximum specialization
- close job definitions, setting out duties, privileges and boundaries
- vertical authority patterns
- decisions based on expert judgement, resting on technical knowledge and on disciplined compliance with the directives of superiors
- separation of policy and administration
- maximum use of rules
- impersonal administration of staff

Weber was simply describing this type of organization, he was not advocating it.

He was followed, however, by the scientific management or classical school represented by Fayol, Taylor and Urwick, who, although they had probably not read Weber, believed that a bureaucratic approach was best. They thought that organizations should minimize the opportunity for 'unfortunate' and 'uncontrollable' informal relations, leaving room only for the formal ones.

In 1938, however, a businessman, Chester Barnard[3] suggested that organizations were co-operative systems, not the products of mechanical engineering or of paperwork bureaucracies. He promoted natural groups within the organization, upward communication, authority from below rather than from above, and leaders who functioned as cohesive forces. He also emphasized the importance of the informal organization – the network of informal roles and relationships which, for better or worse, strongly influence the ways the formal structure operates.

The behavioural science school that followed Barnard developed additional concepts about the basis of formal and informal organizations and the respective roles of the organization, its management and its members.

Douglas McGregor[4] expounded his theory of integration – the importance of recognizing the needs of both the organization and the individual, and the need to create conditions which will reconcile their needs so that members of the organization can work together for its success and share in its rewards.

Rensis Likert[5] devised his theory of organizations from his research, which distinguished between job-centred and employee-centred supervisors, and established that employee-centred supervisors were higher producers than job-centred ones. From his analysis of high-producing managers he found that they were characterized by attitudes of identification with the organization and its objectives and had a high sense of involvement in achieving them. Likert believed strongly in the principle of supportive relationships in organizations:

> In all interactions and all relationships with the organization each member will, in the light of his background, values and expectations, view the experience as supportive and one which builds and maintains his sense of personal worth and importance.

Chris Argyris[6] suggested on the basis of his research into personality developments in organizations that 'The formal organization creates in a healthy individual feelings of failure and frustration, short time perspective and conflict.' To overcome this problem Argyris wanted to emphasize the informal aspects of organization, which will enable individuals to feel that they have a high degree of control over the setting of their goals.

Informal organization, as seen by these commentators, becomes a way of managing and involving people which exists separately from the formal structure. But, as John Child[7] has pointed out, it is misleading to talk about a clear distinction between the formal and informal organization. Formality *and* informality can be designed into the organization in the sense of developing norms and values which become part of the organization's culture (see Chapter 16) and influence the achievement of integration, supportive relationships and the extent to which individuals are allowed to exercise self-control.

The organization as a system

In parallel to the behavioural scientists, systems theorists developed their concepts of how organizations actually function, formally and informally.

Systems theory is concerned with problems of relationship, of structure and of interdependence. There is considerable emphasis on the concept of transactions across boundaries – between the system and its environment and between the different parts of the system.

The basic idea of the organization as a system which transforms inputs into outputs within its environment was extended by the Tavistock Institute researchers Miller and Rice[8] and Trist.[9] They developed the *socio-technical* model of organizations, the principle of which is that in any system of organization, technical or task aspects are interrelated with the human or social aspects. The emphasis is on interrelationships between, on the one hand, the technical processes of transformation carried out within the organization and on the other hand, the organization of work groups and the management structures of the enterprise. The theory also stresses that organizations have to be seen as open systems, strongly influenced by their environment, not simply closed systems consisting of various internal structures and processes of interaction. This approach was further developed by the contingency school of organizational researchers and theorists. And in case anyone reacts negatively to the word 'theory', remember that there is nothing so practical as a good theory, one based on properly conducted research and analysis of what is actually happening.

Contingency theory

Contingency theory, as developed by Silverman[10] with his 'action theory' approach, suggests that the internal structure and systems of an organization will be strongly influenced by its environment, which consists of its markets, its technology, the economy and the degree to which innovation is necessary. This environment will affect not only structure but also managerial plans and actions and organizational performance.

The contingency school of writers developed this theme empirically by a series of research projects. Their analyses of a number of organizations produced the conclusion that organizational structures and methods of operation are a function of the circumstances in which they exist. They do not subscribe to the view that there is one best way of designing an organization or that it is helpful to produce simplistic classifications of organizations as formal or informal, bureaucratic or non-bureaucratic.

Burns and Stalker[11] based their concept of mechanistic and organic organizations on their research into a number of Scottish firms. They established that in stable conditions highly structured or 'mechanistic' organizations will emerge with most of the characteristics of the bureaucratic system. But when the environment is more volatile, the organizational structure becomes 'organic' in the sense that it is a function of the situation in which the organization finds itself, rather than conforming to any predetermined or rigid view of how it should operate. They emphasize, however, that they are not suggesting that either system is superior under all circumstances. The optimum system is one that fits the organization's purpose and environment.

Joan Woodward[12] conducted her research in Essex and established that different technologies demand different structures and procedures and create different kinds of relationships.

Lawrence and Lorsch[13] developed their contingency model on the basis of research into firms in the American plastics industry. They defined organization as the process of co-ordinating different activities to carry out planned transactions with the environment, namely, the market, the technology (the tasks that have to be carried out) and research and development. Organization, as they see it, is a process first of *differentiation*, segmenting different activities in relation to the environment and the various tasks that have to be carried out, accompanied by *integration*, linking the different parts of the organization together to achieve its overall purpose. Successful organizations achieve the optimum balance between differentiation and integration. They have to include specialisms and allow for different approaches, but it is equally necessary to weld these together into a cohesive whole.

Organization therefore becomes a continuous management process of defining different and new tasks in relation to changes as they occur or as they are anticipated, and developing a coherent approach to guiding, co-ordinating and controlling these activities so that they become an integrated whole.

Different Types of Organization and Functional Roles

As we have seen organizations can be described as formal or informal, bureaucratic or non-bureaucratic, organic or mechanistic. But these labels are dangerous in that they oversimplify the complexity of organizational systems operating in different environments and having to differentiate and integrate their activities in a variety of ways.

It is possible, however, to distinguish between different types of structure and the different roles carried out within them.

Different structures

The main types of structure that exist in organizations are:

1   A centralized structure in which any subsidiary companies, divisions or geographically separated activities are subject to rigid control from the centre. Such structures, as illustrated in

Figure 12, may have strong corporate functions which control related activities in the divisions or subsidiary units.

Figure 12
A centralized structure

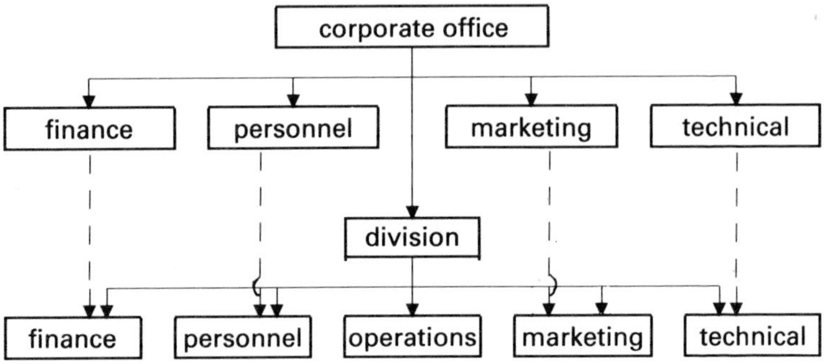

2   A decentralized or divisionalized structure in which authority is delegated to the subsidiaries or divisions to manage their own destinies, with only very broad directions from the centre or corporate office in certain fundamental aspects of finance, human resource management and legal affairs. Authority may remain in the corporate office over longer-range plans, annual budgets, and major capital investments or disinvestments. The implementation of agreed strategies and plans will be monitored from the centre although much of the control will be exercised on an exception basis. This means that only variances from the budget will be reported in any detail. More comprehensive reports may, however, be required for annual, half-yearly or quarterly reviews. Some corporate functions such as finance, personnel, legal and the company secretary's department may remain at the centre, but they are there to provide policy advice and support services and to monitor policy implementation, rather than to exercise control over divisional operations. This type of structure is illustrated in Figure 13.

3   A unitary structure, which may be found in subsidiaries, divisional units or smaller companies where the organization under the chief executive or general manager is divided into

Figure 13
A decentralized or divisionalized structure

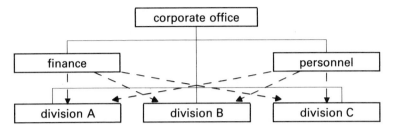

different functions, the heads of which report direct to the top. A typical unitary structure is shown in Figure 14.

Figure 14
A unitary structure

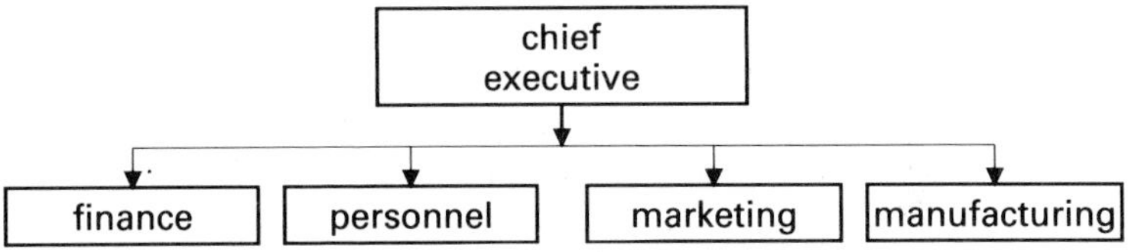

```
                    ┌──────────────┐
                    │    chief     │
                    │  executive   │
                    └──────────────┘
      ┌───────────┬──────┼──────┬───────────────┐
      ▼           ▼      ▼      ▼               ▼
┌──────────┐ ┌────────────┐ ┌───────────┐ ┌───────────────┐
│ finance  │ │ personnel  │ │ marketing │ │ manufacturing │
└──────────┘ └────────────┘ └───────────┘ └───────────────┘
```

Functional roles

Within each of these structures, functions or activities will have different tasks to fulfil, as we will see in Chapter 17. They may also have different roles in that some will be directly involved in delivering the results required for the organization by, for example, manufacturing and selling its products. Others will be more concerned with providing various support services to the chief executive or the operational functions.

The operating roles are sometimes described as 'the line' while the support roles may be designated as 'the staff'. But these militaristic terms are no longer very useful today, when organizations are operating much more on a team basis, and when everyone, especially at the top, exists for only one purpose, to further the objectives of the enterprise. Each function has its role but they are all interdependent. The divisive and sometimes derisory description of functions and people as 'line' or 'staff' is no longer so appropriate.

There are, of course, still functions which are directly involved in income generation, while others are providing the guidance, support and services which will enable income to be maximized. But these functions may often be combined in one department or individual. Marketing, for example, supports sales by conducting research and developing methods of merchandizing and distributing the product. The head of marketing, however, will be mainly concerned with the overall contribution his or her function can make to profitability; in other words, how it can generate income.

Personnel departments are indeed there to support other functions by providing them with the human resources they need, but they are, or should be, equally concerned with their contribution to the bottom line (see my book on this subject)[14] by developing a positive culture and environment and by taking a direct interest in methods of improving organizational effectiveness and performance.

Organization Design

Organization design determines who does what. It deals with the structural aspects of the organization and aims to analyse roles and relationships so that collective effort can be explicitly organized to achieve specific ends. The organization structure will be contingent upon the environment and technology of the organization and the design or design modification process will have to take account of:

- the fact that the organization is a system, constantly redefining its relationship to its environment and subject to continuous change
- the informal processes that enable the organization to function but which must be conducted within a logical framework which indicates the overall authority and communication relationships between individuals and departments

- the need to differentiate between functions but also to integrate them so that they play their part in achieving the common purpose
- the need to obtain the commitment of the members of the organization by providing supportive relationships, enabling them to participate and feel involved, and giving them the maximum opportunity to exercise self-control and self-direction
- the need to establish lines of authority, often referred to as 'lines of command', so that everyone knows who is responsible to whom for what. This presents one of the many dilemmas facing those who are responsible for organization design – 'how do we reconcile the need for flexibility with the need to exercise authority and control

Organizational guidelines

The classical theorists developed a set of principles of organization, but the suggestion that they were universally applicable is no longer tenable. The principles were in any case often inconsistent. There are, however, a number of guidelines which should be taken into account, although their application will depend on the circumstances. These are:

1 *Allocation of work.* The work that needs to be done has to be defined and allocated to the appropriate job holders or departments. Related activities should be grouped together to avoid unnecessary overlap and duplication of work. Matters requiring a decision should be dealt with as near to the point of action as possible, and managers should not try to do too much themselves. Nor should they exercise too close a supervision.

2 *Levels in the structure.* Too many levels of management and supervision inhibit communication and create extra work (and jobs). The aim should be to reduce the number of levels to a minimum, bearing in mind always that organizations are like rubber – if you squeeze them they will expand sideways, so that at some levels the number of subordinates directly reporting to one manager will increase. There is an increasing tendency for organizations to become flatter, partly to reduce the

unnecessary layers which existed because of the existence of traditional hierarchies, and partly because of the spread of advanced forms of information technology which reduces the need for middle managers to act as communication links. As Peter Drucker points out, in many organizations which have not rethought their structures in the light of the availability of new technology, whole layers of management neither make decisions nor lead. Instead their main, if not their only function is to serve as 'relays' – human boosters for the faint, unfocused signals that pass for communications in the traditional pre-information organization.[15]

Reducing the number of levels to create flatter structures does, however, impose a much more stringent requirement to improve teamwork, delegation and methods of integrating activities when spans of control are much wider and middle managers with a co-ordinating role no longer exist.

3   *Span of control.* There are limits to the number of people anyone can manage or supervise well, but these vary considerably between different jobs. Most people can work with a far greater span of control than they think they can, as long as they are prepared to delegate more effectively, to avoid getting into too much detail, and to develop good teamwork amongst the individuals reporting to them. In fact wide spans of control are beneficial in that they can enforce delegation and better teamwork and free the higher-level manager to spend more time on policy making and planning. Limited spans of control encourage managers to interfere too much with the work going on beneath them, and therefore constrain the scope that should be given to their subordinates to grow with their jobs.

4   *One person, one boss.* Generally speaking, employees should report to only one boss. This avoids conflicting orders being given to one person. If managers bypass immediate subordinates when issuing instructions, it can cause confusion, and it undermines authority. If it happens too often you will need to question the abilities of the manager and his or her subordinate, and the existence of the intermediate layer of management. Of course, there will be occasions when a manager has to be bypassed to deal with an emergency, but these should be exceptional.

The exception to the 'one person, one boss' principle is the case of 'functional authority'. For instance, the finance director may lay down methods of preparing budgets and pass instructions on budgeting direct to managers in other departments. But functional authority should only be exercised as a means of getting company-wide policies which have been agreed at top level implemented consistently.

As long as the nature of the authority is understood by all concerned, there should be no confusion. If, however, people feel that they have received an unreasonable request from a functional manager, they are at liberty to appeal to their own managers.

5   *Decentralization.* Authority to make decisions should be delegated as close to the action as possible. Profit centres should be set up as strategic business units which operate close to their markets and with a considerable degree of autonomy.

6   *Optimize the structure.* Design the ideal organization by all means, but also remember that you may have to modify it to fit in the particular skills and abilities of key individuals.

7   *Relevance to organizational needs.* Organizations today increasingly have to be:

- flexible
- more responsive to change
- innovative
- entrepreneurial
- leaner (smaller numbers of non-productive staff)
- flatter
- project-orientated – with an emphasis on teamwork
- capable of gaining and keeping the commitment of the fewer but more highly qualified and versatile staff they need.

The organization structure has to be developed or amended to meet these needs. Inevitably this means a tendency towards more flexible structures, with greater responsibility given to individuals and an extension of the use of task forces and project teams to deal with new opportunities or threats. This implies an informal, non-bureaucratic, organic approach to organization design.

Defining and Describing the Organization

Organizations are usually defined by means of organization charts and job descriptions, which are sometimes incorporated into organizational manuals. All these can be helpful in clarifying relationships and responsibilities as long as it is understood that they can only provide an impression of how the organization functions, and as long as they are kept up to date, an onerous and frequently neglected task.

Organization charts

Charts are sometimes useful in planning and reviewing large organizations. They indicate how work is allocated and how activities are grouped together, they show who is responsible to whom and they illustrate lines of authority. Drawing up a chart can be a good way of clarifying what is currently happening – the mere process of putting the organization down on paper will highlight any problems. And when you come to consider changes, charts are the best way of illustrating alternatives.

The danger with organization charts is that they can be mistaken for the organization itself. They are a snapshot of what is supposed to be happening at a given moment. They are out of date as soon as they are drawn and they leave out the informal organization. If you use little boxes to represent people, they may behave as if they were indeed little boxes, sticking too closely to the book of rules.

Job descriptions

Like organization charts, job descriptions can be too rigid and stifle initiative. If kept brief (one side of one sheet of paper) they have their uses: to define the purpose of the job and its principal accountabilities; to describe the sort of job for which you are recruiting, and the sort of person you want to find; to provide a basis for training programmes and performance appraisal and to help slot jobs into a pay structure.

Job Design

Organization design will involve not only structuring the organization but also designing individual jobs. The aims in job design will be, first, to ensure that the activities which the position is expected to cater for are properly covered and, secondly, to provide for the jobs to be intrinsically motivating, i.e. for the job holders to be motivated by the work itself as well as by extrinsic factors such as pay and other forms of reward.

To design jobs which are intrinsically motivating it is necessary to provide for the following:

- *Feedback.* Individuals must receive meaningful information about their performance, preferably by evaluating it themselves and defining the feedback required. This implies that they should work either on a complete product, or on a significant part of it which can be seen as a whole.

- *The use of abilities.* The job must be perceived by individuals as requiring them to use abilities they value in order to perform the job effectively.

- *Self-control.* Individuals must feel that they have a high degree of self-control over setting their own goals and defining the paths to these goals.

Of course, these principles cannot always be applied in full to the more routine jobs, but an attempt can and should be made by using one of the following job design techniques:

- *Job enrichment*, which aims to provide more opportunities in jobs for personal achievement and recognition, more challenging and responsible work, and more opportunities for individual advancement and growth

- *Autonomous group working*, which creates self-regulating groups who work with the minimum of supervision

- *High-performance work design*, in which autonomous groups are formed where multi-skilling is encouraged (i.e. job demarcation lines are eliminated as far as possible), new technology and equipment is deployed flexibly and with the full involvement of the group, and goals and standards are agreed by all concerned

Introducing Organizational Change

The following ten steps should be taken when introducing organizational change.

1   Base the change on a thorough organizational analysis of the needs of the existing organization, and its ability to meet those needs.

2   Involve those concerned in the analysis.

3   If the change is forced on the company, explain why and how it may affect people.

4   Consult people about other methods of dealing with the situation. Try to get them to 'own' the solution as theirs, and not something imposed upon them.

5   Accentuate any positive existing benefits.

6   Mitigate any problems for the people concerned by retraining, redeployment or generous outplacement benefits for those for whom there are no internal opportunities.

7   Be prepared to modify the ideal solution to cater for reasonable points made by those concerned.

8   Define the new organization carefully and introduce training programmes to help people to adjust to their changed responsibilities.

9   Involve the people concerned in managing the organizational change programme.

10   Consider using external 'change agents' to facilitate change.

Features of an Effective Organization

The following are recipes for organizational success as advocated by leading writers and practising managers.

- The organization 'needs change masters, helping and guiding its management and all that work in it to manage and, indeed, to exploit and triumph over change'.

- Effective organizations 'develop a culture of pride and a climate of success'.

- Organizational success 'depends on the skill of corporate leaders, the ultimate change masters, to envision a new reality and aid in its translation into concrete terms'.

- 'Successful companies provide the freedom to act which arouses the desire to act.'

Rosabeth Moss Kanter[16]

- 'The excellent organizations are both centralized and decentralized. They push decisions and autonomy as far down the organization as they can get into individual units and profit centres. But they are fanatic centralists around the few core values they hold dear.'

Peters and Waterman[17]

- 'The successful firms of the 90s will be users of highly trained, well motivated, flexible people as the principal means of adding value.'

Tom Peters[18]

- 'Nothing will happen unless everyone down the line knows what they are trying to achieve and gives of their best to achieve it.'

- 'The whole of business is about taking an acceptable risk.'

- 'The process of deciding where you are taking the business is the opportunity to get the involvement of others, which actually forms the motive power that at the end of the day will make it happen.'

John Harvey-Jones[19]

- 'The traditional model for management is to establish order and to achieve efficiency in the application of the work force.

This is being replaced by the commitment strategy in which performance expectations are high and serve not to define minimum standards but to provide "stretch objectives", emphasise continuous improvement and reflect the requirement of the market place.'

Richard Walton[20]

- In the effective organization, 'The total organization, the significant sub-parts and individuals manage their work against goals and plan for the achievement of goals.'

- 'Communication laterally and vertically is undistorted. People are generally open and confronting. They share all the relevant facts and their feelings.'

Richard Beckhard[21]

- 'Effective organizational change is most apt to occur when the top managers of the organization are involved and when they indicate their commitment to the change effort.'

Lawrence and Lorsch[13]

- 'Successful organizations develop clear plans or courses of action over time to reach identified goals.'

Pascale and Athos[22]

These messages are fairly consistent. From them and other analyses of organizational effectiveness the following ten factors (not in order of importance) appear to be relevant.

1 Strong visionary leadership from the top

2 A powerful management team

3 A well-motivated, committed, skilled and flexible workforce

4 Effective teamwork throughout the organization

5 A continuous pressure to innovate coupled with the ability to manage and thrive on change

6 Clearly defined goals and strategies to accomplish them

7 A positive corporate culture

8 A value system which emphasizes performance, quality and the responsibilities of the organization to its stakeholders –

shareholders, managers, suppliers, customers and the community

9   An ability to get into action fast

10 A sound financial base

Organization Development

Organization development programmes tend to concentrate on the following areas for improving organizational effectiveness:

● implementing changed systems and structures (see Chapter 12 and above)

● developing positive cultures and value systems (see Chapter 16)

● achieving integration (see below)

● team development (see below)

● improving inter-group relations and resolving conflict (see below)

Achieving integration

The integration of organizational activities is necessary as a means of counteracting the tendency for diversification and differentiation to detract from the achievement of unity of purpose in the attainment of the organization's goals.

Integration is partly a structural matter. It is facilitated if activities are grouped logically together, if lines of communication are short and well defined and if managers do not have unwieldy spans of control. But there are other approaches which can be used, such as:

● *voluntary integration* to encourage people to communicate with each other and to integrate their activities without reference to higher authority

● *meetings* to deal on a continuing basis with planning operational matters requiring integration

● *project teams*, task forces or working parties to deal with specific issues or problems outside the normal routine

- improving the quality of *communications*, which includes making the best use of information technology to keep people informed

- setting up *planning* procedures which involve people in different areas and at different levels in jointly formulating action programmes which they will be responsible for implementing

- *value systems* or sets which guide people on how they are expected to work together on problem solving and provide them with a framework within which they can adopt a cohesive approach to dealing with issues as they arise.

Team development

Team development activities aim to create working groups which satisfy the criteria given in Chapter 11. A team development programme may be carried out by the manager of the group, but it is often better to use a 'facilitator' to intervene independently and objectively in the group processes involved. The facilitator can stand back and help the group to identify and resolve its problems, thereby improving its effectiveness. Such a programme might comprise:

- a group meeting in which issues are explored and agreement is reached on what the team development exercise should achieve

- the discussion and identification of what needs to be done in such areas as structure, systems, relationships and methods of operation and communication

- an analysis of the effectiveness of the group in working together and resolving problems – this may involve exercises in which the group's processes are observed and conclusions drawn as to how well they function

- the joint preparation of action plans to deal with identified needs and improve team working.

Inter-group relations

Inter-group relation activities deal with conflicts or problems relating to communications or roles which may lead to conflict. They may also be concerned with the conflicts or misapprehensions that arise when two companies or departments have to be merged.

Conflict resolution is the basis of most inter-group relations work. The simplest and crudest approach is a confrontation meeting in which the two parties get together, with a third party on the sidelines to help them work through their differences.

A more refined version of this approach is first to get the third party to hold discussions with each of the groups separately to agree on the issues and on an agenda for discussion. The third party then acts as a facilitator at a joint meeting for which a framework has been provided within which the issues can be resolved.

The Organizational Dilemma

There are no easy routes to organizational success. There is no one right way to design an organization. There is always a choice. Organization design is a balancing act between what appear to be a number of equally valid choices. As Rosabeth Moss Kanter[23] has pointed out, organizations face escalating and seemingly incompatible demands:

- Get 'lean and mean' through restructuring – while being a great company to work for and offering employee-centred policies, such as job security.

- Encourage creativity and innovation to take you in new directions – and 'stick to your knitting'.

- Communicate a sense of urgency and push for faster execution – but take more time to deliberately plan for the future.

- Decentralize to delegate profit and planning responsibilities to small, autonomous business units – but centralize to capture efficiencies and combine resources in innovative ways.

These dilemmas mean that organization design and development will always be an empirical process in which 'the law of the situation' will finally prevail. An analytical approach and attention to the guidelines will help but they will not provide the final answer. That will depend on the judgement of those involved, although this judgement will best be exercised against the background of an understanding of the organizational processes described in this chapter.

References

1   LUPTON Tom. 'Best fit in the design of organizations'. *Personnel Review.* Vol. 4, No. 1, 1975
2   WEBER Max *in* GERTH H. H. and MILLS C. W. *eds. From Max Weber.* Oxford, Oxford University Press, 1946
3   BARNARD Chester. *Functions of the executive.* Cambridge, Massachusetts, Harvard University Press, 1938
4   McGREGOR Douglas. *The human side of enterprise.* New York, McGraw-Hill, 1966
5   LIKERT Rensis. *New patterns of management.* New York, McGraw-Hill, 1961
6   ARGYRIS Chris. *Personality and organization.* New York, Harper, 1957
7   CHILD John. *Organization, a guide to problems and practice.* London, Harper & Row, 1977
8   MILLER E. and RICE A. K. *Systems of organization.* London, Tavistock Publications, 1967
9   TRIST E. L. *Organizational choice.* London, Tavistock Publications, 1963
10 SILVERMAN D. *The theory of organization: a sociological framework.* London, Heinemann, 1970
11 BURNS T. and STALKER G. M. *The management of innovation.* London, Tavistock Publications, 1961
12 WOODWARD Joan. *Industrial organization.* Oxford, Oxford University Press, 1968
13 LAWRENCE P. R. and LORSCH J. W. *Organization and environment.* Cambridge, Massachusetts, Harvard University Press, 1967
14 ARMSTRONG Michael. *Personnel and the bottom line.* London, Institute of Personnel Management, 1989
15 DRUCKER Peter. 'The coming of the new organization'. *The Harvard Business Review.* January–February 1988. pp 45–53

16   KANTER Rosabeth Moss. *The change masters*. London, Allen & Unwin, 1984
17   PETERS Tom and WATERMAN Robert. *In search of excellence*. New York, Harper & Row, 1982
18   PETERS Tom. *Thriving on chaos*. London, Macmillan, 1988
19   HARVEY-JONES John. *Making it happen*. London, Collins, 1988
20   WALTON Richard. 'From control to commitment in the work place'. *Harvard Business Review*. March–April 1985. pp 77–84
21   BECKHARD Richard. *Organization development: strategy and models*. Reading, Massachusetts, Addison-Wesley, 1969
22   PASCALE Richard and ATHOS Anthony. *The art of Japanese management*. London, Sidgwick & Jackson, 1986
23   KANTER Rosabeth Moss. *When giants learn to dance*. London, Simon & Schuster, 1989

16

Corporate Culture

Managers have to operate within the corporate culture of their organization, and a strong culture can considerably influence the behaviour that is expected of them.

Definition of Corporate Culture

Corporate culture is the pattern of shared attitudes, beliefs, assumptions and expectations which shape the way people act and interact in an organization, and underpin the way things get done.

Manifestations of Corporate Culture

Corporate culture encompasses the norms and core values of an enterprise and manifests itself in the form of organization climate and management style.

Norms

Norms are the unwritten rules of behaviour which strongly influence climate, management style and how people work together, conduct themselves and carry out their tasks.

The norms of an organization may, for example, produce behaviour which is relaxed and friendly. There is a lot of informal chat (perhaps too much), walking about, drifting in and out of offices, and *ad hoc* meetings, which may often appear to be inconclusive but still get things done. Alternatively, the norms may result in behaviour where relationships are formalized, distances are maintained between levels, meetings are highly structured and everything is recorded on paper.

Core values

Core values are the basic beliefs about what is good or best for the organization, and about what management thinks is important, what should or should not happen. There will be a value system or set which will be accepted by management who will say, in effect, these are the things we believe in. The core values may or may not be expressed formally in a value statement, and this may or may not be shared or accepted by the members of the organization.

Organization climate

Organization climate is the working atmosphere of the organization as perceived by its members. It is shaped and influenced by norms, values and the behaviour of the chief executive and managers, which sets the 'tone' of the organization.

Management style

Management style describes the way in which managers set about achieving results through people. It is how managers behave as team leaders and how they exercise authority. Managers can be autocratic or democratic, tough or soft, demanding or easy-going, directive or *laissez-faire*, distant or accessible, destructive or supportive, task-orientated or people-orientated, rigid or flexible, considerate or unfeeling, friendly or cold, keyed-up or relaxed. How they behave will depend partly on their natural inclinations, partly on the example given to them by their managers, and partly on the norms, values and climate of the organization.

Organization behaviour

Organization behaviour is the way in which people act in the organization, individually or in groups. This embraces the extent to which they are motivated, committed, indifferent, co-operative, intractable, energetic or lethargic. It also includes the various processes in the organization such as planning, innovating, coping with change, delegating, co-operating, involving, interacting, communicating, measuring, appraising and rewarding. These processes will critically affect the way things get done and the results achieved. They will be strongly influenced by the other aspects of corporate culture: norms, values, climate and management style.

Structure and systems

Corporate culture will affect the ways in which the organization is structured and operated. These will include the amount of rigidity or flexibility allowed in the structure, the extent to which informal processes of interaction and communication override or replace formal channels, the amount of authority that is devolved from the top or the centre, and the degree to which jobs are compartmentalized and rigidly defined. It may affect the number of layers of management, the spans of control of managers and the extent to which decisions are made by teams rather than by individuals.

The development and use of systems will also be affected by the corporate culture and will in turn help to shape it. A bureaucratic or mechanistic organization will attempt to govern everything through systems or manuals. An organic approach will only allow systems which are functions of the situation in which the enterprise finds itself rather than conforming to any predetermined and rigid view of how it should operate. In some organizations, people follow systems to the letter, in others, people take pride in 'bucking the system' and cutting corners to get things done. Systems can be used as control mechanisms to enforce conformity or they can be flexed to allow scope for responding to new situations as they arise.

The Importance of Culture to Organizations

Corporate culture is a key component of the achievement of an organization's mission and strategies, the improvement of organizational effectiveness and the management of change. It is important because it is rooted in deeply held beliefs. It reflects what has worked in the past, being composed of responses which have been accepted because they have met with success.

Corporate culture can work for an organization by creating an environment which is conducive to performance improvement and the management of change. It can work against an organization by erecting barriers which prevent the achievement of strategic goals. These barriers include resistance to change and lack of commitment.

The Significance of Corporate Culture to Managers

Managers have to learn to live with the corporate culture, although they can play their part in changing it, if that is necessary. To a large extent, whether they like it or not, there will be established norms and values governing their behaviour. In a bureaucratic, highly structured organization these norms are likely to be strong and difficult to ignore. In a more loosely formed 'organic' organization the norms will be flexible, but they will still exist. After all, if the norm is to behave informally it takes courage and strength of character to deviate from it to any great extent.

If you want to live comfortably within your organization's culture, you have first to understand it and then take whatever steps you can to manage it.

Understanding Corporate Culture

Norms and values

As we have seen, corporate culture is expressed in the norms and values of the organization. You therefore need to find out what they are by observation and by analysing behaviour.

The norms you should analyse will include:

- how managers treat subordinates and how subordinates relate to their managers
- the prevailing work ethic, e.g. 'Work hard, play hard', 'Come in early, stay late', 'If you cannot finish your work during business hours you are obviously inefficient', 'Look busy at all times', 'Look relaxed at all times'
- status – how much importance is attached to it; the existence or lack of obvious status symbols

- ambitions – naked ambition is expected and approved of, or a more subtle approach is the norm
- performance – exacting performance standards are general; the highest praise that can be given in the organization is to be referred to as very professional
- power – recognized as a way of life; executed by political means, dependent on expertise and ability rather than position; concentrated at the top; shared at different levels in different parts of the organization
- politics – rife throughout the organization and treated as normal behaviour; not accepted as overt behaviour
- loyalty – expected, a cradle-to-grave approach to careers; discounted, the emphasis being on results and contribution in the short term
- anger – openly expressed; hidden, but expressed through other, possibly political means
- approachability – managers expected to be approachable and visible; everything being done behind closed doors.
- formality – a cool, formal approach as the norm; Christian names used or not used at all levels; unwritten but clearly understood rules about dress.

Core values

The core values of the organization may be expressed in a written statement – in which case, you should try to establish the extent to which they are acted upon at all levels. In the absence of a written statement, the areas in which you should seek to establish what the organization's values are or whether they exist at all include:

- care and consideration for people
- care for customers
- competitiveness
- enterprise
- equity in the treatment of employees

- excellence
- growth
- innovation
- market/customer orientation
- priority to organizational rather than to people's needs
- performance orientation
- productivity
- provision of equal opportunity for employees
- quality
- social responsibility
- teamwork

Organizational climate

Your analysis of the climate or working atmosphere of the organization should assess the extent to which it is:

- flexible or bureaucratic
- formal or informal
- hierarchical or loosely structured
- friendly or distant
- co-operative or individualistic
- status-conscious or free and easy
- relaxed or stressful
- reactive or pro-active
- innovative or 'stick-in-the-mud'
- political or apolitical
- profit-conscious or cost-conscious
- action-orientated or *laissez-faire*
- results-orientated or process-orientated

Management style

When you analyse management style you should consider the extent to which it can be described as any of the following:

- *autocratic*, relying on authority exercised according to rank within a defined hierarchy, and on the disciplined compliance of subordinates to the orders of their superiors
- *impersonal*, expecting people to perform their duties in accordance with strictly defined terms of reference, rigidly applied rules and detailed directives
- *participative*, sharing decision making with employees by such means as prior consultation, working parties and project teams
- *informal*, relying more on informal interaction between managers and subordinates or between colleagues and work groups rather than on impersonal definitions and directiyes
- *Laissez-faire*, allowing things to drift
- *Benevolently despotic* – autocratic with a human face

Types of culture

The culture of an organization is best analysed under the above headings. Attempts to develop a range of overall culture types are in danger of oversimplifying a complex concept.

The most useful typology has been developed by Charles Handy,[1] who distinguishes between four varieties of culture.

1 *The power culture*, which depends on a central power source in an entrepreneurial organization. It is tough and abrasive but morale is often low and it can easily fall apart.

2 *The role culture*, another name for a bureaucratic organization (mechanistic in Burns and Stalker's terms[2]), which works by logic and rationality. It offers security and predictability but can be frustrating to individuals who want to get results quickly.

3 *The task culture*, which is job- or project-orientated. It is adaptable and appropriate where flexibility and sensitivity to the market or environment are important. People on the whole

like working in task, or, as Burns and Stalker[2] call them, organic, cultures, but they can induce feelings of insecurity (role ambiguity and conflict) if things go wrong.

4   *The person culture*, where the organization exists to serve the people in it, as in professional partnerships.

As Handy points out, none of these cultures is right or wrong. Any one of them could be right in particular circumstances. This rule applies generally when analysing cultures. It is neither possible or desirable to impose on an organization a culture which is inappropriate to its needs.

Although using a 'typology' approach to analysing your own culture can be dangerous, it is sometimes useful to attempt a summary of the corporate culture as a basis for further analysis or action. For example, after a detailed study which involved the use of 'focus groups' (consultant-led discussions with cross-sections of employees) and an attitude survey, it was possible to summarize the culture of Book Club Associates as follows:

- informal
- opportunistic
- entrepreneurial
- autocratic (it is possible to be informally autocratic).
- professional (a belief in achieving high standards)
- output-orientated

Culture management

What culture management is

Culture management is concerned with:

- *culture change*, the development of attitudes, beliefs, norms and values which will be congruent with the organization's mission, strategies, environment and technologies and will lead to significant changes to climate, management style and behaviour which positively support the achievement of the organization's objectives

- *culture reinforcement*, which aims to preserve and reinforce what is good or functional about the present culture
- *change management*, which is concerned with enabling the culture to adapt successfully to change and gaining acceptance to changes in organization, systems, procedures and methods of work
- *commitment gain*, which is concerned with the commitment of members of the organization to its mission, strategies and values

How it is achieved

Ed Schein[3] has suggested that the most powerful primary mechanisms for culture embedding and reinforcement are:

- what leaders pay attention to, measure and control
- leaders' reactions to critical incidents and crises
- deliberate role modelling, teaching and coaching by leaders
- criteria for allocation of rewards and status
- criteria for recruitment, selection, promotion, and retirement

Because cultures have evolved over the years and are usually deeply rooted, they are difficult to change. It is very hard to get people to alter long-held attitudes and beliefs, and attempts to do so often fail. All you can do is to get them to alter their behaviour in ways which will remove dysfunctional elements in the culture and support the introduction of functional elements.

But changing behaviour is not always easy, although it will happen in traumatic circumstances such as a crisis, a change in ownership or the arrival of a powerful, autocratic, charismatic and visionary leader. Behaviour can be changed by:

- leadership setting the example
- the issue of mission and value statements which explicitly state where the organization is going and the values it adopts in

getting there – but these statements must represent reality and must be followed up by workshops, training and discussions which translate the words into deeds

- workshops to get people involved in discussing new values and ways of behaviour and practising their application; as in the British Airways 'Putting People First' programme which involved all 38,000 staff attending an intensive three-day workshop encouraging them to think about and accept the importance of customer service

- education and training programmes to extend knowledge and teach people new skills

- performance management programmes which ensure through the mechanisms of objective setting and performance appraisal that the values, norms and behaviours which the cultural change programme is developing are absorbed and acted upon as part of the normal process of management

- reward management systems which reward people for behaviour which is in accord with the values built into the culture change programme

Such programmes can be used not only to change but also to reinforce a culture. They are most effective on an organization-wide basis. But individual managers have a vital part to play. First, they need to understand their culture (using the checklists set out earlier in this chapter). Secondly, they should get involved as far as possible in the definition of the aims and constituents of a culture management programme. And finally, they should play their part by practising the required behaviour themselves, developing it in their staff, and instilling or reinforcing the value system of the organization throughout their department.

For References see over

References

1 HANDY Charles. *Understanding organizations.* Harmondsworth, Penguin Books, 1985
2 BURNS T. and STALKER G. M. *The management of innovation.* London, Tavistock Publications, 1961
3 SCHEIN Ed. *Organization culture and leadership.* New York, Jossey-Bass, 1987

17

Organization Functions

Overall Functions

Organizations exist to fulfil a defined purpose and the functions carried out within them will vary according to that purpose. However, all organizations will have:

- an overall leader; for example, a chief executive, chairman, managing director, secretary-general, general manager

- operational functions which are there to achieve the main purposes of the organization, be it to provide a public service, to administer an activity (including those of sport and the arts), to service its members, to provide aid, to develop, manufacture and sell a product, or to provide a private service for profit

- support or service functions such as finance, management services, personnel and administration

Non-profit making organizations

Non-profit making organizations will exist to provide certain services in defined areas of activity and to achieve laid-down standards of performance within a budget. The roles of the chief executive and the main service departments such as finance and personnel may be broadly similar to those in the private sector, but the operational functions will vary widely according to the purpose of the organization. I will therefore concentrate more on the functions within profit-making organizations where there is common ground between different enterprises, although the presence of these functions and their role and organization will, of course, vary widely.

Profit-making organizations

Under the chief executive or general manager, a profit-making organization will have three major functions:

1 *Policy formulation, co-ordination and control* as carried out by the board or an executive committee.

2 *Operational activities* (sometimes referred to as line activities), which cater for what the organization exists to do as a commercial enterprise. These comprise:

   ● *Business generation* – innovation (the development of new products or services), marketing and selling

   ● *Demand satisfaction* – manufacturing the product or providing the service to meet demand, and distributing it to the customer. Feedback from the customer in the form of new or repeat orders and reaction to the product or service will affect the business-generating activities.

3 *Support or service activities* (sometimes referred to as staff activities), which ensure that operational activities can take place by:

   ● giving a sense of direction through planning and budgeting

   ● providing finance and the means of planning and controlling expenditure

   ● providing personnel support and services

   ● providing management services which include information technology, organization and methods, and operations research

   ● providing other support services such as supplies (buying or procurement), legal, property, maintenance and administration

   ● conducting research which can be fed into the operational activities of development and marketing.

The interrelationships between these functions are illustrated in Figure 15.

Figure 15
The functions of general management

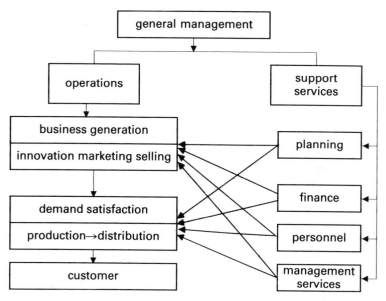

The various functions of management in a manufacturing or profit-earning service organization are described in this chapter under the following headings:

- the chief executive
- the board
- marketing
- production
- inventory control
- distribution
- research and development
- finance
- personnel

- supplies
- management services

The Chief Executive

Chief executives are accountable directly to their shareholders, trustees, members or any individual or body which controls the organization. The amount of control over them varies considerably. In some cases the financial institutions such as insurance companies, who hold large blocks of shares will exert a lot of influence, either directly or through directors whom they have nominated to sit on the board.

The chief executive's responsibilities will include:

- obtaining for the owners of a profit-making organization the maximum return on their investment and providing for the long-term profitable growth of the business (in a non-profit making organization this responsibility might involve ensuring that the organization achieves its objectives within its financial budgets)
- continually developing a vision of what the business should become and taking whatever steps are required to turn that vision into reality
- defining and, as necessary, redefining the mission of the business
- formulating corporate policies as guidelines on how the mission will be accomplished
- developing strategies and goals for achieving the mission within the framework of corporate policies
- ensuring that the human, financial and physical resources required by the business are available
- developing a value system and organizational climate which will help the business to achieve its goals
- exercising visionary leadership which will inspire innovation, committed effort and high standards of performance
- creating a sound organization structure

- building a powerful management team
- directing the various planning and budgeting processes required to achieve strategies and financial targets
- co-ordinating the business generation, demand satisfaction and support or service activities required
- continually monitoring key control information and initiating action as necessary to exploit opportunities, deal with problems or correct variances
- representing the company to the outside world and maintaining good relationships with all the stakeholders of the business, i.e. shareholders, employees, key suppliers, customers and the public at large
- ensuring that the company's social responsibilities to its stake-holders are fulfilled
- ensuring that business is conducted ethically and that the legal obligations of the firm are met in full

In many companies, this role of chief executive is split between the chairman and a managing director. Chairmen are likely to spend a large proportion of their time in looking outside the company, building good relationships with shareholders and the City generally and dealing with major issues created by government policies and edicts. But they will also chair the board and have the overall responsibility for co-ordinating the development of policies and strategies. In addition, they will set the tone of the company by their management style and leadership qualities and may be directly concerned with the acquisition, development or use of key resources, including people and money.

Managing directors reporting to chairmen will concentrate more on the internal management of the business. They will be accountable to the chairman and the board for planning, directing, co-ordinating and controlling all activities and for delivering results.

The board

Boards are there to advise and assist chairmen to carry out their duties. The members of the board will be involved in formulating policies and strategies, reviewing and approving plans and budgets,

monitoring performance, especially financial performance, and
initiating action. Certain key decisions such as the approval
of budgets, major capital investments or disinvestments, key
appointments and the remuneration of directors and senior executives may be reserved to the board.

The board will consist of executive directors, each of whom,
with the exception of the chairman and managing director, will
usually be responsible for a major function. They will in effect be
representing that function on the board, thus bringing their
particular expertise to bear on any decisions and problems as well
as making major proposals and reporting on matters concerning
their area of activity. But as directors, their main role is collectively
to help the chairman run the business. Managing their functions
is not their only consideration when they sit on the board.

Many companies have non-executive directors, who may be
appointed by shareholders or may be brought onto the board by
the chairman with the agreement of board members. These
non-executive directors can play an important role in bringing
independent judgement and a wider range of experience to bear
on issues confronting the business.

Marketing

Definition

Marketing is 'the management process responsible for identifying,
anticipating and satisfying customer requirements profitably'.
(Institute of Marketing)

Objectives

The overall object of marketing is to ensure that the company
obtains the revenues it needs to achieve its profit targets.

As defined by Philip Kotler, marketing management is:

> the analysis, planning, implementation, and control of pro-
> grammes designed to create, build, and maintain beneficial
> exchanges and relationships with target markets for the
> purpose of achieving organizational objectives.[1]

According to Theodore Levitt,[2] 'The purpose of a business is to get and keep a customer.' Marketing aims to decide what companies should do to achieve that purpose and then to ensure that it is done.

The marketing concept

Kotler[1] says, 'The marketing concept holds that the key to achieving organizational goals consists in determining the needs and wants of target markets and delivering the desired satisfactions more effectively and efficiently than competitors.' The target market is defined as the set of actual and potential buyers of a product.

Marketing is not just about selling. As Levitt says:

> Selling focuses on the needs of the seller: marketing on the needs of the buyer. Selling is preoccupied with the seller's need to convert his product into cash: marketing with the idea of satisfying the needs of the customer by means of the product and the whole cluster of things associated with creating, delivering and finally consuming it.[3]

The marketing concept expresses the company's commitment to consumer sovereignty. The company produces what its consumers want, and in this way maximizes consumer satisfaction and earns its profits.

Levitt sums up the marketing concept thus:

> The organization must learn to think of itself not as producing goods or services but as *buying customers*, as doing the things that will make people *want* to do business with it.[2]

The marketing process

The marketing process is based upon the company's objectives and strategies as set out in its corporate plan. Marketing is very largely concerned with planning and analysis, with a considerable input from research and development activities. The plans lead to action which is monitored to ensure that it produces the desired results.

Marketing activities

The main marketing activities are:

1 *Marketing planning.* This is the central marketing process. It ensures that corporate objectives are achieved by setting sales targets and budgets and preparing action plans for achieving results. The plans use the outputs of market research, sales forecasts and market analyses, which include product life-cycle analysis, gap analysis and the analysis of competitors' activities. This data enables the company to focus on:

   - analysing market opportunities to identify where the company would have a competitive advantage for introducing new products, improving existing products and entering new markets
   - selecting target markets which are appropriate to the skills and resources available to the company. If the company is not in the mass marketing business, i.e. offering one product to attract all types of buyers, consideration has to be given to which products need to be differentiated to offer variety in the market and to distinguish them from their competitors. Decisions have also to be made on the segments of the market to be targeted.

2 *Product development and planning.* This involves searching for new product ideas and concepts and screening and testing them to ensure that they meet a consumer need and are potentially profitable.

3 *Sales planning.* Producing detailed field or outlet sales targets and the plans for achieving them.

4 *Media planning.* Deciding on the media to be used in advertising campaigns is an important marketing activity.

5 *Marketing research.* This is the assembly of information on the company's actual and potential markets and on users of the goods or services marketed by the company.

6 *Sales forecasting.* Assessing the sales potential and market trends for the products marketed by the company.

7 *Analysis.* This involves the analysis of the product life cycle,

which describes and forecasts the pattern of sales, the identification of any areas in the market which are not filled by competitors' products and could be exploited by the company, and the analysis of competitors' activities generally.

8 *Target marketing.* This is the more detailed definition of the different groups that make up a market (segmentation), followed by decisions on where marketing effort should be targeted (i.e. which segments should be penetrated). These decisions lead to further decisions on the market position the company wishes to establish in the target market in relation to its competitors. This is called 'positioning'.

9 *Developing the marketing mix.* This is the set of controllable variables that the company blends to produce the response it wants in the target market. The mix comprises the following elements:

- product
- price
- place
- promotion

10 *Marketing and sales operation.* These operations implement the marketing plans, and include advertising and promotion campaigns, new product launches, field sales operations and campaigns, and distribution.

11 *Marketing and sales control.* Performance needs to be monitored to ensure that targets will be achieved within expenditure budgets.

12 *Feedback.* The plan should be amended as necessary in the light of the results achieved.

The interrelationships between these activities are shown in Figure 16.

Figure 16
Marketing activities

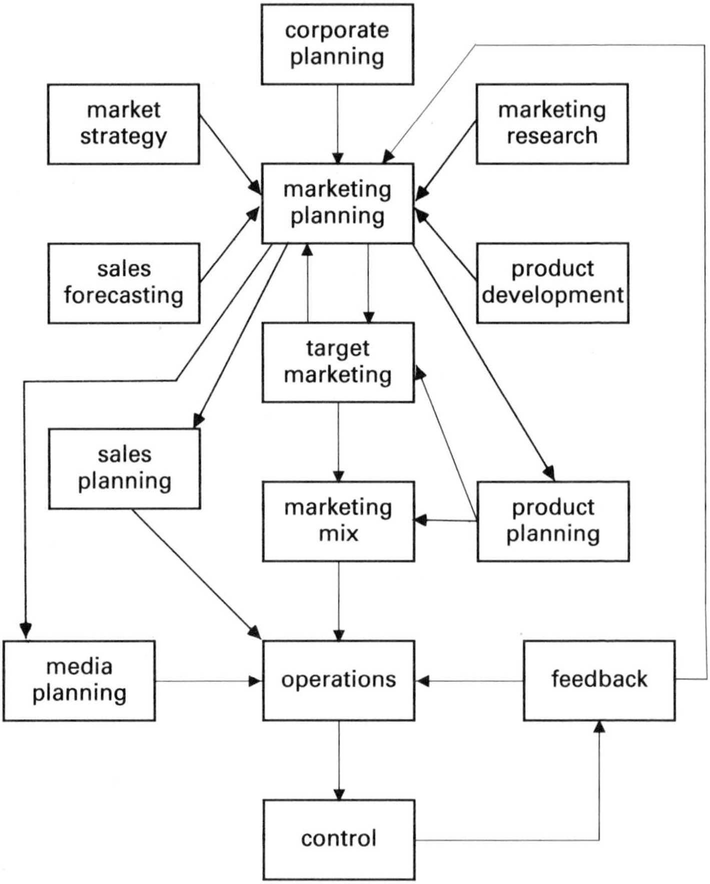

Production

Definition

Production plans and controls the use of people, materials, plant and machines to achieve the company's objectives for output, manufacturing programmes, quality and productivity.

Activities

The main production activities are:

1 *Production engineering*, which specifies and plans the manufacturing process. Within production engineering, the main activities are:

- process planning, which determines how the product or part should be manufactured by referring to the components and assembly drawings and:
  - drafts an operations sequence for each component
  - specifies the machines, hand tools, fixtures, gauges and labour to be used
  - designs manufacturing layouts

- production planning, which analyses sales forecasts and decides on the manufacturing resources and production programmes needed to meet sales demand

- production control, which schedules and monitors production to ensure that production programmes are achieved

2 *Methods engineering*, which uses work study (work measurement and methods study) and productivity planning techniques to record systematically and examine critically existing and proposed ways of doing work, as a means of developing and applying easier and more effective methods and reducing cost

3 *Quality control*, which ensures that during design, production and servicing, both work and materials are within limits that will produce the desired product performance and reliability

4 *Planned maintenance*, which draws up in advance plant, equipment or building maintenance programmes to ensure that they operate or remain trouble-free for a predetermined period

5 *Manufacturing*, which is the actual process of producing the goods or articles

The interrelationships between these activities and their links with inventory control, supplies and distribution (which will be defined later in this chapter) are illustrated in Figure 17.

Inventory Control

Definition

Inventory control ensures that the optimum amount of inventory or stock is held by a company so that its internal and external demand requirements are met economically.

Objectives

Inventory control has four objectives:

1   To minimize the costs of ordering and holding inventory, which is often the largest single investment a manufacturing company makes.
2   To maintain acceptable levels of customer service by minimising stockouts, i.e. goods not being available from stock when required.
3   To maintain a flow of materials and bought-in parts which will enable manufacturing to proceed according to plan.
4   To reconcile the potential conflicts between the objective of minimizing stock and that of maintaining high levels of service.

Inventory control techniques

The main inventory control techniques are:

- *demand forecasting*, which analyses past demands and sales in order to forecast future requirements
- *categorization of inventory items*, which is based on the so-called Pareto's Law which states that where a large number of items are contributing to a result, only a small proportion of these items will make a very considerable impact on the outcome. This is also called the 80/20 rule because, frequently,

Figure 17
The process of production

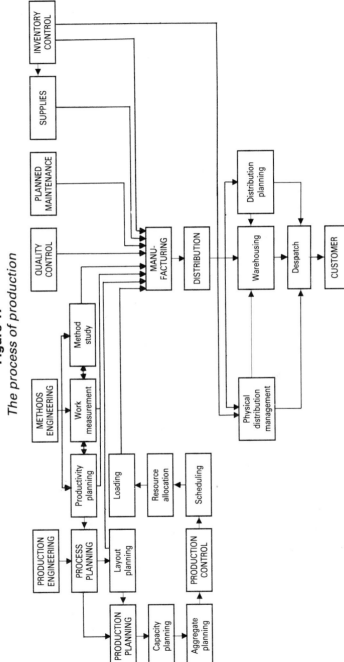

20 per cent of the items account for about 80 per cent of the results. This rule is applied in the categorization of inventory items in order of decreasing importance, starting with A items, which are the key 20 per cent which amount to 80 per cent of usage or turnover, on to the B and C items where usage is progressively lower. These categorizations determine review and reordering policies.

- *reorder level* – reordering systems ensure that replenishment is achieved at minimum cost while meeting service requirements. Policies will be determined for the minimum buffer or safety stock levels which have to be maintained and for economic order quantities.

- *materials requirement planning*, which schedules the provision of component materials and component parts and assemblies so that the customer's requirement is satisfied on time. This is often a production engineering function which is linked to inventory control.

- *just-in-time systems*, which sequence operations so that a supplier or associated manufacturing unit delivers to the next unit on one day the exact quantity it needs for the following day's production. This reduces not only inventory holdings but also the amount of work-in-progress, both of which can create considerable costs to the company because of excessive stock and delays in realizing sales.

Distribution

Definition

Distribution management ensures that finished goods are stored and then delivered efficiently to wholesalers, retailers or direct to the customer.

Distribution activities

Distribution activities consist of:

- *physical distribution management*, which uses quantitative techniques to achieve the best balance between inventory investment, expediting action and shipping frequency, having taken into account the likely incidence of stockouts and their impact on customers and, therefore, on sales

- *distribution planning* which takes the marketing and production plans, analyses them and decides on the distribution resources required and the operational schedules required to satisfy customer demands. The process of distribution planning is illustrated in Figure 18.

- *warehousing*, which is concerned with storing and despatching articles either centrally or in depots

- *delivery*, which ensures that goods or articles are delivered using the company's own transport fleet or other means.

Research and Development

Definition

Research and development (R & D) is responsible for the design and development of new products or the modification of existing ones in order to create or satisfy customer needs and wants now and in the future.

Activities

The main R & D activities are:

- *basic research*, which is sometimes called 'blue skies' research, in which scientists are delving into such things as the basic properties of materials. Their aim will be to achieve break-throughs in the discovery of new applications which can be developed for the manufacture and sale of the product. For example, the basic research carried out at Pilkingtons into the properties of glass led to the development of float glass.

- *applied research*, which is either the application of the discoveries of basic research to its possible use in manufacturing, or the development of a product or service.

Figure 18
The process of distribution planning

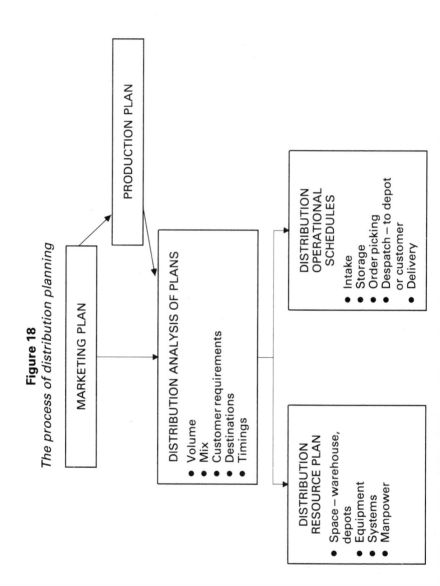

- *development*, which takes a concept or idea originating from research (either scientific and technical research or marketing research) and develops it as a process or product for use or sale.

- *design*, which works in conjunction with development, production or marketing to design the final process or product. In the latter case, design will involve not only the structure of the product but also its shape and its packaging, as required.

Finance

Definition

The finance function is responsible for advising on and managing the financial affairs of the business with regard to financial planning, keeping the books (financial accounting), measuring and analysing financial performance (management accounting) and managing cash (the treasury function).

Financial affairs

The finance function will advise the board on methods of raising finance from the City or by other means. The head of the function in a large public company will probably spend a lot of time liaising with the City – the merchant and joint stock banks, the insurance companies and the 'market makers' – to ensure that the company's reputation as a viable operation is maintained. Effective liaison is also required to enable the company to take pre-emptive action if a predator looks like making a takeover bid.

Financial planning

The finance function is responsible for producing financial forecasts for the long, medium and short term. These will be based on sales forecasts and projections of revenue expenditure (i.e. running costs and capital expenditure). It will also co-ordinate the preparation of annual budgets and reforecasts.

Financial accounting

Financial accounting records the revenue received and the expenditure incurred by a company so that its overall performance over a period of time and its financial position at a particular point can be ascertained.

The financial accounting system classifies, records and interprets in monetary terms transactions and events of a financial character.

The purposes of financial accounting are to meet:

- the external requirements of shareholders, potential investors, financial analysts, creditors, trade unions, the Registrar of Companies (in the UK) and the Inland Revenue

- the internal requirements of the management of the company who require information on the financial performance of the enterprise as a whole

Financial accounting systems are integrated with management accounting systems, although the latter exist to provide more detailed information to management, not only for control purposes but also as a guide to decision making.

Management accounting

Management accounting provides information to management on present and projected costs and on the profitability of individual projects, products, activities or departments as a guide to decision making and financial planning. It involves:

- *cost accounting* – the recording and allocation of cost data

- *cost analysis* – the classification and analysis of costs to aid business planning and control

- *absorption costing* – the assignment of all costs, both fixed and variable, to operations or products

- *marginal costing* – the segregation of fixed and variable or marginal costs and the apportionment of those marginal costs to products or processes

- *standard costing* – the preparation of predetermined or standard costs and their comparison with actual costs to identify variances

- *variance analysis* – the identification and analysis of differences between actual and standard costs, or between actual and budgeted overheads, sales and profits, with a view to providing guidance on any corrective action required

- *cost-volume-profit analysis* – the study of the relationship between expenses, revenue and net income in order to establish the implications on profit levels of changes in costs, volumes (production or sales) or prices

- *sales mix analysis* – calculates the effect on profits of variations in the mixture of output of the different products marketed by the company

- *financial budgeting* – deals with the creation of budgets. The basic form of budget is a static budget, i.e. one which assumes a constant level of activity.

- *flexible budgets* – take account of a range of possible volumes or activity levels

- *zero-base budgeting* – requires managers to justify *all* budgeted expenditure and not to prepare budgets as simply an extension of what was spent last year

- *budgetary control* – compares actual costs, revenues and performance with the fixed or 'flexed' budget so that, if necessary, corrective action can be taken or revisions made to the budget

- *overhead accounting* – directed specifically to the identification, measurement and control of overheads

- *responsibility accounting* – defines responsibility centres and holds the managers of those areas responsible for the costs and revenues assigned to them

- *capital budgeting* – the process of selecting and planning capital investments based upon an appraisal of the returns that will be obtained from the investments

- *risk analysis* – assesses the danger of failing to achieve forecasts of the outcome or yield of an investment

Cash management

The treasury or cash management function manages the cash flow of the company on the principle that although profitability is the overall objective, the immediate aim must always be to ensure that cash in exceeds cash out.

The treasury function will also invest surplus cash on a short-term basis to ensure that it is not lying idle, i.e. that it is making money.

Personnel Management

Definition

Personnel management is concerned with:

- obtaining, developing and motivating the human resources required by the organization to achieve its objectives

- developing an organization structure and climate and evolving a management style which will promote co-operation and commitment throughout the organization

- making the best use of the skills and capacities of all those employed in the organization

- ensuring that the organization meets its social and legal responsibilities towards its employees, with particular regard to the conditions of employment and quality of working life provided for them

There has been an increasing tendency in recent years to rename personnel management human resource management. In many cases the name is different but the function is the same. But as properly defined, human resource management (HRM) adopts a more strategic approach to the acquisition, motivation, development and management of the organization's human resources. People are treated as a key resource to be managed appropriately in the interests of the organization which, in theory at least, will coincide with their interests.

The main personnel activities can be grouped under three headings:

1 Employee resourcing
2 Employee development
3 Employee relations

These are described below and the relationships between them are illustrated in Figure 19.

Employee resourcing

This area covers all aspects of the employment of people; how they are organized, obtained, motivated, treated, appraised and paid; the provision of health, safety and welfare programmes and the maintenance of records. The main employee resourcing activities are:

- *organization design* – developing an organization structure which caters for all the activities required and groups them together in a way which encourages integration and co-operation, and provides for effective communication and decision making

- *job design* – deciding on the content of a job; its duties and responsibilities and the relationships that exist between the job holder and his or her superior, subordinates and colleagues

- *organization development* – planning and implementing programmes designed to improve the effectiveness with which an organization functions and responds to change

- *manpower planning* – forecasting manpower requirements, making plans to achieve forecasts and taking steps to improve productivity

- *recruitment and selection* – getting the number and type of people the organization needs

- *performance appraisal* – reviewing and assessing an individual's performance in order to help him or her to do better and to develop potential

Figure 19
Personnel activities

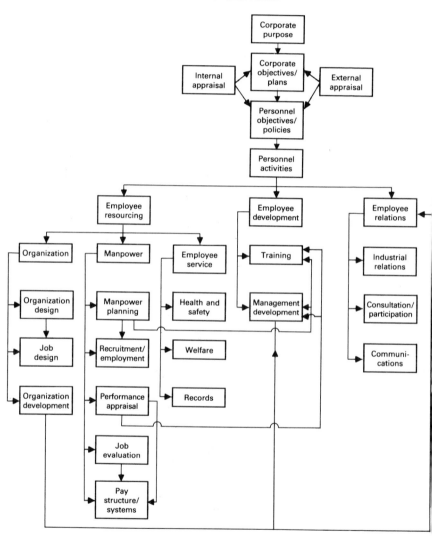

- *employment practices* – conditions of service, deploying and redeploying people, dealing with problems such as discipline and redundancy, ensuring that employment legislation is implemented
- *job evaluation* – establishing the relative value of jobs in a pay structure
- *pay* – developing and administering payment systems
- *health and safety* – administering health and safety programmes
- *welfare* – advising on and assisting with personal problems
- *personnel data* – maintaining information systems for personnel

Employee development

Employee development is concerned with:

- *training* – systematically developing the knowledge and skills required to perform adequately a given job or task
- *management development* – ensuring that the organization has the effective managers it requires to meet its present and future needs

Employee relations

Employee relations is concerned with dealing with employees collectively in the following ways:

- *industrial relations* – co-operating and negotiating with trade unions and staff associations
- *participation* – jointly involving management and employees in making decisions on matters of mutual interest
- *communications* – creating and transmitting information of interest to employees.

Management Services

Management services provide the following facilities:

- *data processing* – the provision of information technology in the shape of computer configurations and the supporting activities of systems analysis, programming and computer operations

- *organization and methods* – the analysis of administrative operations with a view to improving their efficiency and effectiveness

- *operational research* – the provision of management science resources to aid in the analysis of problems and data in order to assist planning and decision making

Supplies

Supplies management (buying or purchasing) involves the procurement of all the materials, plant, equipment and bought-in parts or job-assemblies required by the company. It involves the following activities:

- *supply planning* – using material requirement planning techniques and sales forecasts to develop master purchasing schedules which are exploded into detailed schedules of what components and materials need to be obtained, week by week, over the whole planning horizon

- *materials management*, which is concerned with policies and procedures for reducing purchasing costs, making-for-stock or making-for-customer-order decisions, make or buy decisions (i.e. whether to make the component within the firm or buy it from outside), and the co-ordination of common requirements in different parts of the company

- *quality assurance* – ensuring that the right quality of goods and materials is bought. This involves obtaining proper specifications from user departments on what they require and ensuring through the selection of suppliers and by inspection that the quality conforms to the specification

- *purchasing procedures* for initiating orders, selecting suppliers, negotiating and agreeing contracts and ensuring that deliveries are made on time
- *maintaining stock records* to meet inventory control requirements concerning stock levels, order levels and safety stock
- *reordering stock* as required in accordance with inventory control policies and procedures and purchasing schedules and orders
- *stocktaking* to meet the requirements of the company's auditors for the valuation of stocks and work-in-progress

Administrative Functions

There are a number of administrative functions carried out in most organizations which are either all placed in one administration department, or if they are significant, are catered for in individual departments. For example, property in a large retail organization is a major function, but in a small business might be grouped with other administrative functions.

The administrative service or support activities include:

- *company secretary*, providing the secretarial services required by the board and ensuring that the legal obligations of the company are fulfilled
- *legal*, providing legal services in connection with contractual matters, property, legal issues etc.
- *office services* – telephones, cleaning, catering, office supplies, photocopying, word processing, reception etc.
- *maintenance* – the maintenance and repair of office or factory plant and equipment
- *property* – managing the company's properties, dealing with acquisitions, disposal, extensions, repair and maintenance, and rent negotiation
- *fleet management* – managing the company's transport fleet.

References

1 KOTLER Philip. *Principles of marketing.* Englewood Cliffs, Prentice-Hall, 1983
2 LEVITT Theodore. *The marketing imagination.* New York, The Free Press, 1983
3 LEVITT Theodore. 'Marketing myopia'. *The Harvard Business Review.* July–August, 1960

18

Strategic Planning

What is Strategic Planning?

Strategic planning is a systematic, analytical approach which reviews the business as a whole in relation to its environment. It has two major functions:

1 To develop an integrated, coordinated and consistent view of the route the company wishes to follow
2 To facilitate the adaptation of the organization to environmental change.

The aim of strategic planning is to create a viable link between the organization's objectives and resources and its environmental opportunities. It will therefore determine the future posture of the enterprise with specific reference to its product-market scope (the products it can produce and the markets it can be in), its profitability, its size, its rate of innovation, its relationships both with its stakeholders (shareholders, suppliers, employees, customers and the public) and the external environment generally. Thus, in Igor Ansoff's words:

> Strategy and objectives together describe the concept of the firm's business. They specify the amount of growth, the area of growth, the directions for growth, the leading strengths, and the profitability target. Furthermore, they are stated operationally, in a form usable for guiding management decisions and actions.[1]

Strategic planning is concerned with the formulation of strategies within the framework of company policies. It involves processes of strategic management which, through various operational and project plans, will lead to action and the achievement of goals. The strategic planning process at organizational level will often be formalized by means of a system of corporate planning but will be related to a number of other processes or concepts as illustrated in Figure 20.

Figure 20
The strategic planning process

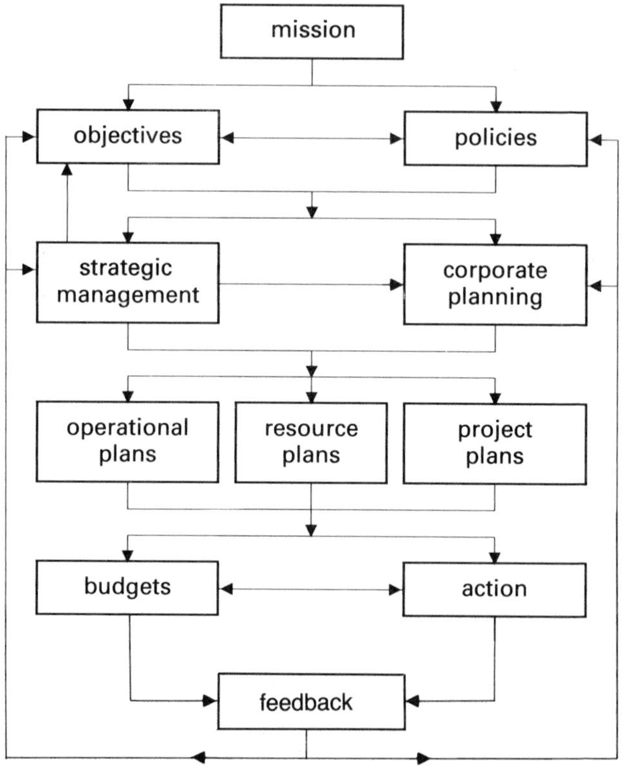

```
                    ┌──────────────────┐
                    │     mission      │
                    └──────────────────┘

   ┌──────────────┐                    ┌──────────────┐
→  │  objectives  │ ◄───────────────── │   policies   │ ◄──
   └──────────────┘                    └──────────────┘

   ┌──────────────┐                    ┌──────────────┐
→  │  strategic   │ ─────────────────► │  corporate   │ ◄──
   │  management  │                    │   planning   │
   └──────────────┘                    └──────────────┘

 ┌────────────┐   ┌────────────┐   ┌────────────┐
 │operational │   │  resource  │   │  project   │
 │   plans    │   │   plans    │   │   plans    │
 └────────────┘   └────────────┘   └────────────┘

   ┌──────────────┐                    ┌──────────────┐
   │   budgets    │ ◄────────────────► │    action    │
   └──────────────┘                    └──────────────┘

              ┌──────────────────┐
              │     feedback     │ ◄──
              └──────────────────┘
```

The strategic planning process starts with the mission of the business, from which is derived its values, policies, overall purpose or objectives, and the critical success factors applicable to achieving its stated aims. These are interrelated and should be made explicit and updated regularly in response to changes in the organization's environment, which will include its markets, competitors, technology and any other external factors.

A continuous process of strategic management and a regular and systematic corporate planning programme can now take place within the framework of the firm's values and policies in order to reach its goals.

These activities lead to the preparation of operational, resource and project plans and related budgets. Action is thus initiated which takes place within budgets, and aims to achieve targets, complete projects or meet standards of performance as laid down in the statement of objectives. Feedback loops are built into the system to monitor progress and performance.

Let us now look in more detail at each stage of this strategic planning process.

Mission

The mission of an organization expresses its sense of purpose – the business the enterprise is in and the broad direction in which it is going. Missions are described in mission statements which may be supported by guiding principles.

The IBM approach

Defining the mission as part of the strategic planning process is essential to the IBM approach at corporate level. This involves the following steps:

1   Define the mission statement.

2   Evolve a corporate strategy which will enable the company to achieve its mission.

3   Define the corporate critical success factors which will determine what issues need to be addressed to achieve strategic aims. (This activity is described in more detail below.)

4   Define within each function the critical success factors which will ensure that it provides the right level of support to co-operative effort.

Functional approach

Managers can and should develop mission statements for their own functions, as in the following example for the personnel department of the International Stock Exchange:

> The mission of the personnel department is to develop and promote the highest-quality personnel and human resource practices and initiatives in an ethical, cost-effective and timely manner to support the current and future business objectives of the International Stock Exchange, and to enable the managers to maximise the calibre, effectiveness and development of their human resources.

Value Systems

A value system expresses basic beliefs in the behaviour which is believed to be good for an organization and in what the organization considers to be important. It is expressed in a value statement.

Uses of value statements

The purpose of a value statement is to help to develop a value-driven and committed organization which conducts its business successfully by reference to shared beliefs and an understanding of what is best for the enterprise. Value statements are therefore an integral part of strategic planning as a means of guiding the direction of effort in the longer term.

Value statements are closely associated with mission statements and like them can be used as levers for change, getting people to act differently in ways which will support the attainment of the organization's objectives.

Content

A value statement defines core values in such areas as:

* care and consideration for people

- care for customers
- competitiveness
- enterprise
- excellence
- flexibility
- growth as a major objective
- innovation
- market/customer orientation
- performance orientation
- productivity
- quality
- teamwork

An example of a value statement is given below.

Book Club Associates – core values

The core values of BCA are:

- *Excellence*. Anything we do well now we can do better.
- *Profitable growth*. We aim to ensure the profitable expansion of the business to generate the return our owners want on their investment and to ensure the continued prosperity and security of our employees.
- *Enterprise*. We thrive by innovation, by creativity and by seizing opportunities whenever they arise.
- *Customer service*. We depend on our customers and maintaining and improving levels of service to them is a continuing priority.
- *Reward*. Achievement brings reward to everyone in the firm.
- *Teamwork*. BCA is an organization which relies on teamwork to get results.
- *Professionalism*. The effective and dedicated use and development of skills is a prime requirement in the firm.

- *Productivity through people*. Higher productivity and therefore profitability is achieved by effective leadership and the development of a committed and well-trained work force.

- *Partnership*. All employees are treated as partners in the enterprise, to be involved in matters that affect them and to be informed of how the firm is doing and of its plans for the future.

- *People*. Employees are treated fairly, and as responsible human beings. They are given the opportunity to develop their skills and careers in the firm, the management of which is constantly aware of the need to improve the quality of working life.

Espoused values

It is important to distinguish between the values a company espouses and the actual behaviour of management and the members of the organization. It is easy enough to produce high-sounding value statements but they are meaningless if management does not practise what it preaches or takes no steps through the development and implementation of supporting policies (see below) to ensure that they are enforced. Management must also do its best to ensure that the values are understood, accepted and followed throughout the organization by example, by education and by insisting that certain standards of behaviour are adhered to.

Policies

Definition

A policy is a statement of principles or common purposes which serves as a continuing guideline and establishes limits for discretionary action by management. Policies may be written or implied and can be identified by the following features:

- They provide a positive but timeless indication of what the company and its management are expected to do or how they will behave in given circumstances.

- They indicate the amount of discretion that can be exercised within defined limits.

- They demonstrate the organization's belief in certain principles of behaviour, thus translating espoused values into action.

- They provide a sense of purpose for the organization which encourages unified action and commitment.

- They provide guidance on answers to the question: 'How do I deal with this important matter in these circumstances?'

Policies are both restrictive and permissive at once. They spell out limits to actions, but at the same time they give freedom to act within the limits specified. Policies should have a degree of stability or they are not policies at all. Stability can, however, be overdone. There is a danger that policies become congealed and are not forward-looking enough. They need to be reconsidered from time to time as the situation changes – circumstances can alter policies as well as cases.

Examples

The following are examples of policy statements:

It is our policy to:
- promote from within
- staff our overseas companies with local nationals
- 'maintain full employment for our staff' (IBM)
- strive towards the achievement of equal opportunity
- be self-financed
- grow through acquisition
- only diversify into fields which are consistent with our distinctive competences
- 'never be knowingly undersold' (John Lewis Partnership)
- continually improve our products
- expand vigorously into Europe
- 'build profitably the highest-quality car sold in Europe' (Nissan)

- lease rather than buy property

- make rather than buy, other things being equal

- not rely upon any one supplier for more than 20 per cent of our requirements for an item

- provide ever-increasing levels of quality and customer service

Distinction between policies, objectives, strategies and plans

As continuing guidelines for action, policies do not inform managers specifically about ends in quantified terms, or about a task to be completed to a certain standard by a certain date. This is the role of objectives and their supporting targets and standards of performance. Nor do policies specify the broad means for attaining the end in terms of the route the organization is to follow. This is the role of strategies. Nor do they indicate the specific programmes or steps required to implement strategies and achieve objectives. This is the role of plans.

Policies will, however, provide guidance on what sort of objectives should be set and the nature of the strategies and plans needed to attain them. They will indicate limits to choices and the parameters or rules to be followed in evaluating and selecting alternative goals, strategies and plans.

For example, a policy only to diversify into activities which are consistent with the distinctive competences of the business would require a firm like Book Club Associates to start its strategic planning cycle with a definition of what they are. They might be defined as being direct-response marketing, buying and mail-order fulfilment. It may then decide that its strategy is to diversify, because of threats to its basic book club business and the opportunities presented to market other types of merchandise. But this strategy would be consistent with diversification policy in that it would be restricted to direct marketing operations using the existing database and fulfilment facilities. Objectives could then be set to achieve a certain percentage of turnover in this type of non-book business by a given date. Marketing plans would be formulated to develop, test and launch new products using well-tried direct-marketing techniques.

Formulating policies

Policies often evolve over a period of time and are shaped by the philosophies of the owners and managers of the business and what has been found to be best for the business in the past. By an osmosis-like process, they seep into the minds of management and are followed almost instinctively – it is recognized without having to be articulated that 'this is the way we do things around here'.

Major policies may be deliberately formulated at the top and passed downwards. But intermediate policies may often evolve at lower levels which are then ratified by senior management.

Changes to the firm's environment or new management may mean that different policies have to be formed. These may be debated in the forum of the board or announced, more autocratically, by the chief executive. Such policies are normally defined in minutes or memoranda.

Implementing policy

A well-established policy will be implemented almost automatically. Everyone knows what to do and exceptions will be noted easily. It does not need to be written down.

Less well-established policies may have to be written and promulgated to all concerned. For example, if it is decided to restrict supplies from any one supplier to no more than 20 per cent of the firm's requirements for a particular item in order to avoid over-dependence on that supplier, then this policy will have to be conveyed to all buyers and the head of supplies will be required to enforce it.

Some companies produce policy manuals, which can be useful. But they are in danger of remaining unread (if voluminous) and of quickly becoming out of date. Even if manuals are not published it is always advisable to ensure that any policy statements or memoranda are accessible for reference purposes.

Objectives

Definition

Objectives set out what is to be attained. They define this in terms of:

- *overall aims or goals* – what the organization wants to achieve with regard to growth, development or diversification
- *targets* to be achieved within a time-scale; for example, increase net profit in real terms by 10 per cent by the end of the financial year. These may be translated into more specific functional targets at a later stage.
- *projects* to be completed, as specified, by a certain time – for example, set up an agency network in Denmark by 1 March which consists of reputable firms which are likely to achieve our sales targets and standards of performance and will cover the whole country
- *standards of performance* to be attained which include how well a task should be done. For example, buyers are expected to maintain an appropriate balance in building inventory between keeping stockouts at an acceptable level while minimizing inventory holding costs.

Corporate objective headings

Peter Drucker[2] has suggested that corporate objectives should be set out under the following headings:

- market standing (i.e. reputation in the market place and market share)
- innovation
- productivity
- physical and financial resources
- profitability – this could be broken down into objectives in such key financial areas as:
  – sales turnover

- contribution to profits and overhead recovery
- overheads
- inventory (stock holding)
- stock turn (the ratio of stock holding to sales)
- return on capital employed (the ratio of profits to capital)
- earnings per share

- manager performance and development

- worker performance and attitude

- public or social responsibility

Hierarchies of objectives

Corporate objectives can be translated into a hierarchy of objectives at each level of management. For example, a corporate objective to launch a new product by a certain date in order to achieve a certain level of sales and contributions to profit and overheads could be translated into sub-objectives as follows:

- *research and development* – design, develop and test a product which meets agreed specifications by x within a cost budget of £y

- *market research* – work in conjunction with R&D to test consumer reaction to the new product and, as necessary, modify its specification

- *marketing* – produce a marketing plan by x covering promotion, advertising, market tests, pricing, packaging and product launch

- *manufacturing* – prepare process plans for the product by x which define how the product should be manufactured, including operations sequences for each component and specifications of the machines, layouts, hand tools, fixtures, gauges and labour to be used

- *personnel* – prepare a plan by x for the training of staff to manufacture and sell the product

- *sales* – prepare, in conjunction with marketing and sales, plans by x for providing sales staff with the necessary product knowledge, and for instructing them in any special sales techniques they may need to use

Formulation of objectives

The overall aims or goals of the organization will be defined at the top by the chief executive and the board by reference to what they believe will satisfy their shareholders, the City, their customers and their employees.

Subsidiary aims in a hierarchy of objectives will be defined by the heads of functions, preferably in full consultation with their key staff.

Targets may be defined by:

- a *top-down* process in which managers are issued targets which they have to achieve which they pass on down the line

- a *bottom-up* process in which functional managers in conjunction with their staff submit targets for approval by higher authority

- an *iterative* process which involves both the top-down and bottom-up setting of targets and a to-and-fro movement between different levels until agreement is reached, although this agreement will have to be consistent with overall objectives. In practice, this is the approach which is used most frequently.

Standards of performance may be laid down in line with policies or in accordance with the wishes of top management. They should preferably be agreed by all concerned. (The setting and agreement of individual objectives was dealt with in Chapter 5.)

Definition of critical success factors

When setting objectives it is important to define the critical success factors which will indicate when they have been achieved. Where objectives are quantified in the form of targets this is easy, but where they are related to task achievement it is even more necessary to take care to spell out the factors that will contribute to successful performance and the standards to be met.

At IBM, the definition of critical success factors is part of the strategic planning programme using a consensus approach with groups of senior managers. This takes place in seven stages, as follows:

1   *Understand the mission*

- The team collectively agrees a mission statement.

- The statement should not be longer than three or four short sentences and should clearly define the circumstances in which the mission will have been successfully accomplished.

2   *Identify issues which will impact on the mission*

- The team focuses on the mission and identifies dominant issues by listing one-word descriptions of everything they think will impact on the mission's achievement.

- The normal brain-storming rules apply, i.e.:
  - everyone should contribute
  - everything is fair game, no matter how crazy or outrageous
  - nobody is permitted to challenge any suggestion
  - the facilitator writes everything down on a flip chart so that the team can see the whole list.

3   *Identify the critical success factor*

- By reference to the list of issues which it is believed will impact on the mission, the team identifies the critical success factors (CSFs). The characteristics of a CSF statement are that it:
  - defines what the team believes *needs* to be done to achieve the mission
  - is not only *necessary* to the mission but also, together with the other CSFs, is *sufficient* to achieve the mission (the necessary and sufficient rule)

- The list of CSFs should:
  - not exceed eight
  - include a mix of strategic and tactical factors

- Absolute consensus must be achieved on what is included in the list.

4 *Identify and define the actions required to meet the CSF requirements*

- Identify and list what has to be done to meet the critical success factors.

- Define the business processes (actions) needed to meet CSF requirements.

- The rules for defining business processes are:
  - The selection should be rigorous in accordance with the necessary and sufficient role.
  - Each description should follow an active verb plus object sequence.
  - Each business process should have an owner, the person responsible for carrying out the process.
  - The owner should be a member of the management team that agreed to the CSFs.
  - No owner should have more than three or four processes to manage.

5 *List CSFs and processes*

- The team draws up a matrix which lists the critical success factors and the business processes relevant to each CSF.

6 *Ensure that CSFs and processes will achieve the desired results*

- The team reviews each CSF to ensure that it is supported by necessary processes which together are sufficient to achieve the results required.

7 *Implement the action plan*

- The team proceeds to confirm the action plan associated with the processes and sets up the implementation programme.

- Monitoring and follow up arrangements are also made.

Strategic Management

Rosabeth Moss Kanter believes that strategic plans 'elicit the present actions for the future' and become 'action vehicles – integrating and institutionalizing mechanisms for change'. She goes on to say:

> Strong leaders articulate direction and save the organization
> from change by drift. . . . They see a vision of the future that
> allows them to see more clearly the steps to take, building
> on present capacities and strengths.[3]

Definition of strategy

A strategy can be defined as a broad statement of where the
organization as a whole, or a significant part of it, is going in the
longer term to achieve its objectives. It defines overall means to
achieve ends and is a declaration of intent which provides for
development and implementation of action plans and programmes.

This definition assumes that the ends or goals have been defined
and that strategy is evolved to achieve them. But the process of
formulating strategy may in itself include the definition of long-
term objectives.

Chandler, for example, defines strategy as follows:

> Strategy is the determination of the basic long-term goals and
> objectives of the enterprise and the adoption of courses of
> action and allocation of resources necessary for carrying out
> these goals.[4]

In practice, the creation of strategy takes place within the framework of the mission, overall objectives, values and policies of the
firm. But the process of formulating strategy is a continuous one
and will produce more specific medium- and long-term objectives
and therefore influence the overall aims.

Definition of strategic management

Strategic management is the process by which an organization
formulates objectives and long-range plans and is managed to
achieve them. It has been defined by Philip Sadler[5] as involving:

- the determination of medium- and long-term objectives – the
  strategic intent
- the selection of a coherent strategy to achieve these objectives
- the direction of the organization so that it moves constantly
  towards their achievement

Organizations and managers who think strategically are looking ahead at what they need to achieve in the middle or relatively distant future. Although they are aware of the fact that businesses, like managers, must perform well in the present to succeed in the future, they are concerned with the broader issues they are facing and the general directions in which they must go to deal with these issues and achieve longer-term objectives. They do not take a narrow or restricted view.

Strategic management is concerned with both ends and means. As an end it describes a vision of what something will look like in a few years' time. As means, it shows how it is expected that the vision will be realized. Strategic management is therefore visionary management, concerned with creating and conceptualizing ideas of where the organization should be going. But it is also empirical management which decides how in practice it is going to get there.

The focus is on identifying the organization's mission and strategies, but attention is also given to the resource base required to make it succeed. It is always necessary to remember that strategy is the means to create value. Managers who think strategically will have a broad and long-term view of where they are going. But they will also be aware that they are responsible first for planning how to allocate resources to opportunities which contribute to the implementation of strategy, and secondly, managing these opportunities in ways which will significantly add value to the results achieved by the firm.

Key concepts in strategic management

The key concepts used in strategic management are:

1   *Distinctive competence* – working out what the organization is best at and what its special or unique capabilities or attributes are, and planning to do these things

2   *Focus* – concentrating on the key strategic issues

3   *Competitive advantage* – selecting markets where the organization can excel and where its distinctive competences give it a competitive edge. Markets are selected where the business can either beat competitors or avoid them. Without competitive edge the business cannot earn a true economic profit.

4 *Synergy* – developing, as suggested by Igor Ansoff[1], a product-market posture with a combined performance that is greater than the sum of its parts. Synergy in sales takes place when products use common distribution channels, common sales forces and administration, or common warehousing. In operational terms, synergy occurs when there is higher utilization of facilities and personnel, spreading of overheads, and bulk purchasing. Management synergy happens if the abilities and skills of individual managers can be used to solve problems and develop strategies better or more comprehensively than they would have been able to do on their own.

5 *Environmental scanning* – scanning the internal and external environment of the firm to ensure that the organization is fully aware of strengths and weaknesses, threats and opportunities.

6 *Resource allocation* – understanding the resource requirements of the strategy (human, financial, plant and equipment) and ensuring that the resources are made available and that their use is optimised.

Components of strategy

Hofer and Schendel define an organization's strategy as 'the fundamental pattern of present and planned resource deployments and environmental interactions that indicates how the organization will achieve its objectives'.[6] They suggest that it has four components:

1 Scope – products, market
2 Competitive advantage to be achieved
3 Resources available and required
4 Synergy expected

Examples of strategy areas

The following are some examples of the areas in which strategies may be formed:

- *corporate*: long-term growth; increased profitability; product-market development; diversification; acquisition; investment and disinvestment

- *marketing*: target markets – the market segments on which the company will concentrate and the marketing position it proposes to adopt in each segment; the marketing mix – the blend of controllable marketing variables which will produce the required response in the target markets and will include new products, prices, promotion, and the placing of sales and distribution activities

- *manufacturing*: the resources required in terms of plant, equipment and any form of new technology to meet market requirements and improve quality and productivity

- *research and development*: the thrust of basic and applied research in the light of assessed market needs; the direction in which development activities should go to support marketing and manufacturing strategies

- *personnel*: human resource management – the acquisition, motivation and development of the human resources required by the organization; organization development – the steps necessary to manage change and create a more effective organization; employee relations – creating constructive and co-operative relationships with employees

- *finance*: the acquisition and utilization of the financial resources required by the firm to its best advantage

- *data processing*: planning the information technology, hardware and software requirements of the firm to meet growth and improve effectiveness

Formulating strategy

A model of the strategic management process is illustrated in Figure 21.

But this model, although theoretically correct, implies that strategy formulation is a rational and continuous process, which it is not, as was pointed out by Henry Mintzberg.[7] He believes that rather than being consciously and systematically developed, strategy reorientations happen in brief quantum loops. He also suggests that, paradoxically:

Figure 21
Formulating strategy

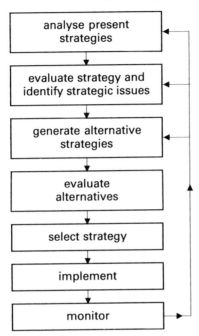

The very concept of strategy is rooted in stability not change.
. . . Organizations pursue strategies to set directions, lay out
courses of action and elicit co-operation from their members
around common, established guidelines. By any definition,
strategy imposes stability on an organization. No stability
means no strategy (no concern for the future, no pattern from
the past). Indeed the mere fact of having a strategy, and
especially of making it explicit . . . creates resistance to
change.

Mintzberg goes on to suggest that most of the time, management
pursues a given strategic orientation. 'Change may seem continuous, but it occurs in the context of that orientation.'

Strategies, according to Minzberg, are not always deliberate. In theory, he says, strategy is a systematic process: 'First we think, then we act. We formulate then we implement.' In practice, 'a realized strategy can emerge in response to an evolving situation'. The strategist can often be 'a pattern organizer, a learner if you like, who manages a process in which strategies (and visions) can emerge as well as be deliberately conceived. . . . To manage strategy . . . is not so much to promote change as to *know* when to do so.'

Corporate Planning

The formulation and implementation of strategies can be conducted without using any formal processes. But a comprehensive approach in the shape of corporate planning can ensure that all factors are taken into consideration, and all the issues are addressed.

Definition

Corporate planning is the systematic process of developing long-term strategies and plans to achieve defined company objectives.

Aims

The aims of corporate planning are to:

- define and plan the long term future of the business
- increase the rate of growth of the enterprise in the long run.
- ensure that the organization can meet the challenge of change and can profit from new opportunities.

The process of corporate planning

Corporate planning consists of the following stages:

1 *Setting objectives* which define what the company is going to do.
2 *Environmental scanning* – conducting internal appraisals of the strengths and weaknesses of the company and external

appraisals of the opportunities and threats facing it. This is the SWOT analysis described in Chapter 7, and the particular areas which should be considered are listed below. The assessment of the present situation would also include portfolio and life-cycle analyses of the various business products as described later in this chapter.

3 *Analysing existing strategies* to determine their relevance in the light of the external and internal appraisal. This will include gap analysis which will establish the extent to which environmental factors might lead to gaps between what could be achieved if no changes were made and what needs to be achieved if objectives are to be reached.

4 *Defining strategic issues* in the light of the environmental and gap analyses. The strategic issues will be the key factors which the organization has to address in developing its corporate plan. They may include such questions as:

- How are we going to maintain growth in a declining market for our most important, i.e. profitable, product?
- In the face of aggressive competition, how are we going to maintain our competitive advantage and market leadership?
- To what extent do we need to diversify into new products or markets?
- What proportion of our resources should be allocated to research and development?
- What are we going to do about our ageing machine tool resources?
- What are we going to do about our overheads?
- How are we going to get our stock levels down?
- How are we going to finance our growth?
- What do we do about improving quality?
- How do we improve levels of customer service?
- How are we going to find and develop the well-qualified, highly motivated people we need in the future?

5 *Developing new or revised strategies* and changing objectives in the light of the analysis of strategic issues.

6 *Deciding on the critical success factors* related to the achievement of objectives and implementation of strategy.
7 *Preparing operational, resource and project* plans to implement strategies in the light of the critical success factors.
8 *Monitoring results* against the plans and amending objectives, strategies and plans or taking corrective action as necessary.

These processes are illustrated in Figure 22.

Figure 22
The process of corporate planning

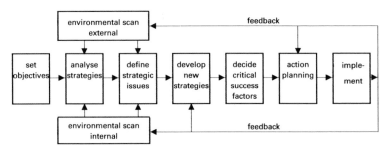

The planning horizon

The planning horizon is the length of time ahead for which plans are made. It will vary according to the type of organization. An oil company, for example might plan as much as 20 years ahead. Manufacturing companies may plan for a period of 3–5 years. A fast-moving enterprise might not want plans to be made for more than a year in advance.

SWOT analysis factors

The analysis of *external opportunities and threats* should cover the following areas:

- economic factors – exchange rates, interest rates, growth rates
- government influences – regulation, deregulation, privatization
- market trends – consumer behaviour
- competitors' behaviour – new products, new processes, mergers
- technological change
- social factors – environmental concerns, health and safety etc.
- supply factors – costs, availability of energy and new materials.

The analysis of *internal strengths and weaknesses* should cover:

- product quality
- product maturity (life-cycle analysis, see below)
- product availability
- cost structure
- market share
- brand strength
- customer loyalty
- management
- organization
- staff
- employee relations
- financial reserves and cash flow
- innovative ability
- flexibility
- quality
- customer service

Portfolio analysis

Portfolio analysis is an analytical approach which asks managers to view companies as portfolios of businesses to be managed for the best possible return. Each business is analysed to assess its unique competitive opportunities and problems and its future capacity for contributing to organizational objectives. Resources are thus allocated or withdrawn from the businesses as appropriate.

The most familiar portfolio matrix is the one developed by the Boston Consulting Group, as illustrated in Figure 23.

Figure 23
The Boston Consulting Group portfolio matrix

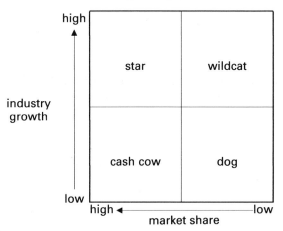

The analysis of businesses into these four categories can lead to prescriptions to withdraw from dogs, milk cash cows, develop wildcats and sustain or maintain the growth and market share of stars.

Product life cycles

Products generally have a life cycle which takes the form of an S-curve which describes performance over time as illustrated in Figure 24.

Product life-cycle analysis is complementary to portfolio analysis, but instead of looking at relative growth rates or market share, it

Figure 24
The product life cycle

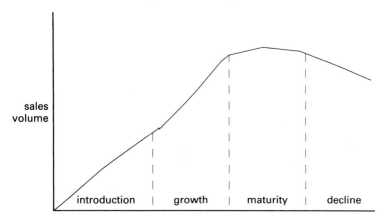

attempts to determine where the product is in the life cycle so that steps can be taken to boost stagnant or falling sales, or to look for modified or replacement products in good time.

Action Planning

Action plans implement strategies and the corporate plan, having taken into account the critical success factors and the resources available. They can be grouped under three main headings:

1 Operational plans for the major operating functions such as marketing and manufacturing
2 Resource plans which programme the acquisition or development of human, financial and material resources
3 Project plans which programme projects for launching new products, introducing new technology, developing new markets etc.

Techniques of planning were discussed in detail in Chapter 4.

Budgeting

Budgets are usually prepared annually but may be updated during the year.

Budgets are needed for three reasons:

1   To show the financial implications of plans

2   To define the resources required to achieve the plans

3   To provide a means of measuring, monitoring and controlling results against the plans

The process of budgeting

The process of budgeting is illustrated in Figure 25. It consists of the following stages.

1   The corporate plan sets out targets.
2   Sales forecasts are prepared.
3   Cost budgets for sales, production, purchasing, administration, research and capital expenditure are produced.
4   A revenue budget for sales is determined.
5   The revenue and various cost budgets are combined to produce the cash balance showing cash inflows, outflows and balances during the year.
6   A master budget consolidating all the above budgets is prepared.

Implementing the Strategic Plan

If it has been formulated properly, a strategic plan will spell out objectives, targets, critical success factors, action plans and budgets.

The implementation of the plan is then achieved by ensuring that everyone knows about those aspects of the plan which affect them and what they have to do to contribute to its achievement. This is the normal management process of organizing and programming work, designating responsibilities, delegating authority,

Figure 25

The budgeting process

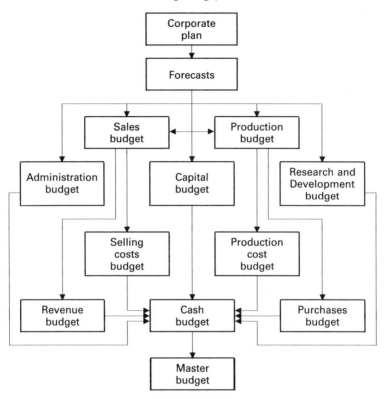

monitoring performance and taking corrective action on the basis of feedback information.

A good strategic plan will not replace the need to manage the task effectively as part of the day-to-day process of management. But it does provide everyone concerned with a much clearer sense of direction and a means of monitoring and measuring performance.

References

1   ANSOFF H. I. *Corporate strategy*. London, Sidgwick & Jackson, 1986
2   DRUCKER Peter. *The practice of management*. London, Heinemann, 1955
3   KANTER Rosabeth Moss. *The change masters*. London, Allen & Unwin, 1984
4   CHANDLER A. *Strategy and structure*. Cambridge, Massachusetts, MIT Press, 1962
5   SADLER P. 'Strategic management'. Address to the Charities Aid Foundation conference, November 1989
6   HOFER C. W. and SCHENDEL D. *Strategy formulation: analytical concepts*. St Paul, West Publishing, 1978
7   MINTZBERG H. 'Crafting strategy'. *The Harvard Business Review*. July–August 1987, pp 66–73

The Social Responsibilities of Business

The demands made on organizations to fulfil their social responsibilities are increasing rapidly. These responsibilities will include the environment, the treatment of minority groups, consumer rights, the supply of safe and healthy goods and services and the quality of working life for employees. Businesses also have responsibilities to their shareholders and those with whom they have purely business relationships.

Social responsibility, however, is not always a clear-cut issue. The question frequently has to be asked – 'socially responsible to whom?' This chapter explores this and other issues under the following headings:

- what is social responsibility?
- the significance of business ethics
- the social responsibility dilemma
- the main areas of social responsibility
- what can be done for the stakeholders in a business – the IBM approach
- the way ahead

What is Social Responsibility?

The social responsibilities of a business are concerned with maximizing the benefits that the business can provide for its stakeholders, and minimizing the detrimental effects on them of its actions. These actions are those which do not have purely economic consequences and which are required of a business under some explicitly or implicitly defined code.

An enterprise is also concerned with business ethics – the manner

in which the organization and its employees conduct their affairs
in relation to accepted standards of business behaviour.

The basis of the belief that business should act ethically and in
a socially responsible manner is expressed by R. Dahl as follows:

> Every large corporation should be thought of as a social
> enterprise, that is, as an entity whose existence and decisions
> can be justified in so far as they serve public or social
> purposes.[1]

This view seems extreme to people such as Milton Friedman, who,
in an article entitled 'The social responsibility of business is to
increase its profits', says:

> In a free enterprise, private property system, a corporate
> executive is an employee of the owners of the business. He
> has a direct responsibility to his employers. That responsibility
> is to conduct the business in accordance with their desires,
> which generally will be to make as much money as possible
> while conforming to the basic rules of society, both those
> embodied in law, and those embodied in social custom.[2]

These are two extreme views, and a balance has to be struck
between them.

However, IBM has no doubt where it stands, as is shown in the
following company policy statement on its social responsibilities:

> IBM is committed to meet or exceed all applicable government
> regulations in any locality and to establish stringent standards
> of its own where government regulations do not exist.

The Confederation of British Industry is also unequivocal about
this issue:

> A company should behave like a good citizen in business.
> The law does not (and cannot) contain or prescribe the whole
> duty of a citizen. A good citizen takes account of the interests
> of others besides himself, and tries to exercise an informed
> and imaginative ethical judgment in deciding what he should
> and should not do. This, it is suggested, is how companies
> should seek to behave. Within its own field of knowledge,
> skill, geographical concern and financial capacity (these are
> important limitations) a company has the duty to be responsive
> to the movement of informed public opinion as well as to the

requirements of authority. A company should, as is indeed the practice of the best companies, pay proper regard to the environmental and social consequences of its business activities, and should not sacrifice the safety or efficiency of goods and services in the interests of expediency and competitiveness. In environmental matters, it is usually the company that is the first to know of a potential hazard or critical situation; it has a duty in such circumstances not only to take all possible remedial measures but also to inform the responsible authorities.[3]

The Significance of Business Ethics

As Pamela Pocock has pointed out:

> Ethical behaviour is necessarily a function of context and will be based on the society in which we live. Different nations and cultures will have different standards by which they judge morality. Thus in the multinational, it may be difficult for some employees to understand why they cannot offer a bribe when such an action to them seems the norm in their country. But, leaving cultural differences to one side, there is also a sense in which some people will adjust their morality to suit the occasion. Rules may be bent for the large client but not for the small. Similarly, within organizations, standards of ethical behaviour may well change as we move into different functions or progress through the hierarchy – what is acceptable in the sales department would not be allowed on the factory floor – and the standards may well become more lax at higher levels in the organization.[4]

Those who are cynical about this subject may remember the, no doubt apocryphal, story of the bishop who said: 'As soon as I hear a businessman talking about ethics, I know it is time to start counting the spoons.' But certain events in Wall Street and the City, and environmental issues, have forced ethical considerations into the consciousness of business people as well as social commentators. Even Sir John Hoskins when he was Director General of the Institute of Directors could say:

> Failure by business leaders to maintain the highest standards of integrity is a form of treason against the enterprise culture.[5]

Codes of business ethics will cover such items as:

- fair dealing – not misleading customers, suppliers or employees
- keeping to the spirit not just the letter of the law
- honesty in presenting reports and advertising products
- prompt payment to small suppliers as well as large ones
- treating employees equitably, according to the principles of natural justice
- loyalty to the organization as long as this is not inconsistent with an overriding ethical principle
- not taking undue advantage of insider knowledge to further one's own interests
- not advancing oneself at the expense of the organization.

These principles would be espoused by most business people but they can be difficult to apply. For example, William Plowden, when he was Director General of the Royal Institute of Public Administration, said in the wake of the Ponting case (the civil servant who followed the dictates of his conscience in revealing confidential information):

> In any organization there is no inevitable congruence between an employee's material self-interest, the dictates of his conscience, the instructions of his superiors, the objectives of the heads of the organization, the interests of the organization's customers or clients and the interests of society at large.

The Dilemma of Social Responsibility

The above quotation sums up the problem of the dilemma between acting responsibly from the point of view of society, and acting responsibly from the point of view of the firm and its owners.

Pamela Pocock has stressed that in this area 'there may be moral ambiguities and any set of reasonable people may well differ over the solution.'[4]

In a Mobil (UK) advertisement published in 1979 the company explained that it had spent around £12 million on equipment in its new refinery on the Thames estuary to curb air, water and noise pollution. But it also felt it had to state in the advertisement that

> Environmental standards are a delicate compromise between what technology can achieve and what society can afford.

The advertisement, however, also declared that:

> Industry's responsibility is to demonstrate a real concern for the environment; to meet government standards without cutting corners; and to use its imagination and skill to meet them at the lowest possible cost to the consumer.

Environmental issues can be fairly clear cut. The government can issue regulations on pollution levels which must be met. Ecological issues are less easily defined. It is clearly right to save the whale and to prevent Brazilian forests being destroyed. But there will be people who will defend as inalienable their rights to kill whales and chop down trees. This sort of dilemma can only be solved by legislation.

Moral issues present even greater problems. Should newsagent chains display soft-porn magazines because their customers ask for them? Or should they listen to the arguments of the Campaign against Pornography, the National Union of Students and the Townswomen's Guild (an unusual but powerful combination) that their display, although legal, is degrading and pernicious? As a leader in *The Independent* commented:

> Like newspapers, newsagents have a vested interest in the freedom of expression as well as in profits and customer satisfaction. . . . It is up to the campaigners to persuade them that such publications are more of a liability than an asset. Ultimately the arguments and how they are put across will decide the outcome.[6]

Most responsible business people would say that they have to adopt a policy of 'enlightened self-interest.' And they would probably agree with A. B. Cleaver, Chief Executive, IBM United Kingdom Limited, who said: 'Business must achieve the right balance between revenue on the one hand and its costs and obligations on the other.'[7]

Areas of Social Responsibility

In each of the following major business operating areas there are social issues which involve management decision processes:

- *product development*: considerations of product safety and use and ecological impact, for example biodegradability, exhaust emissions. This involves management decisions on product feasibility studies and product design, testing and launch
- *manufacturing*: considerations of occupational health and safety and ecological impact, e.g. air and water pollution. Management decisions in this area are concerned with such matters as manufacturing process design and capital investment allocation
- *personnel management*: where consideration has to be given to equal employment opportunities, employment practices, occupational health and safety, the equitable and just treatment of employees and the provision of decent working conditions. This area involves decisions on personnel policies and procedures concerning recruitment, promotion, transfers, training, reward, discipline and terms and conditions of employment generally. It also requires action on work systems and working conditions, especially those which might affect health and safety
- *sales and marketing*: where attention needs to be given to selling and advertising practices, the quality of products and after-sales service and the rights of customers and consumers
- *business generally*: where account needs to be taken of business ethics concerning competition and such matters as settling accounts (especially for small traders)

What can be done for the Stakeholders?

IBM answers this question by considering society as being split into five groups, to each of which it has a specific responsibility. The groups are referred to as IBM's stakeholders and consist of:

1   Shareholders who fund development

2 Employees who run the business

3 Customers without whom IBM could not run the business

4 Business associates – the third parties through whom IBM does business

5 The community in which IBM operates, be it local, national or international

The Chief Executive of IBM United Kingdom Limited, A. B. Cleaver, has defined IBM's philosophy as follows:

> We believe that the establishment of a proper relationship with all five stakeholders is vital to our success and we must therefore recognise and discharge our obligation to each and all of them.[7]

The IBM approach for each of these stakeholders as explained by Cleaver is:

1 *Shareholders.*

- short term – reasonable return on investment
- longer term
  - conduct business legally
  - develop a business fit for the future which they understand
  - explain why we operate as we do and 'explain that our policy of full employment, far from being a management weakness, is a proper investment in the future of the company'.

2 *Employees.* IBM's responsibility to its employees – to develop their skills and abilities and provide full employment – is illustrated by their experience in operating the Greenock plant. Over the years, the technology of this plant has changed progressively, moving from mechanical assembly to electromechanical devices, and from there to electronic systems and then, with the arrival of the personal computer and the low-cost digital display system, to a highly automated, high-volume production plant. 'Throughout this time we have maintained our practice of full employment, continually training and retraining our employees to meet the new challenges as they arise.'

3   *Customers.* One example of IBM's customer care policy is the
    publication of business conduct guidelines which are read and
    formally acknowledged by all employees who come into contact
    with customers.

4   *Business associates.* IBM's approach is that it

    - does not abuse its position of strength

    - pays suppliers on the same basis as it seeks payment from
      its own customers

    - imposes limits on the proportion of a supplier's output that
      IBM represents

    - sets and helps to maintain high standards in its dealers and
      agents

5   *Community.* IBM believes that its responsibility to the com-
    munity is just as important as its obligations to its other
    stakeholders in that 'we require a licence to operate from
    society as a whole'. IBM's activities in this area include:

    - enabling their employees to perform their civic and com-
      munity duties effectively

    - providing equipment and IBM project management to
      worthwhile organizations and causes

    - contributing management training skills for voluntary
      organizations

    - seconding employees to spend one or two years working
      directly in the community

The Way Ahead

To fulfil their social responsibilities organizations need to develop
strategies along the following lines, as suggested by Carmichael
and Drummond.[8]

- *Shareholders.* Manage the company effectively to provide an
  agreed rate of return on their investment and to set objectives
  for each department in order to achieve this.

- *Employees.* Recruit, retain and motivate staff at all levels in line with the strategies of the business; establish participatory career development programmes; provide the best training available towards that end.

- *Customers.* Provide quality products and services at competitive prices; give priority to service and care.

- *Suppliers.* Contract with them to provide quality service to the company and properly to compensate them for so doing.

- *The community.* Ensure that the company is sensitive to the impact of its products on the environment; engage in activities which support and strengthen the community; seek to avoid activities which militate against the community's interests.

References

1 DAHL R. A. 'A prelude to corporate reform'. *Business and society review.* Spring, 1972. pp 373–8
2 FRIEDMAN M. 'The social responsibility of business is to increase its profits'. *Sunday Times.* 13 September 1970, p 32
3 CONFEDERATION OF BRITISH INDUSTRY. *The responsibilities of the British public company.* London, CBI, 1973
4 POCOCK Pamela. 'Is business ethics a contradiction in terms?' *Personnel Management.* November 1989. pp 60–63
5 HOSKINS John. 'Business integrity and the law'. Address at the Human Resources and Development Conference, April 1988
6 *The Independent*, 16 November 1989
7 CLEAVER A. B. 'The social responsibility of business'. *RSA Journal.* September 1987. pp 747–71
8 CARMICHAEL S. and DRUMMOND T. *Good business: a guide to corporate responsibility and business ethics.* London, Business Books, 1989

Glossary of Management Terms

Accountability having to account for one's actions and results to higher authority.

Accountable management holding individuals and units responsible for performance measured as objectively as possible.

Accountable manager one to whom specific authority over part of an organization's resources has been delegated and who is required to answer for the results he or she has obtained from the use of those resources.

Activity, organizational a related set of tasks carried out in an organization to achieve a purpose

Authority (to act) the right to make certain decisions or to act in particular ways within defined limits or constraints.

Authority (to authorise) confirming or agreeing that people can take certain actions.

Authority (to command) giving people instructions or orders.

Budget a statement of the planned allocation and use of the company's resources in terms of the costs that will, or may, be incurred to carry out a certain activity. Budgets may also set out the expected revenues and profits arising from these activities.

Budgetary control compares actual costs, revenues and performances with the budget so that, if necessary, corrective action can be taken or revisions made to the original budgets.

Commitment belief in and acceptance of the organization and its goals and willingness to make efforts on behalf of the organization.

Competency the skills and knowledge, gained through education, training and experience, required to perform a job satisfactorily.

Controlling measuring and monitoring performance, comparing results against plans and budgets and taking corrective action when required.

Core values the basic values (*q.v.*) existing in an organization.

Corporate culture the pattern of shared attitudes, beliefs, assumptions and expectations which shape the way people act and interact in an organization and underpin the way things get done.

Corporate planning the systematic process of developing long-term strategies and plans to achieve defined objectives.

Cost centre departments or units where costs relating to that unit are budgeted for and reported on formally.

Critical success factor a requirement which is essential to the achievement of an objective or the implementation of a plan.

Culture management the process of managing the culture of an organization to achieve change or to reinforce the existing culture.

Data processing the provision of information technology in the shape of computer configurations and the supporting activities of systems analysis, programming and computer operations.

Direction the planning, use and control of resources to achieve a result.

Distinctive competence the particular and relevant knowledge and skills possessed by organizations or individuals.

Distribution the storage of finished goods and their efficient delivery to wholesalers and retailers or direct to the customer.

Duty the responsibility for carrying out an activity or task.

Financial accounting recording the revenue received and the expenditure incurred by a company so that its overall performance over a period of time and its financial position at a point in time can be ascertained.

Function, organizational part of an organization in which various related activities or tasks are carried out to achieve a desired result.

Goal the result the organization or individual wants or is expected to achieve.

Human resource management the strategic approach to the acquisition, motivation, development and management of the organization's human resources.

Inventory control ensuring that the optimum amount of inventory or stock is held by a company so that its internal and external demand requirements are met economically.

Job design the process of deciding on the content of a job in terms of its duties and responsibilities, the methods used to carry out the work and the relationships existing between the job holder and others.

Line managers managers who are responsible for a mainstream activity which directly impacts on the results achieved by an organization.

Line of command the line of authority which descends through an organizational hierarchy.

Management   deciding what to do and then getting it done through the efficient and effective use of resources.

Management accounting   providing information to management on present and projected costs and on the profitability of individual projects, products, activities or departments as a guide to decision making and financial planning.

Management by exception   concentrating on analysing and correcting variances from the plan or budget, or on dealing with out-of-the-ordinary events rather than on spending too much time on monitoring things which are going according to plan.

Management by objectives   a technique in which subordinates agree with their managers their objectives, which are aligned to those of the unit and the organization.

Management science   the use in operational research (*q.v.*) of analytical, statistical and qualitative methods of solving problems.

Management style   the approach managers use in leading their teams and exercising authority.

Management techniques   the systematic and analytical methods such as production control, marketing research, cost-volume-profit analysis, job evaluation and operational research which are used by managers to assist in decision making, and in planning and control.

Marketing   the management process responsible for identifying, anticipating and satisfying customer requirements profitably.

Motivating   getting people into action to achieve the required results and exercising leadership so that they work to the best of their ability as part of a team.

Norms   the unwritten rules of behaviour which influence organization climate, management style, and how people work together, conduct themselves and carry out their tasks.

Objective   a broadly defined statement of what the business or individual is expected to achieve on a continuing and progressive basis.

Organizing   deciding who does what and defining roles and relationships within the organization or unit.

Organization   the design, development and maintenance of a system of co-ordinated activities in which individuals and groups of people work co-operatively under authority and leadership towards commonly understood and accepted goals.

Organization behaviour   the way in which people act in the organization, individually or in groups.

Organization climate   the working atmosphere of an organization as perceived by its members.

Organization design   the process of analysing and determining roles and relationships in an enterprise so that collective effort is explicitly organized to achieve specific ends.

Organization development   improving the overall effectiveness of the organization by integrating activities, team building, developing a more positive culture and handling inter-group relations.

Organization planning   deciding on the future structure of the organization to meet change and/or improve performance, determining the managerial and staff requirements for the future organization and programming the phased introduction of new structures.

Organization structure   the framework for the planning, operational and controlling activities which take place within organizations.

Operational managers   managers who are responsible for a major function such as production or distribution which directly impacts on results.

Operational auditing   the systematic examination of the procedures and management processes of an organization, function or department to determine the extent to which they are operating effectively and to indicate where improvements are required.

Operational research   the provision of management science resources to aid in the analysis of problems and data in order to assist planning and decision making.

Output budgeting   an organizational approach to the preparation, implementation and control of plans to achieve goals and improve performance.

Personnel management   personnel management is concerned with obtaining, developing and motivating the human resources required by the organization, promoting co-operation and commitment, making sure that the best use is made of the skills and capacities of employees and ensuring that the organization meets its social and legal responsibilities towards its staff.

Performance   the process of carrying into effect policies, programmes and plans in order to achieve defined and measurable objectives and the results thereof.

Performance management   increasing organizational effectiveness by improving the performance of managers and staff as individuals or teams.

Planning   deciding on a course of action to achieve a desired result and focusing attention on objectives and standards and the programmes required to achieve the objectives.

Policy a statement of principles or common purposes which serves as a continuing guideline and establishes limits for discretionary action by management.

Portfolio analysis an analytical approach which asks managers to view companies as portfolios of businesses to be managed for the best possible return.

Procedure a method or system for getting things done.

Product life cycle the performance over time of the sales of a product.

Production planning and controlling the use of people, materials, plant and machines to attain the company's objectives for output, and the achievement of manufacturing programmes, quality and productivity.

Profit centres divisions, departments or units which are responsible for the profits arising from their activities. Both revenues and costs will be budgeted and reported on.

Research and development the design and development of new products or the modification of existing products in order to create or satisfy customer needs and wants, now and in the future.

Responsibility the process of taking on particular obligations for performing a job or a task and achieving the required results. Job holders are in a position of responsibility if they are liable to be called to account for what they do.

Role the expectations job holders have about how they should fulfil their responsibilities and perform their tasks by reference both to their own job and also to those of other people.

Standard of performance the level of attainment expected of job holders defined in terms of the observable behaviour that will indicate the extent to which the job or task has been well done.

Staff departments departments whose function is to support and provide services to line departments.

Strategic management the process by which organizations formulate objectives and long-range plans and are managed to achieve them.

Strategic planning a systematic, analytical approach which reviews the business as a whole in relation to its environment and determines the direction to be followed by the company in the longer term.

Strategy a broad statement of where the organization as a whole or a significant part of it is going in the longer term to achieve its objectives.

Success criteria the factors which will be used to measure the results obtained.

Supplies   supplies management, buying or purchasing, involves the procurement of all the materials, plant, equipment and bought-in parts or job-assemblies required by the company.

SWOT analysis   analysing an organization or individual in terms of strengths, weaknesses, opportunities and threats.

Synergy   linking activities so that the results achieved by the whole are greater than the sum of the parts.

Target   a specified result to be attained which will be described in quantified terms.

Values   the basic beliefs about what is good or best for the organization, about what management thinks is important, and about what should or should not happen.

Value system   the set of core values existing in the organization.

Zero-base budgeting   a technique that requires budget managers systematically to re-evaluate all their activities and programmes in order to decide whether they should be eliminated, or funded at a reduced, similar, or increased level.

Bibliography

A further list providing a selection of books on general management is given on page 290.

ADAIR John. *Effective leadership.* Aldershot, Gower, 1983

ALLCORN Seth. 'Understanding groups at work'. *Personnel.* August, 1989, pp 28–36

ANSOFF H. I. *Corporate strategy.* London, Sidgwick & Jackson, 1986

ARGYRIS Chris. *Personality and organization.* New York, Harper, 1957

ARGYRIS Chris. 'T-Groups for organizational effectiveness'. *Harvard Business Review.* March–April, 1964. pp 60–74

ARMSTRONG Michael. *A handbook of management techniques.* London, Kogan Page, 1986

ARMSTRONG Michael. *How to be an even better manager.* London, Kogan Page, 1988

ARMSTRONG Michael. *Personnel and the bottom line.* London, Institute of Personnel Management, 1989

BARNARD Chester. *Functions of the executive.* Cambridge, Massachusetts, Harvard University Press, 1938

BECKHARD Richard. *Organization development: strategy and models.* Reading, Massachusetts, Addison-Wesley, 1969

BELBIN Meredith. *Management teams: why they succeed or fail.* London, Heinemann, 1981

BURNS T. and STALKER G. M. *The management of innovation.* London, Tavistock Publications, 1961

CARLSSON Sune. *Executive behaviour: a study of the work load and the working methods of managing directors.* Stockholm, Strombergs, 1951

CARMICHAEL S. AND DRUMMOND T. *Good Business: a guide to corporate responsibility and business ethics.* London, Business Books, 1989

CATTELL R. B. *The scientific analysis of personality.* Harmondsworth, Penguin, 1965

CHANDLER A. *Strategy and structure.* Cambridge, Massachusetts, MIT Press, 1962

CHILD John. *Organization: a guide to problems and practice.* London, Harper & Row, 1977

CLEAVER A. B. 'The social responsibility of business'. *RSA Journal.* September, 1987. pp 747–71

Committee on the Civil Service. Report, June 1968, Cmnd 3636 Vol 1, para. 150

CONFEDERATION OF BRITISH INDUSTRY. *The responsibilities of the British public company*. London, CBI, 1973

COOPER C. L. 'What's new in stress'. *Personnel Management*. June, 1984

COOPER C. L. and MARSHALL J. *Understanding executive stress*. London, Macmillan, 1978

DAHL R. A. 'A prelude to corporate reform'. *Business and Society Review*. Spring, 1972. pp 373–8

DRUCKER Peter. *The practice of management*. London, Heinemann, 1955

DRUCKER Peter. *The concept of the corporation*. Boston, Beacon Press, 1960

DRUCKER Peter. *The effective executive*. London, Heinemann, 1962

DRUCKER Peter. *Managing for results*. London, Heinemann, 1963

DRUCKER Peter. 'The coming of the new organization'. *Harvard Business Review*. January–February, 1988. pp 45–53

FAYOL Henri. *General and industrial administration*. London, Pitman, 1949

FOLLETT Mary Parker. *Creative experience*. London, Longman, 1924

FOLLETT Mary Parker. *Dynamic administration*. London, Pitman, 1941

FRIEDMAN M. 'The social responsibility of business is to increase its profits'. *Sunday Times*. 13 September 1970. p 32

GARRETT John. *The management of government*. Harmondsworth, Penguin, 1972

GENEEN Harold. *Managing*. London, Granada, 1985

GILDER George. *The spirit of enterprise*. New York, Simon & Schuster, 1984

GOMBRICH Ernst. *Meditations on a hobby horse*. London, Phaidon, 1963

GOWER Sir Ernest. *The complete plain words*. London, HMSO, 1977

GULLICK Luther. 'Notes on the theory of organizations' *in* GULLICK Luther and URWICK Lyndall *eds*. *Papers on the science of administration*. New York, Columbia University Press, 1937

HANDY Charles. *Understanding organizations*. Harmondsworth, Penguin, 1985

HARVEY-JONES John. *Making it happen*. London, Collins, 1988

HELLER Robert. *The naked manager*. London, Barrie & Jenkins, 1972

HERZBERG F. W. *The motivation to work*. New York, Wiley, 1957

HOFER C. W. and SCHENDEL D. *Strategy formulation: analytical concepts*. St Paul, West Publishing, 1978

HOSKINS John. 'Business integrity and the law'. Address at the Human Resources and Development Conference, April 1988

JAY Antony. *Management and Machiavelli*. London, Hodder & Stoughton, 1967

KAKABADSE Andrew. *The politics of management*. Aldershot, Gower, 1983

KANTER Rosabeth Moss. *The change masters*. London, Allen & Unwin, 1984

KANTER Rosabeth Moss. *When giants learn to dance.* London, Simon & Schuster, 1989

KOTLER Philip. *Principles of marketing.* Englewood Cliffs, Prentice-Hall, 1983

KOTTER John. 'Power, dependence and effective management'. *Harvard Business Review.* July–August, 1971

LATHAM G. P. and LOCKE F. A. 'Goal setting – a motivation technique that works'. *Organizational Dynamics.* Vol 8, 1979

LAWRENCE Peter. *Management in action.* London, Routledge & Kegan Paul, 1984

LAWRENCE P. R. and LORSCH J. W. *Organization and environment.* Cambridge, Massachusetts, Harvard University Press, 1967

LAWRENCE Paul and LORSCH Jay. *Developing organizations: diagnosis and action.* Reading, Massachusetts, Addison-Wesley, 1969

LAZARUS R. S. 'The concepts of stress and disease' in LEVI L. *ed. Society, stress and disease.* Vol 1. Oxford, Oxford University Press, 1971

LEAVITT H. J. 'Some effects of certain communication patterns on group performance'. *Journal of Abnormal Psychology.* 1951

LEVITT Theodore. 'Marketing myopia'. *Harvard Business Review.* July–August, 1960

LEVITT Theodore. *The marketing imagination.* New York, The Free Press, 1983

LEWIN K. *Field theory in social science.* New York, Harper & Row, 1951

LIKERT Rensis. *New patterns of management.* New York, McGraw-Hill, 1961

LUPTON Tom. 'Best fit in the design of organizations'. *Personnel Review.* Vol 4, No 1, 1975

McCLELLAND David. *Power, the inner experience.* New York, Irvington, 1975

McCLELLAND David and BURNHAM David. 'Power, the great motivator'. *Harvard Business Review.* March–April, 1976

McGREGOR Douglas. *The human side of enterprise.* New York, McGraw-Hill, 1966

MASLOW A. H. *Motivation and personality.* New York, Harper & Row, 1954

MAYO Elton. *The human problems of an industrial civilisation.* London, Macmillan, 1933

MILLER E. and RICE A. K. *Systems of organization.* London, Tavistock Publications, 1967

MINTZBERG Henry. *The nature of managerial work.* New York, Harper & Row, 1973

MINTZBERG H. 'Crafting strategy'. *Harvard Business Review.* July–August, 1987. pp 66–73

PASCALE Richard and ATHOS Anthony. *The art of Japanese management.* London, Sidgwick & Jackson, 1986

PEDLAR Mike, BURGOYNE John and BOYDELL Tom. *A manager's guide to self-development.* Maidenhead, McGraw-Hill, 1986
PETER Lawrence. *The Peter principle.* London, Allen & Unwin, 1972
PETERS Tom. *Thriving on chaos.* London, Macmillan, 1988
PETERS Tom and AUSTIN Nancy. *A passion for excellence.* London, Collins, 1985
PETERS Tom and WATERMAN Robert. *In search of excellence.* New York, Harper & Row, 1982
POCOCK Pamela. 'Is business ethics a contradiction in terms?' *Personnel Management.* November, 1989. pp 60–3
PORTER L. W. and LAWLER E. E. *Managerial attitudes and performance.* Homewood, Illinois, Irwin-Dorsey, 1968
REDDIN Bill. *Management effectiveness.* London, McGraw-Hill, 1970
SADLER P. 'Strategic management'. Address to the Charities Foundation conference, November 1989
SAYLES Leonard. *Managerial behaviour.* New York, McGraw-Hill, 1964
SCHEIN Edgar. *Process consultation: its role in organization development.* Reading, Massachusetts, Addison-Wesley, 1969
SCHEIN Ed. *Organization, culture and leadership.* New York, Jossey-Bass, 1987
SILVERMAN D. *The theory of organizations: a sociological framework.* London, Heinemann, 1970
SLOAN Alfred P. *My years with General Motors.* London, Sidgwick & Jackson, 1986
STEWART Rosemary. *The reality of management.* London, Heinemann, 1963
STEWART Rosemary. *Managers and their jobs.* London, Macmillan, 1967
TORRINGTON D. P. and COOPER C. L. 'The management of stress in organizations and the personnel initiative'. *Personnel Review.* Summer, 1977
TOWNSEND Robert. *Up the organization.* London, Michael Joseph, 1970
TRIST E. L. *Organizational choice.* London, Tavistock Publications, 1963
WALTON Richard. 'From control to commitment in the work place'. *Harvard Business Review.* March–April, 1985. pp 77–84
WEBER Max *in* GERTH H. H. and MILLS C. W. *eds. From Max Weber.* Oxford, Oxford University Press, 1946
WILLIAMSON E. E. and OUCHI W. C. 'The markets and hierarchies programme of research: origins, implications and prospects' *in* FRANCIS A., TURK J. and WILLMAR P. *eds. Power, efficiency and institutions.* London, Heinemann, 1983
WOODWARD Joan. *Management and technology.* London, Her Majesty's Stationery Office, 1958
WOODWARD Joan. *Industrial organization.* Oxford, Oxford University Press, 1968

WOODWARD Joan. 'Resistance to change'. *Management International Review*. Vol 8, 1968

General Texts on Management

ARMSTRONG Michael. *A handbook of management techniques.* London, Kogan Page, 1986

ARMSTRONG Michael. *How to be an even better manager.* London, Kogan Page, 1988

CHILD John. *Organization: a guide to problems and practice.* London, Harper & Row, 1977

DRUCKER Peter. *The effective executive.* London, Heinemann, 1962

DRUCKER Peter. *Managing for results.* London, Heinemann, 1967

DRUCKER Peter. *The practice of management.* London, Heinemann, 1955

GENEEN Harold. *Managing.* London, Granada, 1985

GILDER George. *The spirit of enterprise.* New York, Simon & Schuster, 1984

HANDY Charles. *Understanding organizations.* Harmondsworth, Penguin Books, 1985

HARVEY-JONES John. *Making it happen.* London, Collins, 1988

HELLER Robert. *The naked manager.* London, Barrie & Jenkins, 1972

JAY Antony, *Management and Machiavelli.* London, Hodder & Stoughton, 1967

KAKABADSE Andrew. *The politics of management.* Aldershot, Gower, 1983

KANTER Rosabeth Moss. *The change masters.* London, Allen & Unwin, 1984

KANTER Rosabeth Moss. *When giants learn to dance.* London, Simon & Schuster, 1989

LAWRENCE Peter. *Management in action.* London, Routledge & Kegan Paul, 1984

MINTZBERG Henry. *The nature of managerial work.* New York, Harper & Row, 1973

PASCALE Richard and ATHOS Anthony. *The art of Japanese management.* London, Sidgwick & Jackson, 1986

PETERS Tom and WATERMAN Robert. *In search of excellence.* New York, Harper & Row, 1982

PETERS Tom and AUSTIN Nancy. *A passion for excellence.* London, Collins, 1985

PETERS Tom. *Thriving on chaos.* London, Macmillan, 1988

SLOAN Alfred P. *My years with General Motors.* London, Sidgwick & Jackson, 1986

STEWART Rosemary. *The reality of management.* London, Heinemann, 1963

TOWNSEND Robert. *Up the organization.* London, Michael Joseph, 1970

Index